Prison Riots in Britain and the USA

Robert Adams
Head of Social Work and Professional Studies,
University of Humberside, Hull

Jo Campling
Consultant Editor

MACMILLAN

First edition 1992
Second edition 1994

Published by
THE MACMILLAN PRESS LTD
Houndmills, Basingstoke, Hampshire RG21 2XS
and London
Companies and representatives
throughout the world

A catalogue record for this book is available
from the British Library.

ISBN 0–333–54947–3 hardcover
ISBN 0–333–62505–6 paperback

Printed and bound in Great Britain by
Antony Rowe Ltd
Chippenham, Wiltshire

PRISON RIOTS IN BRITAIN AND THE USA

Also by Robert Adams

A MEASURE OF DIVERSION: Case Studies in I.T. (*with S. Allard, J. Baldwin and J. Thomas*)

PROBLEM SOLVING THROUGH SELF-HELP GROUPS (*with G. Lidenfield*)

PROTESTS BY PUPILS: Empowerment, Schooling and the State

SELF-HELP, SOCIAL-WORK AND EMPOWERMENT

To James and Rosa Adams

Contents

Preface to the Second Edition

I welcome, and thank my publishers, for the opportunity to make minor corrections in producing this new edition, and add the appendix chronicling prison riots. Unfortunately though, it is easier to update the text of this book than to refashion the fabric of penal policy and penal institutions.

In the year since this book was first published, prison riots in both Britain and the USA have continued to claim their share of media attention, and rioting prisoners have attracted the customary knee-jerk responses from many politicians and officials – all too often in the recommendation of more prison-building and tougher conditions inside prisons.

If Britain's incarceration rate remains high – higher than that of any other country in Western Europe – the proportion of the population of the USA imprisoned is three times higher, the highest rate in the world. The cost of imprisonment is climbing, in absolute and relative terms. The USA now spends more on incarcerating and supervising criminals than on benefits to unemployed people. It is cheaper to send a young person to university than to prison. Texas has one-third of the population of Britain, but locks up almost 60 000 offenders, compared with about 45 000 in England and Wales. Places are being built in Texas to house more than 35 000 additional prisoners. Imprisonment in both Britain and the USA is increasingly a source of profit to private entrepreneurs. In Britain there are plans to expand private provision rapidly. In 16 states of the USA, around 20 000 prison places are managed by private agencies. A tenth of all proposed new prison places will be provided by private contractors.

Officials have continued to blame riots on drug-taking, excessive association, no-go areas for staff, the violent tendencies of prisoners in general and a small number of agitators in particular. But the fact remains that riots are a resilient feature of penal institutions, resistant to simplistic explanation as well as to prevention. Their incidence appears to be as unaffected by tougher responses as by reforms. They occur in every part of penal systems. No institution is immune from them, whether run by private or public corporations. Despite government efforts to present privatization as synonymous with progress, rioting in The Wolds remand centre, Britain's first privately-run prison, was reported in some newspapers in June 1992 and again in June 1993.

In 1993, I accepted an invitation to attend a reunion of staff, on the 150th anniversary of the building of a prison. I came away with the anecdotes of prison officers ringing in my ears – as clear a reminder as ever of the tendency for the grimmest feature of prison – its culture of hierarchy, discipline, *machismo* and violence – to be transmitted not just through the inmate culture but through the memories shared and handed down by generations of staff. If there is to be significant change in prison systems in Britain and the USA, to say nothing of those elsewhere in the world, it will necessitate a cultural revaluation – a revolution in attitudes and values.

Whether even that would be sufficient to affect the incidence and character of riots is doubtful. The fact that riots occur in progressive and well-resourced as well as reactionary and ill-provided institutions attests to the reality that prison riots remain as much a comment on the condition of imprisonment, as on conditions inside prisons.

Robert Adams

Preface to the First Edition

The purpose of this book is to examine the history, nature, origins and outcomes of prison riots and responses to them, and to assess their significance and implications for penal policy and practice. It by no means tells the whole story of this complex subject, but complements the case studies of a handful of specific riots carried out in recent years.

The starting point for the book was the realization that to date no study had been undertaken which set alongside each other the broad experiences of prison riots in Britain and the US over the past two centuries. A number of major prison riots had led to official inquiries, and sometimes also to investigations by other groups including prisoners' movements themselves. But as a former worker in the British penal system – both as the most junior 'turnkey' at HM Prison Pentonville, and later as acting governor of a young offenders' institution – I was concerned that the traditional path of researchers into disturbances in prisons was towards confirming the maladjustment of individual prisoners rather than attempting to understand the social dimensions of incidents. Indeed, a sustained attempt at conceptualization of prison riots is notably absent from most inquiries and studies with regard, say, to the definition of riots, their histories in penal systems, the contexts in which riots arise, and the relationship between the actions of rioting prisoners and the responses of other people, including policies and practices by the governments and prison managements.

Otto von Bismarck cautioned against believing anything until it is officially denied. Prison riots are a contested concept, both in their definition and character. When I first declared an interest in prison riots, a senior official in the British Prison Department advised me that riots are not worth researching because there are hardly any real riots in prisons, only disturbances. By the time I had heard the comment repeated three or four times in different ways, my curiosity was confirmed. One of my academic colleagues used to say, once is an accident, twice may be coincidence, but three times is something else. A useful adage in penal research could be that if the authorities deny the value of studying something too strenuously, then it is probably worth examining.

This book focuses in turn on several key issues which need to be addressed, in the examination and interpretation of prison riots. It uses empirical data to that end, rather than filling the book with 'reliable' and 'valid' data on the many prison riots as an end in itself. Daniel Bell, in the classic book on *The End of Ideology*, states that his 'old-fashioned' interest is in ideas rather than in the language of social sciences, with its 'hypotheses, parameters, variables and paradigms':

> I am interested in social description and in explanation, in a sketching of broad reality rather than the controlled, but abstracted, testing of hypotheses. It is not necessarily less 'scientific' than academic sociology. Nor is it really 'literary'. It is sociology as a 'perspective', as a way of becoming sophisticated about the world.
>
> (Bell, 1960, p. 15)

This remark captures the mood of the present book, one intention of which is to set prison riots in their historical and social context and to raise for debate some key issues for people concerned about the past, present and future of prison riots, from wherever they stand.

Throughout the book, unless the specific context makes the use of other words strictly unavoidable, I have used the term 'prisoner', rather than 'inmates' or 'convicts'. This is despite the fact that many former prisons, like those of the California Department of Corrections for example, are now called 'correctional' facilities. For years, convicts were sent to prisons for punishment. When rehabilitative regimes became more common, many custodial staff had their titles changed from 'guards' to 'correctional officers', whose task was then not to punish convicts but to confine prisoners while they were rehabilitated. Over time, prisoners questioned more and more the ineffectiveness of rehabilitation, the hypocrisy of indeterminate sentences and their continual harassment and punishment by the correctional staff. Disillusioned, growing numbers of prisoners adopted an oppositional stance towards staff and convicts remained as a significant and powerful minority among them (Davidson, 1974, p. 47). I prefer to stand outside such shifts and to use the term 'prisoner' as a recognition of the captivity which all prisoners share. 'Similarly, except where the specific context requires otherwise, I use the term 'prison' as the general term to describe penal institutions for adults. This is partly for clarity and partly to counteract the tendency towards such euphemisms as 'facility', 'correctional institution' and 'center'.'

Throughout the book also, I have tried to avoid using the term America, which includes the territories of North and South America, when what is meant is the United States of America. I use the term 'Britain' to include Northern Ireland, Scotland and Wales, as well as England.

I cannot name individually, but acknowledge here collectively, the enormous debt this book owes to conversations and debates over the years with many prisoners. Additionally, I have found invaluable the help of many other people, including Mark Beeson, Jimmie Boyle, Paul Cavadino, Geoffrey Clarkson, Henry Cowper, Roger Dauncey, John Ditchfield, Audrey Lennox, Norman Jepson, Brian Johnson, Gregor Mclennan, Max Morrison, Peter Timms, Adrian Stanley, staff in the libraries of HM Prison Service and Humberside Polytechnic, the Prison Reform Trust, the US Civil Liberties Union Prison Project, Robyn Cohen and Jo Gustafson of the US Department of Justice, and to Belinda Holdsworth and Jo Campling for their continued editorial support. Pat, Charlotte, Kirsty, Jade and George ensure that my household remains a primary stimulus of critical debate.

None of the above people have contributed to any indiscretions or mistakes in this book, which remain solely my responsibility.

ROBERT ADAMS

. . . someday we will look back upon our criminal and penal process with the same horrified wonder as we now look back on the Spanish Inquisition.

Bok, 1959, p. 50

1 Prison Riots: Problems and Perspectives

> The major political and historical event that marks the path of prison history is the riot.
>
> (Berkman, 1979, p. 34)

THE STARTING POINT

From time to time, riots in prisons have come to public attention in the form of dramatic media coverage of a wave of prison rioting or an account of a particularly violent incident in a single institution. But, for most of the two-hundred-year history of the majority of prisons, prison riots have not been in the foreground of debates about penal policy and practice.

In one sense this is not surprising, since the discontinuities in the recorded histories of prison riots point to the likelihood that gaps of several years, or even decades, often elapse between noteworthy single, or waves of, incidents (see Figure 3.1, p. 62). But when riots do occur, it is sometimes with an intensity of violence which makes their relative neglect by researchers and penal administrators over the years somewhat puzzling.

Perhaps because of this neglect, even to the informed commentator on British penal policy, the Dartmoor Mutiny of 1932 is the first significant prison riot which comes to mind, followed by the wave of riots of the early 1970s, the violent Hull prison riot of 1976 and the lengthy rooftop protest of April 1990 at HM Prison, Strangeways, Manchester, Northern England, which led to the evacuation of the entire prison for several months and the eventual rebuilding of much of the main prison complex. In the US, commentators may recall waves of prison riots in 1928–9, 1951–3 and 1968–70 and the violent incidents at Alcatraz in 1946, Attica in 1971 and the bloodiest incident in US penal history, at New Mexico State Penitentiary, Santa Fe in 1980.

This discontinuous record, marked by dramatic incidents interspersed with long silences, raises a number of questions about the character, representation and incidence of prison riots. To begin

1

with, there may be doubt about whether the apparent gaps in the record reflect reality or simply the vagaries of media coverage and the newsworthiness of particular kinds of story. This raises the further question as to whether, and if so why, prison riots have become more noteworthy since the late 1960s. Is this simply a feature of increased newsworthiness? Are there more prison riots than there used to be? Are incidents becoming more serious, in terms of numbers of staff and prisoners injured and killed? Are modern riots more violent and newsworthy than formerly? Is the media coverage of riots actually responsible in some way for encouraging them – copycat-style?

Behind these immediate questions lie further areas for examination. What causes prison riots? Do they arise spontaneously, independently of identifiable causes, or are they the outcome of widespread features of prisons and penal policies and structures? Are they simply indications of the brutality and thoughtlessness of prisoners, or signs of specific ills in the prison system? What is the significance of prison riots? How do the authorities respond to them? What can be learned from comparing the British and US experiences of them? Are there shared regularities in their outcomes?

This book does not set out to say the last word about all of these questions. But, whilst recognizing that many of them are interconnected and pose further questions to which there are no easy answers, it is hoped to address the major issues raised by them, directly or indirectly. In the process, it offers an interpretation of prison riots in prisons in the United States of America (US) and in England, Northern Ireland, Scotland and Wales (Britain). This involves tackling the complex and difficult task of describing and explaining them, a task which is begun here, but is by no means completed in this single volume.

The sources of data are eclectic and mostly secondary, that is research reports, inquiries and investigations into riots, commentaries by penologists, case studies, surveys and sociological analyses of prisons and criminal justice systems. Use is also made of a search of *The Times* and *New York Times* indexes for the period covered by the book. The author draws also on seven years' experience working in the British penal system, through the period of the spread of prison unrest in the late 1960s and early 1970s, first as a prison officer in the HM Prison, Pentonville, London and latterly as Deputy Governor of a penal establishment. The book emerges also from many years of work in seminars and workshops on institutional and intercommunal riots with undergraduate and post-experience students, including prison staff.

The book sets alongside each other the circumstances of imprisonment in Britain and in the US. It is not simply a comparison of immediate characteristics of incidents, any more than it only presents a calendar of events, though these are important components in the development of a perspective on riots. The very concept of prison riots is contested, let alone the status of the rioters. In this light, it is important to examine how prisons, prisoners generally and especially rioting prisoners are seen, what their status is in society, what kinds of changes have taken place in the situation of prisons and in their organization, administration and description over the years and what light this casts on the subject matter of this book. Again, a full treatment of this aspect of the context of rioting is a subject in its own right, but in the present study it will be drawn on as appropriate.

The task is undertaken in three stages, of description, explanation and evaluation. These are inseparable and in many ways overlap throughout the book. But in broad terms the first part of the book in Chapters 1 and 2 tackles the problems of examining prison riots, while Chapters 3 to 5 describe and compare them in Britain and the US. Chapter 6 addresses problems of explaining how prison riots arise and finally Chapter 7 evaluates their future prospects.

PROBLEMS OF RESEARCH

Several features of the field of study of prison riots are noteworthy: the lack of research into them, the predominance of case studies and inquiries into single incidents, and the contested nature of incidents, reflected partly in the mutually conflicting accounts given of riots by different investigators.

The quotation introducing this chapter makes the comparative neglect of prison riots by researchers throughout most of the twentieth century even more remarkable. Since the 1951–3 riots in the US (see Chapter 3), social scientists have become increasingly interested in researching prisons in general. Sykes (1957) and Cressey (1961) initiated this trend (Conrad, 1989, p. 276). Perhaps one reason for the lack of research into prison riots in particular, however, is the prior necessity to unravel definitional, conceptual and procedural problems of carrying it out. The closed nature of prisons as institutions tends to contribute to the secretiveness and defensiveness of the authorities, and compounds these three areas of difficulty.

First, the problem of definition of the field of study has been raised specifically in the area of prisoners' protests (Fitzgerald, 1977) and labour protest more generally (Geary, 1981, p. 6). On the whole, the approach adopted here follows Geary in concentrating on collective protests. This means excluding protests by individual prisoners, such as absenteeism, from consideration in this present study. But the concept of riots is itself problematic and this makes it difficult to maintain the claim of objectivity in their study. The description of prison riots is a problem because the languages used overlap both the 'technical' and 'the transparent world of the ordinary, the everyday'. The difficulty is that 'we forget that these too are constructions of the world, and of ourselves' (Threadgold and Cranny-Francis, 1990, p. 19).

Second, there is the problem of the lack of study of protest by sociologists in particular. On the other hand, related areas such as prisoner violence have attracted much attention, especially in the period since the 1950s when rehabilitation was a popular penal philosophy, and not least from those who see disturbances involving prisoners as signs simply of the pathology of the individual.

With the exception of one notable study of US prison riots since Attica (Useem and Kimball, 1989), the increasing incidence of prison riots, reported in the media, in Britain and the US since 1968, has not been paralleled by the same enthusiasm amongst researchers for macro-sociological study of the character and significance of prison riots. Much research has been like media coverage – reactive, uncritical and atheoretical in nature. There is a notable paucity of studies which attempt at a conceptual level to relate prison riots to other aspects of penal policy and practice, let alone to criminal justice systems and the wider society. In this, the poverty of theory in relation to prison riots simply parallels the marginal place occupied by prisoners as actresses and actors in penal discourse over the centuries. Reid observes that 'most of the analyses of prison riots have consisted of reportings after the fact of a particular riot' (Reid, 1981, p. 204). Specific riots, Attica in the US (New York Special Commission on Attica, 1972) and Hull and Peterhead in Britain, have attracted case studies, perhaps partly in view of the drama and unusualness of the scale of personal violence and damage involved, but also probably for reasons of serendipity. In the case of Hull, for instance, a collaboration between a Hull academic, J.E. Thomas, and a co-founder of Preservation of the Rights of Prisoners (PROP), the prisoners' rights movement in Britain, Dick Pooley, living in Hull, produced the study (Thomas and Pooley, 1980). The Peterhead disturbances of the late 1980s were the occasion for a detailed case study of disturbances in

Scottish prisons during that period (Scraton *et al.*, 1991). Some attention has been given to the growth of prisoners' protest organizations, for example, in Britain (Fitzgerald, 1977) and in Scandinavia (Mathiesen, 1974). In short, there exists no standard text which gives theoretical coherence to the broad study of the nature, incidence, origins and likely future of prison riots as an aspect of protest by prisoners.

Third, there is the procedural problem of getting access to valid data. They are unpredictable, complex and often too large for one observer to encompass. The unpredictability of riots inevitably leads to a dearth of direct data concerning their origins and this applies to the early stages of riots in particular. A good example of the mutual stand-off between researchers and the authorities is the relationship between Cohen and Taylor and the British Home Office, described in their book on prisoners' experiences of long-term imprisonment (Cohen and Taylor, 1972 and well documented by Jupp (1989, pp. 138–48). The issue of power also complicates research into riots. Prisoners and staff do not occupy equal places in discourse about riots, nor do they have equal opportunities to take up subject or object positions in this. The power differential between them helps to produce and sustain consequent differentials in the knowledges, meanings, values and practices concerning the different participants in discourse about prison riots, which research has the difficult task of teasing out.

The fact that riots in prisons were not systematically studied on a significant scale until well into the 1970s parallels a similar neglect of research into intercommunal rioting (Marx and Wood, 1975, p. 36). Smith, an experienced prison medical officer in Britain, argues that the singular neglect of research into other aspects of prison life includes those in which riots occur. Smith summarizes the position in Britain, at the start of an informative and unique series of almost a score of articles in the *British Medical Journal*:

> Usually the scientist and the scientific journalist are presented with an abundance of information, and their task is to sort out what is reliable and what is not. When it comes to studying prisons everything is different. There are a few good scientific studies of what goes on in prisons, but they are very few and mostly old. This is partly because research is difficult in prison and partly because it has not been encouraged.
>
> (Smith, 1983a, p. 1552)

Not surprisingly, therefore, research into prisons and prisoners is difficult to translate into direct benefits for prisoners. We need to qualify this. Whereas research which does not fundamentally challenge the status quo of penal policy and practice often has flourished, *critical* research into British prison conditions has not always received official support. The Official Secrets Act has been argued by some commentators to be one intentional means by which external critical scrutiny of prisons is discouraged (Cohen and Taylor, 1978). Taylor argues that if John Howard had been alive in the late 1970s to request permission to make his tour of prisons and write his report *The State of the Prisons*, the Home Office would have refused him permission (Taylor, 1978, p. 172).

It is arguable that in Britain the dominant management preoccupation with the control of prisoners has tended to be reinforced by the major research concerns of the Prison Psychological Service (Cohen and Taylor, 1972). Collective disturbances, especially the violent ones, tended to be seen through the methodology of positivism and behaviourism. That is, prisoners often have been observed by methods unrelated to their experience, abstracted from what is in their hearts and minds. Till the late 1960s, the story lacked an account of their conduct from what Silverman calls an action perspective (Silverman, 1970, pp. 126–7). What was missing at that stage, and what Cohen and Taylor (1972) interjected in Britain, were their feelings, their impulses and their struggles.

Similarly, in the US the nature of riots as social phenomena has tended to be displaced by research which concentrates upon the characteristics of prisoners. The racist assumptions of some of this research are barely cloaked beneath their surface statements. Thus, Goodstein and Wright comment, 'considerable research on the association of race and inmate adjustment has been conducted in recent years. Black and white inmates have been found to differ in patterns of adjustment in areas such as ethnic/racial solidarity, expression of power and violence, experience of stress, and prisonization' (Goodstein and Wright, 1989, p. 236). In studies of inmate conflict and violence, research has found that blacks are more likely to possess control and influence in daily institutional affairs (Bartollas, Miller and Dinitz, 1976) and be aggressors in conflict situations (Fuller and Orsagh, 1977). Studies relying upon official misconduct figures find that officials charge blacks with assaultive behaviour more frequently than whites (Flanagan, 1983; Poole and Regoli, 1980; Ramirez, 1984). 'In instances of sexual victimization, findings suggest that blacks are perpetrators and whites targets' (Goodstein and Wright, 1989, p. 236). But, as Goodstein and Wright acknowledge:

> Some researchers propose that apparent race differences on aggression may result from discriminatory treatment of blacks by correctional staff, thereby inflating official statistics (Poole and Regoli, 1980; Wright, 1987) and aggravating resistance among the inmates themselves (Goodstein and MacKenzie, 1984).
>
> (Goodstein and Wright, 1989, p. 236)

Useem distances himself from Kimball, his co-author, proposing a Marxist view of prison riots, arguing that they are inextricably linked with the oppression of oppressed groups, notably blacks, over-represented in the prison system (Useem and Kimball, 1989, p. 12).

CONTESTED NATURE OF RIOT INCIDENTS

Whereas in the US since the early 1980s the Federal Bureau of Prisons has collected data specifically on riots, in mid-1991 a senior official in the Home Office in Britain was still able to respond to the author's request for riot data with the comment: 'The Prison Department does not talk about riots, only disturbances, and the problem is that almost any incident can be called a disturbance' (personal communication). Undoubtedly, the difficulty of defining riots contributes to the problems of examining their nature, incidence and origins. This is not just a technical problem. Because of the different and often conflicting social and political standpoints of the major parties to prison riots, they remain a contested concept and a contested subject of discussion among penal commentators and practitioners. It is an over-simplification, but broadly true, that the experience of prisoners in general, and prison rioters in particular, has tended to be swamped by the voices of the authorities in commentaries on prison riots over the years.

Moreover, when set alongside each other, the versions of particular riots put forward by the authorities and the versions of them put forward by prisoners often simply cannot be reconciled. This caricatures to a degree but is a significant feature of the polarization between staff and rioters which needs to be addressed. In particular, there is a need to describe and interpret prison riots, bearing in mind the difficulty, and probably the impossibility, of ever arriving at a final account of what has happened in a particular incident. The different accounts of prison riots all offer different stories. The authorities, the media and the prisoners form only the first triangle of different perceptions. Within each of these groups there are differences of view. To the extent that they differ, they are in competition to construct, or to silence, different interpretations of realities associated with competing psychologies and sociologies of rioting.

Calvert's comment on revolutions applies with equal force to the field of riots: 'Revolution is not a fact, or a set of facts, but a mental construct, a creation of the individual mind, and so has no real objective existence' (Calvert, 1990, p. 23). This is true of the past as well as the present. Hutcheon notes the paradox that history constructs its object and the past is known only through its textual and remembered traces. It is still 'a parody of objectivity' (Hutcheon, 1989, p. 90).

But this should not allow us to regard the prison simply as a social construction, an interaction between the different experiences of those involved in it. However described, the experiences of prisoners all too often involve deprivations. Alongside research literature and the investigations of the authorities, there is a need to feed into the debate about the character and significance of riots the experiences of the rioters themselves. Prison literature, both autobiographical and fictional, provides an important source of insight into the experience of prisoners in general and prison riots in particular. To the extent that this writing addresses the pain, deprivations and isolation of prisoners (Jepson, 1986), it is easy to see its transnational character. However, superimposed on this generality are the specific traumas of particular social and historical circumstances: Soviet prison camps under Stalin (Solzhenitsyn, 1963, 1974), German concentration camps (Levi, 1987) and prisoner-of-war camps in Europe (Reid, 1950) and in the East (Clavell, 1975) in the Second World War, in Northern Ireland (Adams, 1990), Franco's Spanish prisons after 1945 (Gallego, 1990) and memoirs of British prisoners in military detention (Rigby, 1965) and in civilian prisons (Boyle, 1985). More specifically, some riots have generated not just officially-sponsored inquiries but also published memoirs by prisoners and investigatory publications from non-official standpoints (Abbott, 1981; Cleaver, 1968; Hill, 1991).

The problematic concept of prison riots arises partly from the contradictory nature of two of its widespread component ideas: First, that riots are pointless eruptions, often violent, whose main significance is to confirm the mindlessness of prisoners involved in them, and second, that riots are part of the resistance by prisoners to some aspect of their imprisonment. This statement gets near to the heart of the dilemma, which is whether prison riots are simply to be subsumed under the broader discussion of prisoner violence and indiscipline, or whether they may be viewed as an illegal, but nevertheless purposeful, instance of collective, even political, activity by prisoners. Kimball suggests that the term 'rebellion' is preferable to 'riot', since it acknowledges the political nature of prisoners' actions (Useem and Kimball, 1989, p. 269). Significantly, neither the Du Parcq inquiry into the Dartmoor riot of 1932 nor the Woolf inquiry into the Strangeways riot of 1990 used the term 'riot' in its title (Du Parcq, 1932; Woolf and Tumin, 1991).

Discussion of riots, like the broader subject of protests by prisoners, has tended to be regarded as part of the wider category of indiscipline, and thereby disengaged from resistance *per se*. To arrive at this point, the construction of order in the prison is taken as the starting point for the understanding of disorder. The riot appears as the negation of order. It is excluded from the politics of change and relations between prisoners and the authorities and the state.

This has been as true in the late twentieth century as in the mid-nineteenth century, when, for example, in 1855 discussion of the containment of women prisoners in Britain was couched in terms of how to curb their refractoriness rather than how to deal with the problems leading to their actions (McConville, 1981, p. 413). Goodstein and Wright, 150 years later, note that in the US, debates about the influence of prisons as institutions upon inmates have tended to perpetuate this preoccupation: 'Investigations of the increased role of inmate violence appear to have replaced earlier preoccupations with prisonization among criminologists. More recent organizational analyses of contemporary prison life highlight the importance of the expression or threat of violence to the inmate "public culture".' Among others, they quote Irwin: 'Toughness in the new hero in the violent men's prison means, first, being able to take care of oneself in the prison world, where people will attack others with little or no provocation. Second, it means having the guts to take from the weak' (Irwin, 1980, p. 193). They continue: 'These descriptions leave readers with an image of prison as dangerous and damaging to inmates. Within the violent culture of the new prison, inmates must become familiar with violent tactics, or at least maintain the facade' (Goodstein and Wright , 1989, p. 235). In this way, riots in prisons have not been so much viewed in the context of collective protest as subsumed under prison violence. This macho subject matter tends not to be challenged by those discussing it. It tends to be regarded as an un-avoidable feature of the situation.

DEFINITION OF RIOTS BY PRISONERS

The linguistic shift from 'prison riots' to 'riots by prisoners' as the heading for this section denotes how traditionally the language used to describe protests by prisoners and prison riots limits their description. The problem goes deeper than this:

> Our customary language obscures the interdependence of collective violence and everyday social organization. Words such as 'riot', 'disorder', and 'disturbance' reflect the views of authorities, rivals, and unsympathetic observers. They presume that someone has willfully disrupted the normally peaceful social order by acting violently, and thereby justify repression of the 'rioters'. They distinguish sharply between 'force', the use of physical coercion by authorities, and 'violence', the use of physical coercion by people who lack authority. So-called riots, however, almost always involve at least two parties, an aggrieved group of people and representatives of the authorities. When those representatives are police or other armed forces, they often perform the major share of the physical violence, and sometimes initiate it. A routine demonstration, meeting, or market only becomes a 'riot' when a second party challenges the action of the first.
>
> (Tilly, 1989, pp. 62–3)

There is no agreed definition of what constitutes a prison riot. We need to exercise caution in the way we define it, since this will set the parameters of later discussion. What are the essential characteristics of a prison riot in the penal system? Is every riot a protest? What distinguishes a protest from a riot? Does a riot necessarily involve some form of violence?

Berkman refers to the *American College Dictionary* definition of a riot as 'the execution of a violent and unlawful purpose by three or more persons acting together, to the terror of the people', adding that they are associated generally with 'unbridled outbreaks of passion or emotion' (Berkman, 1979, p. 34). This definition illustrates the problem of arriving at a form of words sufficiently general to hold for all riots, yet specific enough to be meaningful. A further problem is the value-laden nature of the descriptors used by commentators. In the definition above, the 'terror of the people' and 'unbridled outbreaks' are expressions of the values of the writer rather than necessary conditions of the existence of a riot.

Shapland argues that prison disturbances fall into two categories: riots and demonstrations. Riots are 'spontaneous, unplanned and triggered by a single event, like a fight or breaking glass'. Demonstrations, such as sit-ins or go-slows are 'planned and used for a more constructive purpose' (Shapland, 1973, p. 19). Again, the difficulty is the presumption that riots are less purposeful than other collective incidents such as demonstrations as forms of protest.

But perhaps prison riots should be seen as incidents which possess the features of protests, with the important difference that they involve prisoners taking over part or all of the regime or the territory of the prison. The character of protests can be defined in terms used in the broader field of industrial relations. A well-established text on strikes by Hyman follows Griffin in defining a strike as 'a temporary stoppage of work by a group of employees in order to express a grievance or enforce a demand' (Hyman, 1984, p. 17). Adapting this to the prison setting produces the following five characteristics of a protest: tem-porariness; interruption to the regime; a group of prisoners acting together; with the purpose either of expressing a grievance or of achieving change in their circumstances. This provides a basis on which we can build.

Colvin defines the prison riot as 'involving fifteen or more inmates who take control of all or part of a prison through force' (Colvin, 1982, p. 449). Thus he excludes 'non-violent inmate strikes and inmate fights that do not result in a prison takeover' (Colvin, 1982, p. 450). This definition has the advantage of narrowing the field to a relatively homogeneous category of incidents in prisons. But by including only violent and forceful acts, this categorization constricts knowledge of the phenomenon and inevitably constrains discussion in the terms of that knowledge. It perpetuates the connection between rioting and macho prison cultures referred to above. In the wider context of rioting, it is all too easy to fall into the trap of regarding rioting as a macho, and therefore as a male activity, as was implied by Gurr in the title of an early book (Gurr, 1970). A more flexible definition is referred to by Wilsnack, who states that 'a riot can be identified as a seizure by inmates of prison territory where they can move freely but staff cannot, plus a presentation of demands that affect more inmates than those actively participating in the disturbance' (Wilsnack, 1976, p. 67). Wilsnack develops this by suggesting that protests which do not involve the seizure of territory do not qualify as riots: 'Nonriot resistance involves similar demands without seizure of territory; the demands are usually backed up by a refusal of inmates to engage in some officially sanctioned activity. Questions based on these descriptions appear to avoid any confusion with mass escapes or brawls among inmates' (Wilsnack, 1976, p. 67).

By this criterion, demonstrations caused by prisoners banging in their cells, reported to the author by officers at Pentonville Prison in London as occurred before the abolition of capital punishment the night before some hangings, would possibly qualify as riots if they interrupted the night routine. The following description of a long, hot night in Liverpool Prison, built for 1,000 in the nineteenth century and now holding about 1,500 prisoners, might also qualify, when 'the prisoners thumped on the walls, the doors, the bars. The whole prison reverberated to this concerted demonstration against the sheer numbers, the heat, the smell, the proximity. The landing shook under the officers' feet, and the noise didn't stop' (Ackroyd, 1979, p. 11).

Omitting Wilsnack's point concerning rioters usually proposing demands on behalf of non-rioters, we can now propose that riots are likely to include seven characteristics:

(a) They are part of a continuum of activities. Rather than riots being viewed as an aberration, they may be regarded as part of the continuum of activities in the prison.

(b) They involve dissent and/or protest. Riots by prisoners represent only the most obvious illustrations of dissent or protest, which itself is one manifestation of a wide range of disturbances in prisons, including riots, fights, assaults, sit-ins, strikes, demonstrations and lock-outs, involving individuals as well as groups. This variety of happenings could be categorized in many different ways, for instance according to the nature of the incident, purpose of the prisoners, number of participants, or the degree of violence used.

Dissent may vary from civil disobedience at one extreme, to terrorism at the other, or any combination of these (Warner and Crisp, 1990, p. 2). Any evaluation of the nature and significance of rioting implies an evaluative position in relation to the authorities against which protest is made. For example, a riot incident may be defined by the prisoners as an act of protest, in which case 'no discussion of the legitimacy of protest can properly be conducted without reference to that of the structures or practices to which objection is made; power is but the other side of protest' (Warner and Crisp, 1990, p. 2).

So, evaluative commentaries on riots need to consider also the nature of that which is rioted against, if that is how the dissent is perceived. This approach to understanding the riot has moved towards the view that it may be an act of protest. Lukes (1978) reminds us of the need to adopt a radical view of the exercise of power which takes in the structures which define the issues and constrain those who act. Beyond interpretations of the structures and interactions of power and protest, or rather embedded in them, are the knowledges which frame the concepts themselves: 'Interpretations of protests reflect the explanatory paradigms in which they rest. These interpretations need to be placed in context and to be viewed critically . . . There is tension, not just between interpretations but between the knowledges which inform them' (Adams, 1991, p. 178).

(c) They involve an interruption to the regime. Undoubtedly, riots as protests act as an interruption to the control by staff of the prison regime at one or more levels.

(d) They involve a takeover by prisoners of all or a part of the prison resources, regime and/or staffing. This may be achieved materially and directly by a sit-in or barricade across a wing, or indirectly by, say, taking one or more staff hostage. It may also be symbolic and involve a struggle over, say, cultural capital in the institution, such as the noisy demonstration by prisoners in their cells described above.

(e) They are temporary. Riots tend to be short-lived. Most occupy less than a day and a good proportion only a few hours at most.

(f) They involve groups of prisoners. Though there is argument about the minimum number of prisoners it takes to riot, undoubtedly rioting is a collective activity. It is likely that below a minimum of, say, five prisoners it would be difficult to justify the use of the term 'riot' to describe an incident.

(g) They are directed towards achieving a change and/or expressing a grievance. Either or both of these elements are invariably associated with rioting.

So, riots by prisoners may be defined as *part of the continuum of practices and relationships inherent in imprisonment, which involves dissenting and/or protesting activities by individuals or groups of prisoners which interrupt their imprisonment, by means of which they take over all or part of the prison resources and either express one or more grievances or a demand for change, or both.*

INCIDENCE

The incidence of prison riots has always been difficult to establish. Official statistics do not make them easy to discern, and they have not always been referred to in the annual reports of the prison department published by the Home Office. When they have appeared, it has usually been under headings such as those associated with issues of discipline and control. There is a long tradition of this. In 1922, the Prison Commissioners classified prison offences in four categories: violence, escapes and attempted escapes, idleness and 'other breaches of the regulations' (Hobhouse and Brockway, 1922, p. 235). This made it very difficult to discern whether or not any collective protests occurred in the guise of these labels. Thomas notes that there had been few riots before the 1960s in Britain, apart from the Dartmoor Mutiny in 1932 and some disturbances on the hulks a hundred years before that (Pooley and Thomas, 1980, p. 5). Until the mid-1980s, with the exception of a minority of incidents dealt with in the early 1970s as though they were control and discipline matters, in Britain it was not easy to find references to prison riots in the annual reports of the prison department (see Chapter 4). But since the mid-1980s, prison riots have become greater sources of media attention and the Home Office has allowed its officials more freedom to comment publicly on them.

The fact that such recorded histories of prison riots are discontinuous and fragmentary raises the question as to whether there are shared regularities in these occurrences, or whether each incident of protest should be understood as a more or less distinct local event. It is misguided to attempt to reconcile the history of riots by prisoners with a view of history which seeks a continuous narrative, to which is attached a simple, uni-dimensional explanation as to their occurrence. There is, as Waskow indicated in a classic study of riots in the US, a question as to whether more general processes are indicated by particular incidents (Waskow, 1967, p. 291).

Riots in prisons may be discontinuous, but it is all too easy to reduce their significance by labelling them as spasmodic outbreaks of disorder which punctuate prison history. Investigations into riots, and general commentaries upon them, have tended to reinforce a loose use of the term 'riot' and a reduction of the historical account to presumptions about the riot as a more or less predictable, but sporadic, if sometimes shocking, reaction to bad prison conditions. All too rarely have official inquiries or the mass media offered an understanding which incorporates an account of the motivations and actions of rioting prisoners.

Rioting by prisoners is not a feature of isolated 'bad' institutions in a minority of 'bad' penal systems. In carrying out the present study, it was noted that the *New York Times* and *The Times* alone report more than 400 prison riots in countries other than Britain and the US in the twentieth century. Prison riots are a repeated part of prison life in prisons all over the world. They can be found in every continent. They are a feature of developed and developing countries. They occur in socialist countries such as Cuba, as well as in capitalist and mixed economies such as the US and Western European countries. By conceptualizing riots as though they only occur in situations where something is defined as amiss, commentators invoke the view that riots have simply no causes and exclude the possible interpretation that prisons by their nature produce riots.

REPRESENTATION

The general lack of research into prisons, prison conditions and prison riots until the last third of the twentieth century is only exceeded by the almost total lack of research into public knowledge and opinion of prisons. Strangely, however, the common assumption of professional commentators that perhaps in consequence the public remains largely ignorant of what happens in prisons is belied by a survey of prison news coverage in newspapers, periodicals and on television in the US for 1976 (Jacobs, 1983, p. 106). A search of *The New York Times* and the *New York Daily News*, a wide range of magazines and all CBS news programmes, revealed a scope and depth of coverage which stood up well against coverage of other news subjects (Jacobs, 1983, p. 107). But in spite of this, only eleven per cent of the total media coverage concerned prison disturbances, thus refuting the assertion that prison violence figures prominently in the treatment of prisons by mass media (Jacobs, 1983, p. 110). Leaving aside the question as to the accuracy and level of the information, it is clear that there is more news coverage on subjects related to penal policy and practice and prison conditions than on escapes, violence and riots (Jacobs, 1983, p. 114). Notwithstanding this, in the US in particular, extensive, detailed press coverage followed the major prison riots of the twentieth century.

Often, reports of prison riots highlight bad prison conditions in the process. Many of the grimmest features of prisons in Britain and the US – overcrowding, excessive locking-up, over-controlling security, inadequate ill-rewarded work, punitiveness and insanitariness – have persisted for two centuries or more often in the same buildings which were built more than a century ago. Despite much publicity about these conditions, these facts must raise the likelihood that such prisons serve some societal purpose as they stand. The most obvious purpose is that of less eligibility: providing a destination of last resort, which is manifestly less desirable to the 'underserving poor' than all other alternatives.

There is a tendency for prison authorities to under-report prison riots. This may be viewed as understandable. The under-reporting of riots is often associated with defensiveness about conditions in prisons and sensitivity about how prison staff lose control and the authorities seem unable to manage institutions effectively.

In contrast, prison riots have often made big news when they have reached the media. Although the advent of television, and news and documentary coverage in particular, have escalated the processes of spectacularizing news events, even as long ago as 1929, when it first broke, news of the prison riot in Auburn, for example, occupied very nearly the whole of the first three pages of *The New York Times* (*New York Times*, 12 December 1929, pp. 1–3). In the 1970s and 1980s, and especially during and after such incidents as Attica in the US in 1971 and Strangeways in Britain in 1990, events in prison became a major focus of the mass media. The development of press and television coverage of the prison riot in the last quarter of the twentieth century highlighted the drama of staff-prisoner interaction and led to the more lengthy incidents becoming spectacular forms of entertainment. In the US, the catalogues of mass deaths and injuries at Attica in 1971 and Santa Fe in 1980 needed no embellishment. But in Britain, the process by which the 25 days of the Strangeways riot became a virtually non-stop television drama, with scores of reporters and camera crews besieging the prison, became the subject of an unprecedented inquiry by the Press Council. 'In the first few days horrific accounts of killings, butchery and torture appeared in many papers. Sensational banner headlines reporting large numbers of deaths, accompanied by detailed accounts of gruesome events within the prison, later proved to be totally unfounded.' (Press Council, 1991, p. 5) Thus twelve local and national newspapers on the day following the riot reported between twelve and twenty deaths. Three editions of the *Manchester Evening News* contained headlines: '20 dead', '20 dead?', 'Mayhem' and 'Sex offenders hanged and castrated as drug crazed inmates go beserk'. (Press Council, 1991, p. 31)

The fact was that not a single person was murdered by a prisoner during this riot. The ready take-up by reporters of unfounded rumours was as striking as the reticence of the Home Office about providing well-informed briefings for the media from the earliest stage of the riot.

So descriptions of some prison riots since 1980 have paralleled some media productions: for instance, the fragmentation of experiences and incidents in the sequences of anticipated further outbreaks of rioting, followed by escalated riots and the aftermaths of incidents, in New Mexico 1980 or Strangeways 1990. Rather than a television feature, Featherstone could have been describing the process of a riot when he says that such reporting 'fragments into a series of perpetual presents, leads to the transformation of reality into images, a breakdown of temporality and a sense of history, and a number of intensities, vivid and powerful experiences' (Featherstone, 1991, p. 58). The prison under riot siege takes on ironically some characteristics of the theme park. The media 'circus' treat Strangeways as the source of nightly news 'entertainment', just as Disneyworld entertains children and families (Featherstone, 1991, p. 59–60). Rioting prisoners take licence to act uncharacteristically, that is not like captives, but like performers, demagogues, media stars and in diametric opposition to everyday reality. Temporarily, they act like politicians, prison reformers or civil rights activists.

All too often, prison riots are represented as though they are 'simple' explosions of collective violence by prisoners. Mostly, this sort of misrepresentation can be laid at the door of the mass media which in the case of the Strangeways riot, incidentally, was later investigated and refuted by the Press Council (Press Council, 1991). But in any case, this is not the whole story. Other commentators on riots are no more independent. The authorities who investigate riots commonly do not begin their inquiries from an independent standpoint. There is typically a divergence between the defensive reports on riots prepared by officials in prison systems and the critical reports produced by prisoners themselves. Is this anything more than an obvious finding, to be expected in a situation where there is a social gulf between custodians and those who are confined? To some extent, the answer to this question depends on the perspective of the commentator on prison riots.

Traditional Views

The starting, and finishing, point for many people is the view that riots arise simply because of the sort of mindless behaviour to be expected of prisoners. Riots do no more and no less than confirm their criminality.

Liberal Views

From a liberal standpoint, rioting by prisoners may be perceived as essentially misguided but understandable. A typical liberal view focuses on the need for prisoners' grievances to be attended to, and prison reforms undertaken. Liberal opinion, however, tends to take for granted the continuance of the structures, principles and of imprisonment, which form the broader context of debates about what goes on in prisons.

Radical Views

Some radical perspectives view riots as part of the continuum of political actions taken by prisoners. Riots may be seen as ways in which prisoners empower themselves temporarily through the riot, though the threat of further rioting may be ever-present thereafter. Berkman presents the history of the prisoners' rights movement in the latter part of the twentieth century in terms of this tension. During this period, prisoners have struggled to extend their intrinsically constrained reach outside the institution: 'Much of the political history of prisoners is the history of connection, coalition, support groups, and the like – attempts to jostle for position in the wider political and social arena' (Berkman, 1979, p. 34).

The fact that an appreciation of the prisoner's perspective on riots is labelled as 'radical' is unfortunate and misleading. It reflects the normative base from which much so-called independent understanding of prison riots starts. The researcher and writer Rubenstein's radical stance does not outlaw terrorism. Far from this, Coleman comments in a review of perspectives on terrorism, that:

[Rubenstein] is not averse to depicting mass violence as in some cases a legitimate instrument of social transformation. He too does not differentiate between state violence and terrorist group violence. But his purpose is neither to defend nor to condemn terrorism. Rather he wants to ask whether terrorism as small-group violence for which arguable claims of mass representation can be made is an effective means to the goal of social revolution.

(Coleman, 1990, p. 220)

PERSPECTIVES ON PRISON RIOTS

Traditional and liberal views dominate the way riots are perceived. The context in which prison riots are studied tends to be framed by the language of order as normal and riots as disturbances of that order. As a description that is strictly accurate, but words such as 'disturbance' are not neutrally descriptive. They embody a normative judgement. In a study of protests by pupils, the author notes:

The centre of gravity of social theory concerning institutions has rested in issues associated with control and order in them. Almost inevitably, resistance and protest by inmates have been relegated to the margins. In some ways, protest is seen thus as an interim, transitional stage in the process of social change. It may even be treated as though it is unusual or abnormal. In the wider field of societal change, Feldman suggests [1964, p. 114] that 'the conception of revolution is derivative from a conception of peaceful politics, and the conception of peaceful politics is derivative from that tame image of the social system.'

(Adams 1991, p. 14)

Just as functionalism has dominated the study of prisons, so resistance to prisons has been relegated to the margins as aberrant in the latter half of the twentieth century. The focus of research into the actions of prisoners has tended to use the language of 'adjustment' (Goodstein and Wright, 1989, pp. 236–8).

Research into prison riots has been characterized by the same convergence between positivism and functionalism which has marked the study of the prison in general. Some researchers (for instance, the studies by Ostfeld and others in Chapter 6) study prisoners as though their collective actions, as observed and tested behaviour, can be researched without any distinction being drawn between social and natural phenomena.

Until the 1970s, the dominant paradigm of research into prisons was functionalism. Bramham's review of relevant research indicates (Bramham, 1980, Ch. 1) that the sociology of the institution has allowed little or no space for protest. Conflict has tended to be viewed as aberrant, dysfunctional or, in left-wing functionalist accounts, 'simply' as inevitable. The first empirical study of the prison community appears to have been conducted by Hans Reimer during the mid-1930s, when he spent three months in a state penitentiary and two weeks in a county jail, covertly carrying out an ethnographic study of these institutions. Reimer's study viewed disorder from the relatively stable and static position of order. He compared the prison community with a 'primitive' society, cut off from the outside world and in a state of delicate equilibrium, which violence from time to time threatened to destabilize (Reimer, 1937). 'Despite periodic eruptions, the "society of captives" tended to return to its delicate balance. It was, paradoxically, a highly static model in a society filled with conflict and contradictions' (Stastny and Tyrnauer, 1982, p. 131).

Weber's theory of bureaucracy has been drawn on to develop the analysis of formal versus informal aspects of life in prison. As Schrag observes, 'there frequently evolves a system of unofficial controls that may have little similarity to the original, rationally planned, official program' (Schrag, 1961, p. 320). Schrag also comments (Schrag, 1961, p. 322) on the logical and empirical defects of theories derived from Weber's theory of bureaucracy (Hartung and Floch, 1956; Sykes, 1958, Ch. 6; Martin, 1955; Ohlin, 1956, pp. 22–6; American Correctional Association, 1953; MacCormick, 1954; Fox, 1956; McGraw and McGraw, 1954).

Since 1978 in the US, the term 'complex enforcement' has been used to describe legal claims, usually by prisoners, beginning with *Holt* v. *Starver* in 1970, that entire prisons and prison systems violate the cruel and unusual punishment standard of the eighth amendment to the Constitution of the US. 'The central feature of the complex lawsuit is its systemic focus, reflected in both the target selected for legal criticism, a system thought to be wrongful, and the nature of the remedy imposed, a remedial plan wide ranging in scope and detail.' (Anon, 1981, p. 626). Similarly, conditions in British prisons were condemned as involving 'inhuman and degrading treatment' of prisoners, by the torture committee of the Council of Europe, after its visit to Leeds, Brixton and Wandsworth prisons in 1991. (*Guardian*, 13.12.91, p. 20)

In the quarter century between Reimer and Goffman, research into prisons in general, and riots in particular, tended to follow this pattern: where order presided, the status quo ruled, prisoners generally conformed, violence being viewed as disruption to the general homeostasis which prevailed. It was a perspective consistent with the dominance of functionalism over sociology during the period. Cressey notes how the critique of the functionalist explanation of prison happenings, in terms of events *within* the prison, was surfacing as Goffman was first producing for discussion in seminars the mimeographed essays on which his book *Asylums* was based ('Introduction' to Irwin, 1980, p. ix).

The Prison Over-conceptualized as a Closed System

With some notable exceptions (Jacobs, 1977; Jacobs, 1983, Ch. 3), sociological studies of the prison have exaggerated features which isolate it as a total institution cut off from society, and underplayed those which link it with society at large. Goffman's pioneering work based on a mental hospital in Washington DC may have contributed to this tendency (Goffman, 1961). Isolating what happens in prisons from external factors is associated with a tendency for some researchers to regard the prison as a relatively closed 'laboratory'. Inevitably, this severely constrains the usefulness of their research.

Jacobs' critique of dominant perspectives on prisoner subcultures counters this feature of the literature (Jacobs, 1983, Ch. 3). In Jacobs' classic study of a maximum security penitentiary for 2,000 prisoners, he describes four active gangs in the prison, demonstrating how they form an active part of the street gang scene of Chicago, to the extent that his informants emphasize how, if the gangs disappeared from the streets, they would also disappear from the prison (Jacobs, 1977). Research since the 1960s, notably the ethnographic tradition exemplified by Moore's study, demonstrates the need to revise Goffman's conceptualization of the prison as a total institution, largely isolated from society at large. As Moore puts it:

> Our view of prisoner adaptations (or the prisoner subculture, if this term is preferred) complements the tendency in recent criminological analysis to focus on prison as an inextricable part of the

social system, rather than as an isolated (if expensive) adjunct to the society that has impact only on the individual prisoner. We are interested in the valid but usually unavailable collective life experiences of men in prison.

(Moore, 1978, pp. 125–6)

Neglect of the Macro-sociology of Prison Riots

Macro-sociology contributes a perspective on the interplay between the prison, and disturbances in the prison, the way they are seen and responded to, and wider economic and social forces in society. Since the Second World War, the study of resistance by prisoners has advanced in the light of studies of prisoner-of-war camps and concentration camps.

Jacobs praises the virtues of two rare studies of the macro-sociology of the prison (Rusche and Kirchheimer, 1968; De Beaumont and De Tocqueville, 1979) but argues that, in the case of the former, there is an emphasis on material conditions at the expense of other factors, and, in the case of the latter, there is an omission of the impact of religious ideas on the history of penal policy and practice. Jacobs sets out to remedy also their neglect of the significance of the concentration camp and the prisoner-of-war camp, alongside other penal institutions (Jacobs, 1983, p. 20). He observes that 'the ways in which the concentration camps served the race ideology of National Socialism and the economic requirements of the German war economy demonstrate the bases for both slave labour and genocide' (Jacobs, 1983, p. 19).

Berkman's painstaking study of prisoners' protests within a California prison in the 1970s is a noteworthy exception to the neglect of the macro-sociology of the prison riot. His research fulfils his realization that:

In order to understand the forces which brought about the group form of politics it was necessary to understand the total political program out of which the group movement grew. In California, that included the challenges that prisoners raised concerning the system of labour within the prison, the system of individual and collective rights, and the ideology of the governing groups which supported these systems within the prison.

(Berkman, 1979, pp. ix–x)

There are striking parallels between the situation of the complaining prisoner in the British penal system, for example, and that of the concentration camp inmate, whose identity is denied. Prisoners who complained and who failed to make their allegations stick were prone immediately to be charged themselves with making false and malicious allegations against an officer (Cohen and Taylor, 1978).

The concentration camp research illustrates the most complete exclusion of the imprisoned from the rights of citizenship. It demonstrates the convergence of political, economic, and social circumstances that make it possible for a society to destroy its prisoners without contradicting law, public opinion, or political leadership.

(Jacobs, 1983, p. 20)

The neglect of the world beyond the total institution has been reinforced by a tendency to focus on prisoners rather than on prison staff. For many years, the singular lack of research into staff who guard prisoners significantly reflects their virtual invisibility to researchers and, perhaps, the assumption that 'prison guards are incompetent and psychologically, morally, and socially inferior' (Jacobs, 1983, pp. 133–4). There are good empirical grounds for examining the connections between staff and prisoner dissatisfactions, for instance associated with the outbreak of various forms of collective disturbances, involving not just prisoners but staff as well. On the contrary, research and official investigations of riots reinforce the public stereotype that they are 'brutal, racist and dim-witted'. The fact that guards in the US are the lowest paid security staff reflects their poor public image (Jacobs, 1983, p. 134). In many senses, the guard is closer to the inmate's world and social position than to that of senior administrative personnel:

The social distance between lower- and higher-level guards is reinforced by the paramilitary organization, whereby information originates below, but initiative and decisions come from above. Discipline parallels that of the military: the line officer is often scrutinized as closely as the inmate under his surveillance. Alleged trafficking in contraband is said to justify periodic shakedowns of the line officers. Lieutenants inspect both guards and inmates to see that they are working properly at an assignment. Just as guards are required to write tickets (disciplinary reports) on inmates' rule violations, so too do superiors, and sometimes inmates, compile reports on guards' infractions of the rules. The disciplinary board for guards is similar to the tribunal that hears inmate cases. Like the prisoners, rank-and-file officers and their unions have pressed, often successfully, for greater procedural and substantive rights in recent years.

> (Jacobs, 1983, p. 139)

The high turnover of staff is paralleled often by the high degree of absenteeism among them at any one time. The inquiry into the Jackson Prison riot in 1952 commented that in the year in which the riot occurred, as many as 40 per cent of the guards were suspended from duty for offences or suspected infractions of the discipline code during the course of the year (Special Committee to Study the Michigan Department of Corrections, 1953). As Jacobs puts it: 'Low prestige, poor pay, unpleasant working conditions, and strict discipline make prisons ripe for unionization' (Jacobs, 1983, p. 139). Despite these conditions, the fact that most guards identify strongly, and hierarchically, with their own senior staff and warden, tends to inhibit the development of even stronger bonds of a unionized kind, for example, within their own peer group or alongside inmates (Jacobs, 1983, p. 139).

The commonality between the overlapping and shared aspects of militaristic and macho staff and prisoner cultures is a significant contributory factor towards prison riots involving violent episodes and confrontational interaction between the authorities and the rioters.

In the 1970s, three main streams of influence directly and indirectly contributed to the growth of a more critical tradition in research into prisons. First, there was more of a climate of collective protest in many sectors of society in 'developed' countries, ranging from feminism to Martin Luther King, to education and anti Vietnam war-draft protests.

Second, there was the impact of what became known as the 'new criminology' and the 'new', that is Marxist, criminologists (Taylor, Walton and Young, 1973). Whereas the functionalist mainstream of research into the prison as an institution flowed between the US and Britain up to the 1970s, thereafter European critical thought regarding deviance and penology in the early 1970s touched on prison riots and protests in several European countries. Salierno's work illustrates the thinking of 'La Nuova Sinistra' and facilitates direct links between critical perspectives on society and penal policy and practice (Salierno, 1972). Beginning in Britain, the new criminologists grew out of the National Deviancy Conference and addressed issues of power in criminal justice. Although the new criminology left many questions unanswered, it did put on the agenda the links between criminal and penal policies and practices and the wider social and political context.

Third, there was a revival of critiques linking prisons with the changing conditions in the labour market. In the 1970s, when the US was acknowledged to have the highest incarceration rates and longest sentences in the 'Western world', critical commentators revived the work of Georg Rusche in the 1930s. Rusche proposed that prisons were less eligible institutions. They functioned as a means of social control. When society's surplus labour needed dumping, they provided living conditions just below those of the lowest working-class people (Rusche and Kirchheimer, 1968).

Since the late 1960s, prisons have been no less protected from challenge by critics and 'consumers' than other social institutions. The changing character, impact and significance of prison riots in the last quarter of the twentieth century can be viewed as one indicator of the crisis of legitimacy of prisons themselves in society. The significance of riots such as Attica in 1971 and Santa Fe in 1980 in the US, and Strangeways in Britain in 1990, is that the clock cannot be put back. They represent changes in the structure of relations between prisoners, staff, the media and society at large, and in the consciousness of issues concerning prisons and rioting, which are irreversible and have to be taken account of in projected penal policies and practices, even if for a time it seems they can be denied.

CONCLUSIONS

Research into what are termed 'total institutions' has contributed, whether accidentally or deliberately, to the impression that prisons are 'total institutions', which are cut off from, and therefore marginal to what happens in, society and that the riots which erupt in them from time to time are somehow peculiar to them. It is more accurate to suggest that prisons are central to society and that incidents in them are mirrored in other aspects of social policy and practice in the health, education, welfare and policing of people's lives.

Rioting as an aspect of protest by prisoners may be seen as a persistent, deep-seated form of resistance by consumers, clients, captives and residents in institutions as a consequence of social stratification and processes which are reflected in the way such institutions function. Researching prison riots involves trying to appreciate the character of resistance by prisoners, not only to their imprisonment, but to wider aspects of their circumstances in society.

But this poses a number of further tasks. In the first place, there is a need for an adequate description of rioting by prisoners, in the past and in the present, in the light of which some of the questions raised in this chapter may be examined further. Different periods in the history of prison riots may be viewed simply as representations of different perspectives on riots themselves. The next chapter examines this question of the different vantage points from which narratives of prison rioting may be constructed, in the light of the necessity to allow space for all participants in riots to be given due weight, and not just the voices of the authorities.

2 Narratives of Imprisonment and Rioting

> Reality is a question of perspective; the further you get from the past, the more concrete and plausible it seems – but as you approach the present, it inevitably seems more and more incredible.
>
> (Rushdie, 1982, p. 165)

MULTIPLE PERSPECTIVES ON NARRATIVES

This chapter locates narratives of histories of prison riots in the context of debates about different perspectives on penal strategies, policies and practices. It was noted in passing in Chapter 1 that the development of a great range of alternatives to imprisonment in the criminal justice systems of Western 'developed' countries does not reduce the centrality of prison in those societies. Cohen observes in a review of the role of prison in society that 'in more senses than the obvious one, the prison is the ultimate depository of changes that happen elsewhere' (Cohen, 1977, p. 217). He attributes to Rothman's study, 'which has revolutionized our thinking about the history of institutions' (Rothman, 1971), the insight 'not so much that such institutions might – as Goffman and others suggest – share common internal features, but that their roots are to be found in common external social developments and values' (Cohen, 1977, p. 217). Foucault dramatizes this image of the prison as a disciplining institution, by attempting to illustrate how it reappears in the hospital, the school, the asylum, the workhouse, the military academy and in industry, thus ensuring in all walks of life the docility of the individual (Foucault, 1977).

Rushdie's comment in the novel *Midnight's Children* which introduces this chapter is a reminder of the sensitive way he preserves as a problematic the so-called facts of the history of civil disturbances from which Indian Independence emerged (Rushdie, 1982). The immediate problem for the commentator on prison riots is that the images of riots which are inherited or not directly experienced have to be viewed as not 'essentially true', either in the past or in the present. Indeed, one person's actual experience of an incident, likely as not, will contradict that of another. Like the story of prisons itself, the history of prison riots can be told from more than one standpoint. There is no essentially 'correct' and 'complete' history of prison riots waiting to be discovered. That is, prison riots do not lie like natural objects, waiting to be discovered and described. They are socially constructed. Just as the definition of what constitutes a riot is likely to be contested, so the narrative of rioting, from the past to the present, with all its discontinuities, areas for controversy and different interpretations, 'needs to be "situated," "contextualized," and "problematized"' (Cohen, 1985, p. 10). Narratives on penal strategies are themselves unfinished. The lack of consensus between different versions of the history of rioting makes it necessary to attempt to minimize misrepresentation in accounts of them, including those which follow here below.

This chapter focuses in turn on the different vantage points from which narratives of prison and rioting history have been, and may be, constructed, and on ways of viewing phases or epochs of rioting over the past two centuries or so. The focus of analysis varies according to the version of prison history which is adopted. The history of prison riots is not understood here simply in terms of the impact on them of the repressive forces of the state. Some of the controlling and shaping systems, mechanisms and influences and processes operate on prisoners 'from above', some from outside the prison system and some 'from below' through the culture of prisoners themselves.

This dichotomy is the beginning rather than the end of the story. Histories of rioting are constructed in terms of further dimensions, each involving tensions between polarized accounts: first, there is the institutional versus the prisoners' version of history; second, there is the emphasis on events and factors internal versus those external to the prison. Berkman's instructive account of the prisoners' rights movement in the US spells out the dichotomy between an 'institutional history . . . conceptualized in terms of administrative and policy changes that molded the complexion of the institution' and the 'actual history' which achieves its richness 'by tracing the patterns of beliefs and activities of the clients – a historical phenomenon usually absent from institutional histories' (Berkman, 1979, p. 33). Berkman also notes that 'it is not always clear whether a particular change or event is the product of an external or an internal spark' (Berkman, 1979, p. 33).

Behind, within or beyond the surfaces of particular versions or accounts of specific riots, however the commentator chooses to regard or disregard them, are the perspectives from which the narratives are written. The narratives of prison riots need to be located in the context of the history of imprisonment itself. Some accounts of the history of imprisonment and rioting amount to a meta-narrative which overarches particular perspectives. This review of narratives shows how post-modernism has brought to sociology a scepticism of the construction of grand totalizing theories, as a mistaken, even misleading enterprise (Hutcheon, 1989). It shows how this critique confirms the impossibility of undertaking a 'final', that is complete, history of prison riots.

The impact of standing outside a view of the relative importance of issues which concentrates most of the significance in the organization and expression of the power of the state can be seen in the careful treatment by Young of the shifts towards criminalizing the militancy of the British suffragette movement (Young, 1990, pp. 142–62). In the process, Young successfully holds back from adopting uncritically a simple hypothesis of repression by the state (Foucault, 1980, pp. 200–1), and the exercise of domination through associated professions, concepts and theories (Foucault, 1978, pp. 9–12), holding onto the idea that 'resistance *is* implied in the operation of power' (Young, 1990, p. 151).

Rothman's brilliant, detailed analysis of the origins of the asylum in the Jacksonian period is the starting point for critical reflection on the revolutionary changes in the US which ensured that institutions for poor, insane and criminal people, which were places of last resort in the eighteenth century, within fifty years became the first resort (Rothman, 1971). An article by Ignatieff which postdates his own case study of the Quaker 'reforms' of the British prison at the turn of the eighteenth century (Ignatieff, 1978) not only casts a self-critical eye on the historical perspective he adopts in his book, but provides a useful framework in terms of which to locate his own history of prisons and those of other people. Ignatieff charts the challenging of liberal histories of imprisonment by different revisionist versions, challenged in their turn by counter-revisionist critics (Ignatieff, 1981).

Liberalism: Narratives of Reform

Until the 1970s, the history of imprisonment tended to be written from within the reformist tradition (see, for instance, Rose, 1961).

What are sometimes termed liberal criminological histories 'emphasized conscience as the motor of institutional change' (Ignatieff, 1981, p. 154). They made the assumption that prison regimes based on reform had to be better than those based on retribution. They concentrated on changes inside the prison as an institution, rather than making any connections with what was going on in the wider social context (Ignatieff, 1981, p. 154).

In the reformist analysis, prison history is the story of the uneven but generally forward march of progress, while prison riots tended to be viewed as occasional, aberrant and generally abnormal phenomena, as is the case with the case study of the Hull prison riot (Thomas and Pooley, 1980).

According to Cohen, Rothman's attempt to stand critically outside the reformist interpretation is only partially successful. His narrative amounts to flawed idealism in its 'implicit identification between the analyst and the historical reformers being analysed' (Cohen, 1985, p. 21). This, coming from Cohen, who in some writings could himself be described as a flawed idealist (Cohen, 1975), seems hyper-critical of Rothman, who, after all, asks at the outset:

> By what criterion is a penitentiary an improvement over the stocks or a system of fines and whippings? And does not the subsequent history of these institutions suggest that their origins cannot be understood a priori as advancements that men of goodwill must automatically support? To describe the asylum as a reform takes for granted precisely what ought to be the focus of investigation.
>
> (Rothman, 1971, p. xv)

The reformist narrative may be rhetorical in character. At any rate, it is likely to use the plight of the victim to make a documentary statement of behalf of the prisoner. Its ideology is likely to be presumptive on behalf of the prisoner rather than liberating. Hutcheon argues that it has parallels in revelatory arts with a message of social criticism. These include movements such as the 1930s social conscience photography, which has been described as arrogantly speaking for poor people, 'without urging them to change their own conditions' (Hutcheon, 1989, pp. 126–7). The exhortatory tone of this commentary by Hutcheon does not address the issue of how to empower powerless people. She accepts Rosher's comment that aesthetically and formalized information is passed on by the artist to the recipient addressed as socially powerful (Hutcheon, 1989, p. 27). This rings true in the penal field where there is a significant overlap between the constituent memberships of both the academic community commenting on penal strategies and the reforming groups which are campaigning for changes in them.

Revisionism: Narratives of Class Conflict and State Power

In the 1970s, liberal reformist histories were criticized and revised from various socialist and radical standpoints (for example, Melossi and Pavarini, 1977 (trans. in 1981); Ignatieff, 1978; Foucault, 1975, (trans. in 1977); Rothman, 1971). Within the ambit of revisionist commentaries of the 1970s, certain shared themes are discernible. For instance, revisionist histories of the growth of systems of incarcerating criminals in Britain and the US speak of change rather than progress and are often still more critical. They agree that changes in the concepts, policies and practices of imprisonment cannot be explained simply in terms of progressive enlightenment through humanitarian zeal:

> The reformer's critique of eighteenth century punishment flowed from a more or less ambitious conception of power, aiming for the first time at altering the criminal personality. This strategy of power could not be understood unless the history of the prison was incorporated into a history of the philosophy of authority and the exercise of class power in general.
>
> (Ignatieff, 1981, p. 156)

Irwin's study of the jail in the US represents it as part of a continuum of prisonizing facilities developed over the past two hundred years to contain what nineteenth-century writers called the 'rabble', the 'dangerous classes' and what he terms 'the underclass' (Irwin, 1985).

The contribution of revisionism has been to locate histories of imprisonment in the explanatory context of narratives of class conflict (Scull, 1977; Melossi and Pavarini, 1981), social control by the state (Foucault, 1987), or a combination of these (Ignatieff, 1978).

At an extreme, even well-documented and critical revisionist histories may tend towards depersonalized functionalism. Scull's account of the decarceration of criminal, delinquent and mentally ill people (Scull, 1977) has been criticized for its tendency to present the complex story of changes in mental health and criminal justice policy in Britain and the US as reductionist and determinist (Matthews, 1979, pp. 100–17).

Melossi and Pavarini present 'the most resolutely orthodox' (Cohen, 1985, p. 23) Marxist analysis. It binds the nature of the prison in a tight cause–effect equation between the changing nature of capitalism, modes of production, fiscal crises and the demand and supply of labour. Melossi and Pavarini reduce the complexities of the narrative to economically determined equations. It is a functionalist account in which the motives of participating people are 'more or less irrelevant or only of derivative status' (Cohen, 1985, p. 23).

Foucault's commentary on the history of imprisonment charts the impact of the vision of Jeremy Bentham on the way prisons were conceived and designed, from the early nineteenth century onwards. Foucault's commentary does not make any explicit references to prison riots, but his work illustrates how the design of prisons – their physical and social architecture – has been influenced by the fears of the authorities about potential disorder in prisons, fomented by that potentially destructive force – a mob of inmates.

Power is expressed in the prison through discipline. Foucault combines the concept of 'discipline' with Bentham's view of the Panopticon, so as to describe how panopticism serves the ends of discipline:

> The celebrated, transparent, circular cage, with its high tower, powerful and knowing, may have been for Bentham a project of a perfect disciplinary institution; but he also set out to show how one may 'unlock' the disciplines and get them to function in a diffused, multiple, polyvalent way throughout the whole social body. These disciplines, which the classical age had elaborated in specific, relatively enclosed places – barracks, schools, workshops – and whose total implementation had been imagined only at the limited and temporary scale of a plague-stricken town, Bentham dreamed of transforming into a network of mechanisms that would be everywhere and always alert, running through society without interruption in space or in time.
>
> (Foucault, 1982, pp. 208–9)

Bentham's dream, in the literal sense, never became widely adopted in the US. The only two prisons modelled on the Panopticon to a significant extent were Western State Penitentiary in Pittsburgh, opened in 1826 and redesigned within ten years, and the twentieth-century Stateville Prison in Illinois, from the design point of view 'one of the worst prisons in America (in that inmate gangs virtually run the place)' (Hawkins and Alpert, 1989, p. 38).

At the level of metaphor, though, Benthamite principles are powerfully and almost universally expressed in the attempts made from the early nineteenth century to the end of the twentieth century to achieve good order and discipline in the prison through its physical and social architecture. The disciplines are seen as 'techniques for making useful individuals' (Foucault, 1979, p. 211). Foucault does not use the term 'discipline' to mean either an institution or an apparatus. He defines it as 'a type of power, a modality for its exercise, comprising a whole set of instruments, techniques, procedures, levels of application, targets; it is a "physics" or an "anatomy" of power, a technology' (Foucault, 1982, p. 215).

The functions of prison staff can be inferred from Foucault's description of the supervisory activities of the police force in French society in the eighteenth century. They act as an intermediary network between the monarch and the lowest levels of the operation of power in society (Foucault, 1982, p. 215), since 'between these different, enclosed institutions of discipline (workshops, armies, schools) . . . extended an intermediary network, acting where they could not intervene, disciplining the non-disciplinary spaces; but it filled in the gaps, linked them together, guaranteed with its armed force an interstitial discipline and a meta-discipline' (Foucault, 1982, p. 215).

Foucault proposes that disciplinary mechanisms in the emerging conditions of the eighteenth and nineteenth centuries can cope with issues and problems outside the scope of their predecessor systems of power. His view of discipline is that:

> It arrests or regulates movements . . . it must also master all the forces that are formed from the very constitution of an organized multiplicity; it must neutralize the effects of counter-power that spring from them and which form a resistance to the power that wishes to dominate it: agitations, revolts, spontaneous organizations, coalitions – anything that may establish horizontal conjunctions.
>
> (Foucault, 1982, p. 219)

Thus, the Panopticon model of prison deals effectively with collective resistance by prisoners:

> The crowd, a compact mass, a locus of multiple exchanges, individualities merging together, a collective effect, is abolished and replaced by a collection of separate individualities. From the point

of view of the guardian, it is replaced by a multiplicity that can be numbered and supervised; from the point of view of the inmates, by a sequestered and observed solitude.

(Foucault, 1982, p. 201)

Foucault's work is couched in an unremitting scepticism of all humanitarian motives (Jones and Fowles, 1984, p. 45). He insists on power as inseparable from knowledge, as a vehicle for change at the materialist level of the relationship between capitalism and the nature of prisons and at the idealist level of concepts (Cohen, 1985, p. 25). There is in Foucault what Cohen refers to as a 'structuralist denial of human agency' (Cohen, 1985, p. 10).

Foucault's critique of liberal reformist histories of imprisonment in some ways illustrates Marxist functionalism (Cohen, 1985, p. 27) and in others moves beyond it. In his attempts to link changes in penal policy and practice to changes in capitalism, he is Marxist (Jones and Fowles, 1984, p. 44; Cohen, 1985, p. 27). But to the extent that his arguments take off into an idealist narrative, where the connection between ideas and events is frail or not even sustained, he is criticized as anti-historical (Jones and Fowles, 1984, p. 38). Where Foucault makes no attempt to reconcile his account with Marxism is at the junctures between capitalism and penal practice, where the prison becomes a micro-system with its own momentum, not driven by the nature of the capitalist system (Cohen, 1985, p. 27).

The centrality of power in Foucault's analysis combines with his view of the dominance of the disciplining activities of the authorities at different levels – the state and the institution, for example – to squeeze out the possibility of prisoners exercising their own determining muscle through rioting.

The revisionist narrative left scope for the examination of prison riots as part of the continuum of protests by prisoners (Fitzgerald, 1977). However, this was still in the context of riots being unusual and somewhat aberrant happenings, whose explanations needed to be seen in terms of the responses of prisoners to the ways they were disciplined by the prison and the state.

Narratives of Fragmentation of Oppressed Groups

In the wake of the collapse of the rehabilitative ideal, different penological philosophies were revisited in attempts to construct a new and acceptable positive penal philosophy as a basis for the practice of imprisonment.

Ignatieff (1981) uses the term counter-revisionism for narratives attempting to incorporate the experiences and the culture of prisoner rioters. Such accounts may be provisional and recognize the contested nature of the concepts to which they relate. Counter-revisionism is a tortuous label which implies, perhaps unfortunately, that revisionists got there first and but for them counter-revisionism would have nothing to say. The counter-revisionist contribution puts back at the centre of accounts of riots and debates about their origins the participants who have been there all along, but whom structural theories have tended to ignore or underrate. Counter-revisionism reflects a questioning of prevailing revisionist currents of prison riot history, which it is maintained undervalues the part played by prisoners in the outbreak of riots. The crucial contribution to this process is the experience of the parties, including the rioters, themselves. As a consequence 'we now get the histories (in the plural) of the losers as well as the winners, of the regional (and colonial) as well as the centrist, of the unsung many as well as the much sung few' (Hutcheon, 1990, p. 66). The term 'fragmentation' more appropriately distances this perspective from revisionism and prepares the way for us to reflect the realities of prison riots in the disparate and diverse settings provided by penal systems which lack a clearly articulated purpose in the post-rehabilitation period.

The 1980s saw growing unease at what were perceived as weaknesses in revisionist narratives of penal policy and practice. During the 1980s, there was a growing recognition of the need for an overhaul of 'strong state' (Corrigan and Leonard, 1978, Ch. 9), as well as Marxist conceptualizations not only of prisons and prison riots, but of deviance and the criminal justice system itself (Sumner, 1990, p. 41). The key to such reconceptualizations is the realization that the modern state does not determine what happens in the prison system. The relationship between the people in and around the system and those who administer and staff it is a contributory factor.

Thompson's commentary on food riots in eighteenth-century Britain criticizes the tendency for some accounts of riots towards economic reductionism and the swamping of the social history of events, thus squeezing out the contribution of the rioters themselves as self-conscious and self-activating rather than being portrayed simply as instinctively responding to economic stimuli (Thompson, 1971, pp. 76–8). Sumner goes some way towards this in the criminal justice field, by proposing that a balance is struck between the perception of criminal law and criminal justice systems either as 'purely class weapons or as "organized class terror" (Pashukanis, 1978, p. 178) . . .

or as resembling any simple "will of the people" (Chambliss, 1974)' (Sumner, 1990, p. 43). Instead, Sumner asserts that 'the criminal justice system will still always be right at the centre of the definition of the public. That breaks both ways: it means that the system defines and represents the public realm, its integrity, value and role, but also that the public defines and regulates criminal justice system' (Sumner, 1990, p. 42).

The prison riot is an apt illustration of an area of criminal justice policy and practice where different power blocs and interests interact. If we accept Sumner's comment that the modern criminal justice system is 'still an arena of contestation between unequal forces' (Sumner, 1990, p. 45), we still must acknowledge that the gains are not all on the side of the authorities. Mathiesen argues that the principle of the 'unfinished' involves protesting prisoners not declaring their reforming or revolutionary agenda too soon, lest they are outflanked by the authorities (Mathiesen, 1974). But they should not be too pessimistic. One outcome of the Strangeways riot of 1990, an overt display of bravado by rioters if ever there was one, was that the prison was scheduled for rebuilding at a cost of some £60m – an objective penal reform groups and prison staff themselves had failed to achieve for a century or more.

The fragmented narrative opens the way for the prison riot to be viewed, like the rest of the continuum of actions by prisoners, as part of the day-to-day practices of the prison institution. The task is formidable. 'The real challenge is to find a model of historical explanation which accounts for institutional change without imputing conspiratorial rationality to a ruling class, without reducing institutional development to a formless ad hoc adjustment to contingent crisis, and without assuming a hyper-idealist, all triumphant humanitarian crusade' (Ignatieff, 1981, p. 157). Sumner clarifies one implication of this statement, in denying the adequacy of saying that the policies and practices of criminal justice are either instruments of class domination or sites of struggles between competing class forces, preferring to say that:

> Because criminal justice is always an effect of, and participant in, fractured social relations of all kinds, and because social relations of all kinds overlap in practice, the class character of criminal justice, in all modes of production, is thoroughly intertwined with, and overdetermined by, its other social features; the exact picture varying with national, cultural and historic context.
>
> (Sumner, 1990, pp. 45–6)

The other essential component, of course, is that referred to above by Young – the contribution of the actions of rioting prisoners themselves.

Through the contribution of post-modernism, we see the influence of art and cultural studies, as critics of the 'totalizing theories' of 'grand designs' which centralize power in the analysis of institutions and resistance to them (Adams, 1991, pp. 19–20 and pp. 177–8). These downgrade the importance of the individual as the shaper of histories. There is a contradiction between proposing that the voices of the unheard are heard, and turning away from any recognizable voice or author/ess to a 'de-authored' plural reality. 'Postmodernism works both to underline and to undermine the notion of the coherent, self-sufficient subject as the source of meaning or action' (Hutcheon, 1990, p. 109).

The strength of the contribution of the post-modern in literature and history – the understanding of the past and the present – is partly its regard for the openness and for the lack of insistence on closure in the narrative. 'To challenge the impulse to totalize is to contest the entire notion of *continuity* in history and its writing' (Hutcheon, 1990, p. 66). Again, this offers the opportunity for 'something different from the unitary, closed, evolutionary narratives of historiography as we have traditionally known it' (Hutcheon, 1990, p. 66). At the same time, it both reflects and reinforces the fragmentation which is a feature of penal history and the history of prison riots from the 1970s. We shall see how some riots point up the case for attempting both to explore and then to transcend this fragmentation.

PERIODS OF IMPRISONMENT AND RIOTING

McKelvey's summary of the history of prisons and rioting is a rough and ready attempt to compartmentalize it into periods:

> American prisons have developed through a succession of fairly clearly defined eras, much like a great unfolding pageant, and the central theme has been the evolution of penological realism . . . Stocks, whipping posts, and grim gallows cluttered the background during the eighteenth-century prologue; the scenes of the first act, running through several decades of the nineteenth century, were staged in front of the massive walls of rival prisons; now in the second act the walls have been pushed aside, and we watch the officers and reformers debating before the open face of towering

cell blocks in which the figures of convicts can be seen crouching silently behind the bars; in the next era the convicts will file out onto the front stage and take a major part in the drama; finally, in an epilogue an individual convict will remain standing in center stage while keepers, teachers, doctors, psychologists, divines, and judges will make up a speechless background.

(McKelvey, 1968, p. 145)

Yet hindsight may lend a view of the flux of history, which imposes more continuity, order and meaning than the happenings themselves can sustain. It is difficult to describe the changes in prisons and rioting over time from a position outside the assumptions and ideologies of particular periods. The attempt to divide history into phases, eras or epochs is no more than a reflection of different perspectives on history, each of which highlights a particular facet of prisons and rioting, its description reflecting merely '"the state of the art" of sociological and historical explanation at the time' (Featherstone, 1991, p. 9). In the process of the narrative, hopefully, the 'raw materials are transformed, given "shape and form" – that is to say, meaning' (Hutcheon, 1989, p. 65).

An appreciation of the hesitance of post-modernists about 'grand narratives' should not prevent us from clarifying the major epochs in the history of rioting. The above review of different narratives emphasizes the requirement that the rioting prisoner as narrator be incorporated into the text. We need also to look behind the rioter and behind other participants and commentators and locate them in terms of their context. In short, we need not only to view what is produced but to gain insight into what forces produce the producers, just as previously we saw that the task was to describe not only what the penal reformer wrote, but what wrote the penal reformer.

As a way of bringing into relief the changing features of prison riots in Britain and the US throughout the history of imprisonment, they are categorized in terms of what are identified below as significant shifts in prison policy and practice. Clearly, this will be an attempt to paint complex realities with a very broad brush, which in the process will gloss over local differences and irregularities in a way which will seem to ignore them. But this is done in the interests of providing a framework for succeeding chapters. It is also being framed in a way which enables both the 'edges' of different periods to be blurred and the entire sequence of changes to be viewed as a cumulative process of transitions.

The rationale for imprisoning people has changed dramatically over the past two hundred years, though Murton makes the useful point that the changes have involved the sedimentation of additional ideological themes rather than the total replacement of former ones. Murton's analysis of the major transitions in penal philosophies over the past two centuries emphasizes throughout the dominance of the work ethic and reformation (Murton, 1979, pp. 9–10). Stastny and Tyrnauer's study of the US prison is more sophisticated. They set out a typology identifying four configurations of regime and power over the past two centuries. They divide the history of penology in the US into five periods: 1790–1830, the early American prisons typified by meditation and moral instruction; 1830–70, the Pennsylvania and Auburn systems characterized by judicial reprieve and probation and the use of religion and discipline in the solitary and silent systems; 1870–1900, the reformatories emphasizing the separation of younger and older offenders, vocational training and education and parole; 1900–40, industrial prisons based on inculcating habits of working; 1940–80, case-work prisons characterized by classification and the rehabilitation of prisoners (Stastny and Tyrnauer, 1982, p. xi). Clearly, the mid-1970s were a watershed in which changes were taking place, witnessed close at hand by these commentators. Looking back, it is possible to confirm *their* sense of fragmentation in the wake of the decline of the rehabilitative ideal and to locate that historical moment with greater certitude in relation to surrounding periods.

From the point of view of the narrative of prison riots, the first four periods of Stastny and Tyrnauer can be grouped together. They can be summarized in terms of the reformative philosophy and those of the beliefs in hard work, control and punishment which were inextricably entwined with it.

The eighteenth century Age of Reason produced utilitarian prison architecture and social relations, welded to the reformative philosophy of imprisonment. Through the nineteenth century, the reformative ideal became tarnished and was supplanted by custodial and management goals. 'Gradually this Utopian vision went sour; custodial and management goals transcended reformative ones; isolation did not work and came to be seen as inhumane; separation and classification broke down *within* the walls. The late-nineteenth century "seminaries of vice" became the "inmate subcultures" of today's closed prisons' (Cohen, 1977, p. 221).

During this period, the increasingly obvious ineffectiveness of penal institutions as reformers of prisoners did not lead to the dismantling of prison systems. On the contrary, some moved towards substitute purposes such as the cultivation of the work ethic and others simply became more punitive and controlling. During this period also, the established reformative philosophies may have been in decay and undermined but the institutional systems of imprisonment remained in place and, in Britain during the mid-nineteenth century and in the US in the early years of the twentieth century, actually underwent significant expansion, exemplified in the 'Big House' prisons of the US.

A second major historical change is noteworthy in the mid-years of the twentieth century, during which rehabilitation was adopted and maintained as a prominent ideal of imprisonment. After the Second World War, 'correctional institutions' began to replace 'prisons'. By the 1950s, most states in the US had replaced Big Houses with correctional institutions based on rehabilitative regimes. Medico-treatment percolated into prisons in Britain, where in the early 1960s several prisons began to involve prison officers in running therapeutic group-counselling for prisoners. A 'psychiatric prison' with a therapeutic regime designed like a mental hospital was opened at Grendon Underwood near Aylesbury.

A third major change involved the decay of the rehabilitative ideal and its lack of replacement in Britain and the US by another single identifiable penal philosophy. In fact, a diversity of expressed penal values and attempts to construct new philosophical rationales for imprisonment around, for example, notions that custody of itself can be inherently positive without being an agent of human change, is a feature of the post-rehabilitative prison system.

Irwin analyses the transition from the Big House of the US prison system through the rehabilitative prison of Period Three to its 'contemporary' successor in Period Four. Irwin's account of the Big House parallels Jacob's study of how the Chicago gangs, such as the Black Stone Rangers, Devil's Disciples and Vice Lords, into the prisons, where gangs and counter-gangs fought between themselves (Jacobs, 1977).

So far, we have deliberately not attempted to ascribe dates to these periods. This avoids the necessity to justify and defend a particular date against other possible choices. Some suggestions about landmarks or milestones in the respective histories of rioting in the US and Britain are, in any case, given in Chapters 3 and 4. At this stage, it will be sufficient to conclude this chapter by describing in more detail the key features of prison riots through these changes.

Traditional Riots

The riots of the nineteenth and early twentieth centuries more often than not were *ad hoc* mutinies by fugitive prisoners concerned with escaping their harsh conditions.

Riots Against Conditions and Consciousness-Raising Riots

The ethic of reformation, of control of the inner state of mind, had been exemplified in the Philadelphia system, focused on internal spiritual insight and rebirth. In the twentieth century, it was transformed into the belief in rehabilitation through control of the outer states of the body presaged in Auburn, focusing on change through external compliance.

Useem and Kimball (p. 9) divide the postwar years into an earlier period of confidence associated with the primacy of rehabilitation (1950–65) and a later period of conflict (1966–75) associated with the decline of rehabilitation as the basis for the prison regime. The problem with this description is that it makes it seem as though the earlier period was relatively free of prison riots, which was certainly not the case.

Berkamn divides the history of postwar prison movements in the US into phases. He distinguishes the early, pre-1960s period from the 1960s and early 1970s by reference to the degree of planning and the political direction of the prisoner movements. This is helpful. Riots by prisoners in this period of the growing dominance of rehabilitation fell into two categories: those which were primarily directed at an aspect of prison conditions *per se* and those which involved an element of consciousness-raising activity by prisoners. In fact, riots against prison conditions began to surface before the rehabilitative philosophy became dominant. They were transitional between the earlier period and this one. So, the riots of this second period tended at first to be directed against aspects of prison conditions and latterly more and more against the rehabilitative philosophy itself. Some of these riots involved 'total' confrontations between entire groups of prisoners and prison staff. A feature of the shift from traditional prison riots was the increased tendency for prisoners to articulate grievances. At first, conditions in the rehabilitative prisons were resisted, but not their penal and social context. Latterly, prisoners became more committed to taking collective action, with a consciousness-raising dimension.

The early 1970s saw in the wake of the exhaustion of the ideology of rehabilitation a decline in many aspects of penal systems in Western countries. In the US, a government report summarized the situation in these terms:

> An increasing number of persons confined in a rapidly deteriorating stock of prisons whose purpose was (and largely remains) uncertain . . . Tragic prison disorders have become relatively common events; judicial supervision of state prison facilities, a routine occurrence.
>
> (National Institute of Justice, 1981, p. 1)

Irwin describes how from the early 1960s in the US, and towards the end of that decade in Britain, 'the old social order with its cohesion and monotonous tranquility' (Irwin, 1980, p. 181) was confronted by prisoners who rioted collectively in growing consciousness of the links to be made between the oppressions they experienced and those of other oppressed groups in their own and third world societies.

The occurrence of riots in the rehabilitationist prison offers both staff and prisoners evidence for the ideology that prison creates the conditions for the contagion of further criminality and collective protest by prisoners.

Consciousness-raising riots of the 1960s have been contrasted with the earlier riots of the 1950s by Pallas and Barber. They chart the shift from the unplanned, spontaneous early incidents which only challenged abuses of power and not their source or its legitimacy, to the more organized 'revolutionary upheavals' of the later period (Pallas and Barber, 1973, p. 341).

The attack on the rehabilitative ethic was partly from the anti-treatment liberal lobby and partly from the 'back to justice' prisoners' rights movement. There was a convergence between radicalism and the New Right in the emphasis on just deserts and punishment.

Post-Rehabilitation Riots

The postwar years have witnessed a shift from outright confrontations between polarized staff and prisoner groups in the Big House institutions, to the more diffuse and fragmented politics of protest and rioting in the last quarter of the twentieth century.

Fragmentation was accentuated by penal policies which emphasized and enforced physical, behavioural and social divisions between prisoners. Cohen traces back to the nineteenth century the tendency of the prison system to isolate some prisoners viewed as particularly dangerous. Whereas in the nineteenth century, the assessment and classification of prisoners was used to further the reformation, through isolation, of the individual, in the twentieth century the impulse to classify led to the segregation of *groups* of prisoners. 'Rehabilitation and correction are believed to be possible only if the prison population is separated out into those who might benefit from such a regime, those who would impede such a regime, those who would be "bad risks"' (Cohen, 1977, p. 221).

In one sense, the post-rehabilitation period has seen the re-imposition of a number of fresh ideological tenets, infused with pathological assumptions. One of these is very much associated with justifying the isolation of so-called 'refractory' prisoners, including rioters and potential rioters. Associated with the security units, segregation units and control units which fragment prisons and prisoners in its wake, is the medical analogy that some prisoners need to be isolated, lest they infect others with their rebelliousness.

Psychotherapy, group and individual counselling, casework, psychiatrically-based treatments, psychological assessment and treatment programmes all were represented in prisons in the 1950s and 1960s. To some extent, these were relatively harmless in that they were found not to work very well, and in any case, because they were relatively expensive in custodial staff time and specialist professional resources, tended to be used on a very marginal basis in prison systems. In Britain, for example, only half a dozen prisons ever introduced group counselling and then only for a few prisoners as an adjunct to an essentially unchanged regime. Already by the end of the 1960s, Nokes suggests that this confirms the lack of commitment of the British Home Office actually to changing prisoners' behaviour (Nokes, 1967). It is equally possible, however, that it simply reflects the somewhat contradictory themes of respect for persons and personal change which are embedded together in the rehabilitative ideal. Only in Grendon Underwood prison near Aylesbury was there a sustained attempt to build an institutional regime around these medically inspired therapeutic concepts – a regime, incidentally, which has survived into the 1990s.

As medico-treatment approaches in general were undermined by research indicating their ineffectiveness as ways of reducing further criminal convictions, these 'softer' styles of treatment on the whole tended to disappear from prison systems in Britain and the US.

Behavioural control based on behaviourist psychology did not disappear, but survived the discrediting of medico-treatment models of rehabilitation, in both Britain and the US. Newer forms of behavioural control were sometimes associated with the use of drugs and sometimes with the total manipulation of regimes.

Cohen notes that behaviour therapy includes positive, operant or negative, aversion therapy, using such drugs as Anectine 'which induces pain and fear through sensations of dying or drowning' to modify sexual behaviour, chemotherapy such as hormone implants, chemical castration or psychosurgery, the use of drugs such as Prolixin 'which produces a zombie-like effect' to curb violent behaviour in prison, and in California, brain surgery, advocated 'in such institutions as the MPDU – the Maximum Psychiatric Diagnostic Unit – to reduce trouble-makers to a state referred to by the California Department of Corrections as "temporarily dormant"' (Cohen, 1977, p. 223).

It is in the total manipulation of regimes, based on behaviour modification, that the parallels between the Benthamite vision and behaviourist psychology are most apparent:

> The way in which the Panopticon replaced Christian redemption by materialist/behaviourist psychology is similar to the replacement of Freudianism (change through insight) by Behaviourism (change through external compliance). For both Bentham and Skinner, pleasure and pain are the driving forces to be manipulated by the environment; both have the same vision of a completely synchronized social system.
>
> (Cohen, 1977, p. 223)

Cohen's modern example of an operant conditioning regime 'in which torture and deprivation are the "negative reinforcements"' is Patuxent Institution, the 'total treatment facility' in Maryland for more than 400 prisoners, where 'the behaviour modification programme consists of promotion from filthy roach-infested punishment cells, through various levels of "reinforcement", up to the final luxury of TV and family picnics' (Cohen, 1977, p. 224).

To summarize this characteristically disparate commentary on the disparate and disjointed state of the post-rehabilitative prison, the ironic consequences of ordering the prison so as to segregate prisoners in small clusters include the risk that they are placed also in settings where riot conditions can foment. But the fragmentation that is a feature of post-rehabilitation riots illustrates the shift of prisoners' interests away from collective activity towards self-interest and individualism.

CONCLUSIONS

This review of different perspectives on narratives of imprisonment and rioting highlights the extent to which the perspective of the narrator interacts with the dominant penal philosophy of the day. No single narrative of the history of imprisonment can be relied on to tell the whole truth. Since every account is written from a vantage point, its theoretical perspective on history itself, as well as on the history of imprisonment and rioting, is necessarily partial. There will be some truth in every account, but certainly not all truths in any one account. Reformist, revisionist and fragmented narratives each produce histories which adopt different perspectives on the origins, nature and significance of rioting by prisoners. It is clear that changes in prisons need to be seen against the backcloth of the changing nature of rioting as a concept and as a happening. The construction of histories of the authorities, rioters and rioting are crucial to the task of describing and understanding prison riots. In the next two chapters, these histories in the US and Britain will be examined.

3 Prison Riots in the US

> Literally and metaphorically, prisons are houses of darkness: dark in their secretness; dark in their filth and overcrowding; dark in their policies, which are premised, at best, on blind ignorance and, at worst, on self-deception and deliberate cruelty; dark in their tenacious refusal to admit the light of law, the illumination of written rules prescribing the rights and duties of keepers and kept.
>
> (Orland, 1975, p. 141)

INTRODUCTION

The history of prison riots in the US falls into four main periods, each characterized by a prevalent form of riot. This is not to say that other kinds of riot did not occur in each period. In fact, the advent of a new form of riot should be seen as part of a cumulative process, which adds to, rather than replaces, existing forms of rioting. Thus, for example, riots against conditions continued after the early 1960s when some prisoners had begun also to protest about the ideology of rehabilitation.

Until 1929, prisoners resorted to riots largely as a traditional means of confronting or escaping from the rigours of the prison; from 1930 to the early 1950s riots were mainly protests against conditions within prisons; from the early 1950s to the mid-1970s increasing numbers of riots involved collective consciousness-raising among prisoners who often were making more broad-based protests, for instance against the ideology of rehabilitation itself; finally, from the mid-1970s until at least the early 1990s riots in the post-rehabilitation period took on a fragmented character.

From the eighteenth century to the end of the twentieth century, prisons for criminals and suspected criminals in the US remained a heterogeneous rather than a centralized, unified system. For example, the increasing numbers of new jails being built before the year 1900 supplemented rather than replaced many other means of curbing recalcitrant citizens. For example, major industries such as mining and the armed services maintained their own systems for dealing with criminals. It was not until 1895 that the Federal Government took on responsibilities for prisons formerly subcontracted out

46

to the states, and as late as 1905 only two federal prisons had been built – near Fort Leavenworth, Kansas, and at Atlanta, Georgia, both based on the Auburn system. In 1930, several acts of Congress gave the federal prison system the authority to establish the Bureau of Prisons and formulate and implement its policies. An 'individualized system of discipline, care and treatment' through 'an integrated Federal penal and correctional system' was thereby established (US Bureau of Prisons, 1949, p. 40). By the end of the Second World War, the federal prison system included 26 establishments, catering for all categories of offenders. Friedman's comment aptly applies to the entire period: 'The legal system is still a patchwork of power, a rug made of rags' (Friedman, 1973, p. 570). Many institutions have been created in the spirit of make-do and adapt, rather than being purpose-built. Thus, for the best part of a century, there have been several levels of administrative responsibility for different kinds of prison: federal prisons, prisons in the 50 States, those in the District of Columbia and the Commonwealth of Puerto Rico, and jails and other institutions in the 3047 counties. Each level of government operates independently of the other levels. Thus, the Federal Government does not directly control State prisons. The States usually are responsible for prisons and parole. Courts in counties usually control probation, but counties do not have jurisdiction over jails operated by cities and towns. Commonly adult and juvenile administrations have been separate, as institutional and community arrangements have been. Eighty per cent of the 121 000 people employed in corrections in 1965 were involved in custody (US President's Commission, 1967, p. 162).

TRADITIONAL RIOTS: BEFORE 1929

Traditional riots were simple, isolated *ad hoc* incidents, during which the motives of the rioters invariably remained unarticulated. The first recorded prison riot occurred in the US even before independence was declared in 1774 (Mahan, 1982, p. 65). There are records of riots and mass escapes at that time, in the improvised prison in the copper mine of Simnsbury, Connecticut (Teeters, 1953, p. 15).

In fact, imprisonment and prison riots are twin features of the history of the US. It is only a modest exaggeration to suggest that all major changes in penal policy and practice in the US have been predicated at least in part on the prevention of collective violence, including rioting, by prisoners. During the late eighteenth and early nineteenth centuries, most States shifted from virtual independence from institutions as a means of dealing with poor, mentally ill and criminal people, to great reliance on them (Rothman, 1971, p. xiii). Ironically,

> the prison, America's contribution to efforts to stem criminality, came into existence in the early nineteenth century under rather curious circumstances – as the result of efforts to lessen the harshness of capital and corporal punishment. The prison was thus viewed as a reform of the system. But almost since its inception, there have been ongoing attempts to reform the 'reform'.
>
> (Murton, 1979, p. 9)

The penitentiary had its roots in the religious and secular principles of penology espoused in the wake of the Enlightenment. These equated goodness and truth with reason. The punishment of the prisoner combined rehabilitation and deterrence. In the late eighteenth century, a movement began in Philadelphia, involving Quakers and people from puritanical religious backgrounds, which led to criminals being moved from the stocks and pillories into prison cells where it was hoped they would reflect on their misdeeds and thereby be spiritually improved (Erikson, 1966, p. 199).

Norval Morris notes that:

> The jail, the workhouse, the almshouse, the reformatory, and the convict ship all antedate the prison. The castle keep for the political personage out of favour or office and the church's cell for retreat and penance were part of the genesis of the prison, but they were established for different social classes and different political purposes.
>
> (Morris, 1974, p. 4)

He argues that although confinement in various institutions was known earlier, the prison was actually an invention of the Pennsylvanian Quakers of the US, in the last decade of the eighteenth century. The alleged evils of indiscriminately housing different groups of prisoners together were reported on in Pennsylvania in 1788 and led to the setting up of the Pennsylvanian system (Barnes, 1968, pp. 87–91).

The design of churches, cathedrals, factories and schools testifies to the use of architecture to convey social, religious and moral beliefs and values. Nowhere is this more clearly demonstrated than in discourse about the design of prisons, in the two centuries from Jeremy

Bentham onwards. Bentham, the originator of rationalist and utilitarian principles of prison design and operation, intended that the architectural features of the prison would determine that its regime would 'grind rogues honest'. His vision of the Panopticon was originally that of a factory, but later was adapted to provide, as the word suggests, an omnipresent, all-seeing and supervising, central presence and the guarantee of good order and discipline in the radial prison, with centrally-placed staff able to see down the entire length of, and height of, the cells ranked on each wing.

The impact of such utilitarian thinking about the penal code and practice on prison history in the US is less easy to determine, and according to official histories of prison architecture, played a secondary role in favour of 'reforms' by indigenous Quakers (US Bureau of Prisons, 1949, p. 20). More critical historians, such as Rothman, locate the rationale for harsh conditions, hard work, collective discipline and individual reform clearly in the utilitarian tradition (Rothman, 1971).

The penitentiary was the epitome of the total institution. Its walls were intended to isolate the prisoner from the world at large and its cells to protect the offender from the risks of others' criminality. In such a situation, the likelihood of collective protests by inmates was remote, since 'this society approximates an undifferentiated collection of persons unconnected with each other except for their presence within the same institutional construct. They are effectively barred from interacting or communicating or aggregating into groups' (Stastny and Tyrnauer, 1982, p. 13).

In 1790, a cell block was erected in the yard of the Walnut Street jail, based on the Norfolk system (McKelvey, 1968, p. 6). In this way, men convicted of felonies could be kept in solitary confinement. But overcrowding was so bad by 1815 that 'a series of riots compelled the authorities to consider measures of reform' (McKelvey, 1968, p. 7). At that time, legislation which changed Walnut Street from a county jail to a state penal institution led to ambiguities in its role, overcrowding and worsening circumstances for prisoners. 'Riots, mass escapes and deadly assaults on the keepers by the embittered convicts resulted from these wretched conditions' (Teeters and Shearer, 1957, p. 15).

At the turn of the eighteenth century, many states were revising their criminal codes. In particular, imprisonment was substituted for the death penalty for many offences. In Newgate, New York in 1796, Charlestown, Massachusetts and Baltimore, Maryland in 1804, and Windsor, Vermont in 1809, the Walnut Street jail was copied. But unfortunately these copies provided communal rooms rather than individual cells. Richmond penitentiary in 1800 was modelled on Ghent. The prisons of Frankfort, Kentucky in 1798 and Columbus, Ohio and Concord, New Hampshire in 1812 were not models of careful planning. Connecticut continued to use a former copper mine as its prison. Most remaining states which abolished corporal and capital punishment still used the county jails. For a period, Newgate prison in New York was run on Quaker lines but its governor resigned in 1803 when the state passed its industries to a private contractor. 'Serious overcrowding and the consequent disruption of industry and discipline rapidly converted all these prisons into riotous dens of iniquity and roused a wave of popular indignation that in turn prepared the way for a new era of prison reform' (McKelvey, 1968, p. 7).

The indignities and cruelty of the Auburn system, originally imported to the US from Europe, led finally to its abandonment. The exploitation of prisoners by labour contractors was attacked by reformers and labour unionists themselves, for their own distinctive reasons. 'Inmates worked together but under an unmitigated rule of silence, the breaking of which resulted in prompt and often cruel punishment. Rebellion smoldered in many prisons' (McKelvey, 1968, p. 7).

When purpose-built prisons began to emerge from the conjunction of religious and social ideas about reforming penal practice, the two major influences – the Quaker colonists in West Jersey and Pennsylvania and ideas and plans imported from Europe – were not powerful enough to extinguish in prisoners the motivation towards rebellion. But even prior to the establishment of the Auburn system, prison riots occurred in Maine and Massachusetts prisons 'and, in fact, almost everywhere, from the beginning of prisons in this country' (Teeters, 1953, p. 14).

But at first, the penitentiaries successfully enforced discipline. The virtual absence of collective prison riots from the early penitentiaries is unsurprising, considering the enforced segregation of each individual prisoner. The Pennsylvania reformers eagerly pursued John Howard's purpose of ensuring prisoners were induced to reform through solitary reflection and penitence. In 1829, the principle of separate confinement was embodied in the opening of the Eastern Penitentiary of Philadelphia, at Cherry Hill. When Charles Dickens encountered it in about 1842, he recoiled in horror:

Over the head and face of every prisoner who came into this melancholy house a black hood is drawn; and in this dark shroud, an emblem of the curtain dropped between him and the living world, he is led to his cell from which he never again comes forth, until his whole term of imprisonment has expired. He never hears of wife or children; home or friends; the life or death of a single creature. He sees the prison-officers but with that exception he never looks upon a human countenance or hears a human voice. He is a man buried alive; to be dug out in the slow round of years; and in the meantime deaf to everything but torturing anxieties and horrible despair.

(Dickens, 1906, pp. 155–6)

The penitentiary was born in England but implemented and developed most extensively in the US. The philosophy of the penitentiary involved 'a critical shift in the meaning of punishment: that persons should be sent to prison *for* punishment via penal discipline rather than just sentenced *as* punishment for a crime committed. It was then a small, logical step to the concept of indeterminate sentences' (Hawkins and Alpert, 1989, p. 39). At the same time, the principle of classification of the offender on the basis of detailed case studies of background and behaviour in the ideal setting would determine the precise nature of the prescription for reform. The purpose of the solitary and separate confinement exemplified in the Pennsylvania system was reformative, that it would encourage reflection and reformation. Prison labour, also, was valued so that prisoners could be turned from idleness and crime towards the habit of hard work and the prospect of employment through a useful trade. The Pennsylvania system was imitated in Pentonville prison in London, opened in 1842.

The Auburn system was a regime which originated in the Pennsylvania system, but developed a distinctive character based on daytime congregate work, buttressed by rigidly enforced rules of silence and lack of eye contact whenever prisoners were outside their cells. The Auburn system became more popular than the Pennsylvania system in the US, partly because workshop-based industries proved more profitable than cell-based work and the building of 'Auburn' prisons was less expensive than 'Pennsylvania' prisons.

Sing Sing prison was the archetype of Auburn-style architecture, consisting of five tiers of internal cells ranked in long dark corridors, which, as in the third Western Penitentiary of Pennsylvania opened in 1892, with their factory-like external facades flanking the gatehouses to the prison, often became substitutes for the prison wall itself and have been described as 'the curse of prison construction for the following century' (US Bureau of Prisons, 1949, p. 32).

In the Walnut Street jail, the Pennsylvania system, and later the Auburn system, were first worked out. Later, these were much copied in Europe and the US. The Pennsylvanian design was based on cellblocks radiating out from a centre, derived from Ghent prison. The Auburn design was based on the rectangular cellblocks of the hospital of Saint Michael in Rome. The only notable architectural change in the design of prisons in the following century was the introduction in 1898 of the 'telephone-pole' layout of cellblocks along a central corridor in Fresnes, France. This was adopted in the US by the end of the Second World War as 'the basis of the most modern and satisfactory prison structures of our day' (US Bureau of Prisons, 1949, p. 25) in institutions later to be disrupted by major riots, such as the Rikke Island prison of New York City.

Walnut Street had facilities for only sixteen cells for individual prisoners. The rest followed the dominant trend until well into the nineteenth century of housing prisoners in communal rooms and dormitories, so much so that many of the early prisons were known as 'Newgates' after their infamous English counterpart (US Bureau of Prisons, 1949, p. 26). Thus, the first New Jersey state prison at Trenton was congregate on its opening in 1799, its first individual cellblock was not built until 1820 and complete cellular confinement was not established until 1836, when the new state penitentiary was opened at Trenton.

Despite the energetic debates at the time between rival advocates of the congregate system of New York and the solitary system of Pennsylvania, they shared a preoccupation with ensuring the complete isolation of prisoners from each other. While in Cherry Hill prisoners stayed totally apart, in the Auburn system they worked together but in total silence. In Auburn, rioting was practically impossible, as was observed at the time, since:

[Prisoners] are united, but no moral connection exists among them. They see without knowing each other. They are in society without any intercourse; there exists between them neither aversion nor sympathy. The criminal, who contemplates a project of

escape, or an attempt against the life of his keepers, does not know in which of his companions he may expect to find assistance.
(De Beaumont and De Tocqueville, 1979, p. 58)

It is ironic that the Auburn system became the dominant prison design in most state prisons and many federal prisons in the US, despite the fact that the Auburn system and the penitentiary movement were judged failures before the end of the nineteenth century (Hawkins and Alpert, 1989, p. 46). Between 1830 and 1930, the authorities became obsessed with prison security. They improved and refined the construction of the Auburn-style prison to reduce as far as possible the risk of prisoners escaping.

In 1835 a Committee reported that prisoners had been kept in darkened cells on bread and water for as long as forty-two days and had been brought out delirious; they had been ducked in ice-cold water; they had been deprived of food for three days on end or of their main meal in the day for three weeks; with their arms and legs strapped and wearing handcuffs they had been placed in the 'mad chair', a box made of planks in which it was impossible to move; strait-jackets had been laced so tightly that when released the men's necks were black with congealed blood; gags of wire and chain had cut men's mouths and tongues open; their hands in leather gloves had been drawn so tightly up behind their backs to chains round their necks that some prisoners had been strangled.
(Hibbert, 1966, p. 169)

In 1912, a former prisoner at San Quentin recorded that a similar strait-jacket was still in use: 'a piece of canvas about four and a half feet long, cut to fit about the human body. When spread out on the floor it has the same shape as the top of a coffin, broad near the end for the shoulders and tapering either way. Big brass eyelets run down the sides. It is manufactured in various sizes, and is designed solely as an instrument of torture' (Hibbert, 1966, p. 193). Even after prisoners had been asphyxiated in it, the rules governing the strait-jacket were modified rather than its use abandoned, with prisoners being released for a brief respite every six hours before being laced up again.

Subsequently, the efforts of the authorities to enforce the rules of isolation and silence led to the use of punishments as vicious as those outlawed by reformers half a century earlier. 'Men and women were flogged for offences no more serious than looking up when they should have had their eyes fixed on their work' (Hibbert, 1966, p. 181). 'The whip became common in Auburn, Charleston, and Wethersfield; Pennsylvania used the iron gag; Maine preferred the cold shower' (Orland, 1975, p. 27).

In the eighteenth and early nineteenth centuries, a paternalistic view of slaves had maintained them as developmentally equivalent to children. After about 1830, the social inferiority of black people could no longer be taken for granted. The economy of slavery shifted from its location in relation to primarily domestic labour to a model more appropriate to the expanding base for agricultural and industrial production. Darwinist theories and Lombrosian criminology converged to redefine the position of black people in terms of evolutionary inferiority. Franklin provides evidence that this inferiority was also considered to be constitutional. That is, 'negroes' were assumed to be a subspecies of humanity (Franklin, 1982, p. 8).

As the 'fugitive slave' literature challenged the basis of slavery, so did the fictional adventures of the escaping black convict. In the US, 1850 saw the passing of the Fugitive Slave Act. If the setting for the drama of the fugitive slave was the black communities of the southern states, the audience for their stories and mythologies was white and cultured members of the northern states (Franklin, 1982, p. 6).

The slavery of the black prisoner was central to the US narrative of resistance to prisons. Slaves tended to be invisible up to a point in the US, and even more so in Britain. The 'slave' narrative of the prison was at its zenith in the US before the Civil War, paralleled in the writing of Nathaniel Hawthorne, Poe and Fenimore Cooper (Franklin, 1982, p. 4). It was blatantly racist. It downgraded the aspirations of black people. To the extent that it was taken for granted, it was corroborated in the nineteenth century by Lombrosian and a century later by Eysenckian criminology.

Lincoln's proclamation during the American Civil War that slaves were to be emancipated took effect from 31 December 1862 and marked the end of one struggle but the beginning of another – for equality, freedom from segregation and discrimination and for social justice in society. After the Thirteenth Amendment to the United States Constitution abolished slavery, prisoners may have remained to fill the gap left by this change. Perhaps prisoners provided a cheap source of labour on farms, railroads and publicly funded utilities such as mines, rivers and roads. At any rate, the case of *Ruffin* v. *Common-*

wealth explicitly recognized that prisoners were 'slaves of the state' (Martin and Eckland-Olson, 1987, p. 5). Most traditional riots were adjuncts to the flight from such slavery.

From the late 1860s, the Irish and Elmira systems were introduced in the US increasingly, as the progressive successors to the widely criticized Auburn and Pennsylvania systems (Barnes, 1968, p. 400). Thus, remission for good behaviour, staging and parole began to spread in the US.

By 1870, the penitentiary system was overdue for reform. It was realized that as reforming agents penitentiaries were failures. They had long lapsed into a custodial habit, increasingly punitive and constrained by lack of money to run them efficiently (Hawkins and Alpert, 1989, p. 48). Prison systems in search of a mode of operation which was above reproach increasingly adopted the military style of management (Hawkins and Alpert, 1989, p. 50). The new reformatories which began to be built in the US from 1876 offered jobs to many former Unionist and Confederate veterans. The convergence of militarism and prison management provided the rationale for the Draconian responses to rioting soon to be adopted as logical and natural by federal and state authorities alike.

If reforming efforts in the US aimed partly to replace the disorder of early custodial measures with the rationally ordered repression of more efficient, reformed and reforming prisons, they were unsuccessful. Prison riots continued to be as much a feature of the new prisons as they were of their antecedents. Even as early as 1815 Massachusetts prison guards 'were exhorted to think of the prison as a volcano filled with burning lava, which, if not restrained, would destroy both friends and foes' (Teeters and Shearer, 1957, pp. 228–9). The Auburn prison riot of 19 January 1857 ended peacefully when the authorities gave in to the demands of the prisoners (Fox, 1956, p. 46). After the riot in Ludlow Street jail, New York, in April 1895, Sheriff Tamsen said that inmates rioted when he locked up the Horse Market Gang (Fox, 1956, p. 43).

After the industrial depression of the 1890s, restrictive labour laws in Pennsylvania culminating in the Muelbronner Act (1897), largely brought about by pressure from the labour unions, led to a dramatic decline in numbers of prisoners working productively. By 1915, efforts were being made by prison staff to introduce arts and handicrafts as a productive alternative (Teeters and Shearer, 1957, p. 149). But simultaneously they were arming themselves to deal summarily and violently with collective disorder.

Prison discipline seemed to be within reach of its goal in 1900. 'Major prisons in all parts of the North were turning to the methods of the reformatory; even in the South and the West the omens were propitious. The system seemed on the verge of attaining the destiny so hopefully mapped out by the inspired leaders of 1870' (McKelvey, 1968, p. 225). But demographic and industrial changes combined with a mood of intransigence among staff close to complacency (McKelvey, 1968, p. 227). The end of the nineteenth century and the early decades of the twentieth witnessed widespread industrial turmoil, culminating in the National Labour Relations Act of 1935 which guaranteed the right to unionize and stated that it was an 'unfair labour practice' to interfere with this right. In the 1930s also, the New Deal introduced attempts to counter the worst impact of the Great Crash of 1929, through introducing safety nets of welfare, unemployment, insurance, old-age pensions and public housing (Friedman, 1973, p. 575).

However, the abandonment of the rules of silence 'greatly simplified the job of discipline in one respect but opened the way for favouritism and intrigue and encouraged the development of espionage' (McKelvey, 1968, p. 163). Undoubtedly, some of these reforms, tokenistic though they were, served to release some of the pent-up frustrations of prisoners in the form of protests. Often, the authorities abolished harsh disciplinary measures only to find them continuing informally.

> A few years after New York abolished corporal punishment in prison an investigation at Clinton revealed the frequent use of paddling, tying up by the wrists so that the toes barely touched the floor, confinement in dark cells, and the like. Warden Howard was dismissed in Indiana when evidence leaked out proving that he had made frequent and sometimes cruel use of the 'cat' although it had been abolished six years earlier. When Ohio prohibited the lash and the 'shower bath,' the authorities invented the 'humming bird,' a device for administering electric shocks, which was even more fearful than the former tortures. The correct punishment was not, in fact, a simple matter to be determined by a legislative majority. Thus, it frequently happened that riots and fires broke out, and old grudges were settled in bloody frays in which officers were sometimes killed when the prisoners learned of the abolition of punishments they had feared.
>
> (McKelvey, 1968, p. 163)

Hostage-taking was not a noteworthy feature of prison riots until the twentieth century, though barricades reminiscent of the Civil War were used in the Plattsburgh riot in New York in 1907, when the authorities broke down the barricade built by 300 prisoners using guns and water-hoses (Garson, 1972, p. 412). Most incidents, like the revolt at Rahway reformatory in 1907 (*New York Times*, 2 December 1907, p. 7:6), the uprising at New Jersey reformatory in 1909 (*New York Times*, 26 October 1909, p. 7:6) or the mutiny in which two prisoners were shot at Bushy Mountain mines, Tennessee state prison in 1911 (*New York Times*, 2 October 1911, p. 7:6), were more straightforward confrontations.

In the Southern states, the old contract system combined with racism to ensure the continued oppression of black prisoners (McKelvey, 1968, p. 224):

> The prisoners were, in fact, gaining a voice in their control, they wrote as never before, describing the corruption and the horrors that still remained, but especially the stupid 'slouching about their sterile tasks' that had become the prime factor of the prison environment . . . The silent opinion of the mass of the convicts was even more influential, forcing the authorities to admit practically all prisoners to the top grade and its privileges, inducing the parole boards to release men automatically at the end of their minimum sentences, and encouraging the officers to develop a more lenient discipline. But this mass opinion was not always silent, and for the first time in the age of penitentiaries a wave of prison riots broke the monotonous routine.
>
> (McKelvey, 1968, p. 227)

Optimism informed by hindsight, leads McKelvey to comment:

> More than ever before the wardens had to bid for the confidence and co-operation of their prisoners. The experiments with self-government that were to gain so much notoriety at the end of the period were not the sorts of prison development they were sometimes considered to be, but the result of a union between idealistic officers and the upsurging desire of the mass of the criminals for more tolerable conditions. The prison populations had acquired a new character, whether as a result of changing social conditions outside or because of the disappearance of the Auburn restraints, and this new character played its part in the development of the

modern prison customs under which almost everything but violence is tolerated.

(McKelvey, 1968, p. 227)

In 1912, 350 prisoners lynched a black prisoner in Wyoming State
Prison, this being the prelude for the escape of 20 prisoners and the
death of three guards (Garson, 1972, p. 412). This was not an isolated
occurrence. In April of that year, prisoners in three departments of
Sing Sing prison went on strike (*New York Times*, 25 April 1912,
p. 10:6). In June, a food riot broke out at San Quentin prison,
California (*New York Times*, 10 June 1912, p. 20:4) and three months
later the National Guard was called in to suppress a riot at Jackson
prison, Michigan (*New York Times*, 4 September 1912, p. 1:2).

The somewhat discontinuous history of prison riots to a degree
reflects the fact that the authorities have traditionally viewed them
from the vantage point of the light they cast on management and
practice in the prison, either playing them up or down accordingly.
Sometimes it may have paid to emphasize the seriousness of damage
done by prisoners, where the implication for management was not
negative. More often though, incidents were played down, or where
possible, not reported. Thus, Warden Clancy called the $150 000
damage caused by the Sing Sing prison riot of July 1913 'a trivial
affair' (Fox, 1956, p. 44) even though the fire destroyed four buildings (Garson, 1972, p. 413).

Sometimes a change of warden, and therefore a change of management style, usually in the direction of tightening up, brought
about rioting. Thus, there was speculation that the 1914 prison riot at
Blackwell's Island, New York City, was caused by a loss of drugs after
a new warden tightened up on trafficking (Fox, 1956, p. 45). In the
spring of 1914 another riot at Sing Sing followed staff changes, and in
July the prisoners at Trenton State Prison mutinied and attacked the
keeper (*New York Times*, 14 July 1914, p. 5:1).

The military model of management and practice outlasted other
more precarious rationales for imprisonment, such as the betterment
of prisoners (Street, Vinter and Perrow, 1966). One consequence was
the restriction of the guards' roles largely to custodial activities. The
fact that guards became an armed force, often totally cut off from
informal interaction with prisoners, made more likely a harsh and
immediate reflex response to prison riots. Whether or not the outbreak of the First World War emphasized this trend, in November
1915 the prison farm at Milledgeville was issued with a machine gun

and the warden was ordered to use it if any attempts were made to remove prisoners (*New York Times*, 11 November 1915, p. 9:5). Earlier that year, on 2 July 1915, a riot had accompanied the transfer of 79 prisoners to Auburn (Fox, 1956, p. 44) and prisoners in the Bronx county jail had rioted when their water supply was cut off (*New York Times*, 12 September 1915, II, p. 12:5).

Unsurprisingly, given the way prison managements were armed and oriented towards 'first strike' tactics, the authorities often suppressed such riots with great violence. Deaths among prisoners were an increasingly common outcome of incidents throughout the history of traditional prison riots in the US. 'Most of the riots that occurred between 1865 and 1913 involved escape attempts and often resulted in the death of one or two prisoners' (Garson, 1972, p. 412). Prisoners rioted in New York City's Bronx county jail in 1916 over the curtailment of visiting privileges (*New York Times*, 3 April 1916, p. 8:5) and the following year black prisoners mutinied at Cook county jail, Illinois (*New York Times*, 4 July 1917, p. 5:2), but the riot a month earlier in 1917 at Joliet penitentiary, Illinois (*New York Times*, 6 June 1917, p. 7:1) involved 900 prisoners rioting in response to what they saw as more restrictive prison rules (Fox, 1956, p. 45). 'As prisoners set fires and attacked firemen, the warden called in troops. The inmates were driven back with bayonets, and one was clubbed to death' (Garson, 1972, p. 413). Four hundred prisoners refused to go back into their cells in a mass revolt at Clinton prison in June 1919 (*New York Times*, 17 June 1919, p. 19:5). That same year, the military prisoners at Leavenworth went on strike (Fox, 1956, p. 45). The announcement of proposals for reform to the system of military imprisonment (*New York Times*, 23 July 1919, p. 10:3) was followed a few months later by a further strike of about 1800 men (Fox, 1956, p. 46). Later in the summer, a prisoner was shot dead (*New York Times*, 5 August 1919, p. 32:1) during a disturbance in a Connecticut shirt factory at the state prison (Fox, 1956, p. 46).

The relative quietude of the immediate postwar period was not reflected in punishments meted out to rioters. The rioting at Banner coal-mining camp in the autumn of 1923 led to seventeen prisoners being flogged (*New York Times*, 19 September 1923, p. 3:5). 1927 was a bleak year for violence in prison riots. The riot in June of that year in the Kansas mine followed the refusal of the warden to allow prisoners to have cigarettes (Fox, 1956, p. 46). A prison riot in Illinois on 13 June of that same year was associated with an attempt by four prisoners to storm the gate and escape. One of the bloodiest battles of the 1920s between prisoners and the authorities occurred when the riot in Folsom jail in November 1927 was quelled with tanks and National Guardsmen, at a cost of the deaths of nine prisoners and two guards, with 31 prisoners and three guards seriously injured (Fox, 1956, p. 47).

In the criminal justice and prison systems, the tensions between decentralized diversity and local control and centralized uniformity have been continuing threads through the culture of penal policy and practice in the US into the twentieth century. Prohibition may not have stopped people drinking from 1919 to 1933. But it brought about significant changes in the criminal justice system. It filled to overflowing the federal courts and federal jails (Friedman, 1973, p. 568). It encouraged the growth of federal responses to policing, for instance, in an increasingly urbanized world grown smaller through improved road, rail and air communication. In absolute terms, state and local government budgets continued to grow. They paid for roads, schools and the local welfare system. But in relative terms, the federal system grew more important, taking over areas of education, interstate highways and institutional building, including the growing number of federal prisons.

Despite the reforms of the late nineteenth century, conditions in most prisons in the US remained squalid. In 1924, almost three-quarters of the prisons in Georgia were filthy, with no running water and no separate accommodation for prisoners with contagious diseases (Hibbert, 1966, p. 172). Increasing overcrowding made these conditions worse.

RIOTS AGAINST CONDITIONS: 1929 TO EARLY 1950S

In 1929–30, some of the more corrupt, filthy, overcrowded and unruly prisons of the US provided the touchpaper for the first explosive wave of prison riots which swept across the country at the time of the great stock market crash.

Prison architecture displays a central irony of prison history: the retention of the physical structure of the penitentiary and the reformatory, long after the discrediting of their concepts. 'This "edifice complex", a basic acceptance of large prisons in spite of their history of failure, resulted in the construction of twenty-seven Big House prisons after 1900' (Hawkins and Alpert, 1989, p. 54). The design of correctional facilities in the US exhibit two characteristics: expensive

investment in ever-more futile materials and technologies for the
control of prisoners and, often equally expensive, attempts to extend,
repair and restyle existing obsolescent buildings. The consequence
was that by the end of the Second World War, over a third of the
prisons in the US were more than 70 years old and only 17 had been
built since 1900 (US Bureau of Prisons, 1949, p. 37). At the end of the
1980s, 61 prisons in the US, built before 1900 and housing half the
100 000 prisoners who were in maximum security, were still in use
(Hawkins and Alpert, 1989, p. 54).

The fortress prison was the apotheosis of the paramount priority
attached to prison security after the 1930s. A number of such prisons
were built, with cellblocks which were designed to be as far as possible
tool-resistant. Fortress prisons soon attracted critics on account of
their huge size, enormous cost and above all the consequences for
staff working in them, their worst feature, allegedly, being:

> . . . the effect on the mentality of the warden, who inevitably
> becomes the commander of a fortress – the 'captain of the guard'
> – concerned mainly with counting and locking inmates, with little
> time or regard for his primary duty of seeking to reform offenders.
> Either by original planning or by subsequent additions, these ab-
> surdly secure and expensive prisons also came to be increasingly
> larger, but usually were just as promptly overcrowded.
>
> (US Bureau of Prisons, 1949, p. 33)

After 1945 in the US there was no national policy regarding the use
of prisons *vis-à-vis* incarceration and its alternatives, the nature of
prisons, their administration, ways of working and standards of operation. The federal nature of the US made it inevitable that different
states would respond differently to the policing of crime, sentencing
and imprisonment of criminals. This fact was complicated by the
existence of the federal system of imprisonment, administered by
Congress, whose policies and practices interacted with the various
state systems of imprisonment.

Between 1923 and 1940, the average annual population of 150
state and federal prisons increased from 84 761 to 191 776 (Hibbert,
1966, p. 172). In the era of prohibition, the Mafia and other gangs
ruled many towns, corruption flourished. An account of life in San
Quentin, corroborated as typical of many other prisons, indicates that
in the 1930s, poor prisoners suffered while 'apart from being able to
live a life of comparative ease in prisons such as this, drinking, smok-
ing, buying the bodies of young prisoners, and even apparently of

women brought in and out by the guards, rich and influential criminals could continue to exercise their power over warders whose positions rested upon political favours' (Hibbert, 1966, p. 198).

As late as the 1940s, it was still estimated that while in California
guards were recruited for the prison service on merit, 'elsewhere the
evil of politics is still evident and still operating in the selection of
candidates. In 1947 it was estimated that three quarters of the country's thirteen thousand prison guards had been "selected unscientifi-
cally"' (Hibbert, 1966, p. 419).

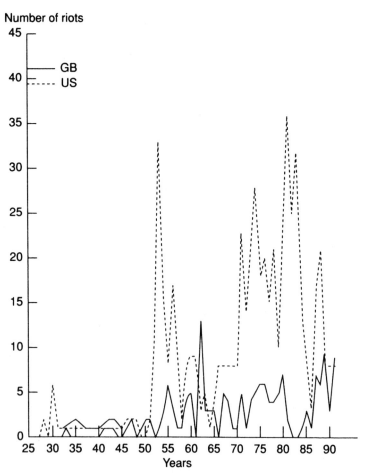

Figure 3.1   Incidence of prison riots in Britain and the US, 1925–90 (based
on newspaper and official reports).

First Wave of Riots: 1929

The first recorded wave of prison riots swept the US during 1929 (see Figure 3.1). It began on 22 July with the riot at Clinton prison, Dannemora, New York, continued with Auburn on 28 July, Leavenworth on 11 August, Colorado on 3–4 October and the further riot at Auburn on 11 December 1929 which was the occasion for extensive coverage in the *New York Times* (12 December 1929, pp. 1–3). Fox makes general reference to these incidents, listing Holmsburg which does not get major coverage in the *New York Times* (Fox, 1956, pp. 48–50), but omits mention of the series of minor riots which escalated in August of that year, including incidents when five prisoners escaped in a riot at Alabama state prison on 2 August, and 100 prisoners at the State Narcotic Hospital, Spadra, California, revolted and 16 escaped.

The initial riot, at Clinton, appears to have been suppressed by state troopers at a cost of three lives (*New York Times*, 12 December 1929, p. 3:5). Auburn, where the next disturbance occurred, opened in 1817 and was the oldest prison in New York State. With a cell capacity of 1,226, by July 1929 it housed 500 prisoners in excess of this figure. Conditions were described as atrocious (*New York Times*, 12 December 1929, p. 3:5). The first riot there on 28 July led to four guards being shot, two prisoners being killed and two escaping. On 11 December, renewed rioting at Auburn led to the deaths of eight prisoners and the chief keeper. The riot at Leavenworth prison, Kansas was reportedly the fifth in its history. It erupted in the mess hall after lunch and involved all the 3,758 prisoners. The warden ordered the guards to shoot at once, one prisoner being killed and several wounded when it was quelled by machine-gun fire. In the two-day Colorado state prison mutiny by 150 prisoners, three guards were killed outright and four others taken as hostages and killed before cell walls were demolished with dynamite. At first the explosive had no result, but then with successive blasts of explosive the prisoners were driven back to their cells, five of them being killed in the process. On 21 April 1930, the greatest loss of life occurred in a prison riot in the US. Two thousand prisoners in Ohio State Penitentiary were loose in the exercise yard and in the associated burning of prison buildings, staff refused to unlock the cells, so 317 prisoners were reported to have died (Fox, 1956, p. 22).

Investigations into these riots indicated a groundswell of discontent among prisoners about prison conditions and led to the reorganization of the US federal prison system and the establishment of a new Bureau of Prisons (Wilson and Barnes, 1952, p. 138). In the year of these riots, attention was drawn in a prisons and reformatories handbook to three suggested causes: over-long sentences, changes in a New York law regarding earning 'good time', and sparing use of parole authority (*Handbook of American Prisons and Reformatories*, 1929, quoted in *New York Times*, 24 November 1929, p. 16:1). But conditions in prisons did not improve enough to prevent further disturbances. In any case, prison staff joined others calling for the use of quick-acting tear gas to incapacitate rioters (*New York Times*, 11 April 1930, p. 29:2). The following year, the authorities in New York State were known actually to be considering plumbing in gas pipes for the direct use of tear gas in the mess halls at Auburn and the new prison at Attica (*New York Times*, 1 June 1931, p. 19:3). A riot at Howard state prison, Rikers Island, reportedly the sixth there in nine months, on 19 April 1930 (*New York Times*, 20 April 1930, p. 2:2) was followed by a very violent incident in 1931 when a riot by more than 1000 prisoners in Joliet penitentiary was forcibly suppressed by officers with guns and tear gas, at the cost of the death of one prisoner and injuries to three more (Garson, 1972, p. 414).

Appalling prison conditions occurred in the context of general barbarity and anarchy in the provision of local facilities for punishing and locking up offenders. It was 1937 before the stocks were abolished in Georgia as a means of punishing prisoners on chain gangs (*New York Times*, 14 March 1937, p. 16:2). Later that year, a curb on visitors led prisoners in the county jail at Anderson to mount a sit-down strike (*New York Times*, 20 June 1937, p. 3:1). In the following year, in Disney, Oklahoma, we get a glimpse of the crude 'justice' meted out to the 'Okies' of whom Steinbeck wrote in *The Grapes of Wrath*, the absence of a jail in the town stimulating the officials simply to tie offenders to a local tree and leave them there (*New York Times*, 25 October 1938, p. 6:4).

Several 'minor riots' took place in the US through the 1930s and early 1940s. Fox refers to incidents at Marquette prison in Michigan, Pennsylvania, New York, Texas, Jackson, Sing Sing, Arkansas, Duval County in Florida and Atlanta, this last in 1944 (Fox, 1956, p. 23). There was a strike at Alcatraz penitentiary early in 1936, following which 100 prisoners were sent to solitary confinement (*New York Times*, 25 January 1936, p. 9:4). In 1942, prisoners at San Juan prison, Puerto Rico, undertook a five-day hunger strike over the state of the food (*New York Times*, 17 February 1942, p. 3:5). In 1944, a riot

occurred at Atlanta federal prison (Fox, 1956, p. 49) when 125 prisoners barricaded themselves in and took four guards hostage in protest
at being quartered with alleged Axis spies (*New York Times*, 8 December 1944, p. 23:2). Despite these incidents, the 1940s were memorable
mainly for the riot in 1946 at Alcatraz.

The 'Battle' of Alcatraz

The postwar period began with a single event in Alcatraz, the island
fortress federal penitentiary in California, which marked the confrontational and violent style of riots by prisoners, and of their violent
suppression by the authorities. But Alcatraz may have marked a watershed in this respect, since the tough official reactions to prison riots
characteristic of the previous half century were softened in a policy of
restraint by the authorities in the decade which followed. To that
date, they could hardly have been less restrained.

Alcatraz, a place of confinement for military prisoners from the
late 1850s, was also used as a health resort as late as 1900 (Johnston,
1949, p. 7). In 1933, the military authorities handed the island over to
the Department of Justice and Alcatraz became a federal penitentiary,
run by Warden James Johnston, who was still in charge during the riot
of 1946. This incident, known as the 'Battle of Alcatraz', began with a
mutiny and attempted escape on 2 May and ended two days later with
two officers and three prisoners dead (Johnston, 1949, p. 221). The
prisoners were armed in this incident and in their efforts to regain
control of the institution the staff used demolition bombs, anti-tank
shells and rifle grenades with the help of officers from the Sixth Army
headquarters (Johnston, 1949, p. 233).

Late in 1946, the New York Correction Officers Benevolent Association was reported as seeking pay increases for its personnel and
predicting prison escapes and riots (*New York Times*, 26 October 1946).
The year after Alcatraz, disturbances continued in Southern states. In
Georgia, a riot in a convict highway camp at Brunswick in July was
soon followed by the announcement by the State Corrections Board
that the highway convict camp system was to be abolished (*New York
Times*, 12 August 1947). In Wanpun state prison, Wisconsin, 69
prisoners held four guards hostage in a sit-down strike during which
they barricaded themselves in the laundry (*New York Times*, 25 November 1947).

What was described as a 'jail outbreak' in Columbia, Tennessee,
resulted in two black prisoners killed and two other people injured

(*New York Times*, 1 March 1945). Early in 1948, a riot was reported in Mexico City penitentiary (*New York Times*, 24 February 1948). Prisoners in Margette prison attempted to use visiting governor Williams as a hostage in a jail break in July 1950 (*New York Times*, 9 July 1950). Later that year, prisoners in New Jersey state prison went on strike in protest against the small size of food allowances (*New York Times*, 2 November 1950). This was still rumbling on a month later (*New York Times*, 1 December 1950). A riot by a hundred prisoners in the state prison of New Mexico was quelled by the state police (*New York Times*, 21 November 1950). One convict later admitted planning the riot as a reprisal against one of the guards (*New York Times*, 22 November 1950).

The Riot Wave of 1951–3

The unprecedented number of riots in American prisons occurring between 1951 and 1953 was noted by the Committee on Riots in its report (American Correctional Association, 1953).

In the 1950s, recorded crime was falling. The population of state and federal prisons fell by 8000 to 166 000. The rising tide of rehabilitation was symbolized by the decision of the American Prison Association in 1954 to change its name to the American Correctional Association. The wave of prison riots in 1951 to 1953 dented but did not destroy the optimism of the 1950s and early 1960s (Useem and Kimball, 1989, p. 11). Far from these riots raising doubts about the validity of rehabilitation, the disturbances were actually viewed as justifying greater efforts towards the rehabilitation of the prisoners who were involved (Useem and Kimball, 1989, p. 10).

In February 1951, ten prisoners of the state prison farm in Angda, Los Angeles, slashed their heel tendons in protest at alleged brutal treatment (*New York Times*, 27 February 1951) and the following day six more prisoners followed suit (*New York Times*, 28 February 1951). In March, 29 prisoners were jailed for a hunger strike in Mobile, Alabama, in protest at meals being served by blacks *New York Times*, 24 March 1951). In the summer of 1951, a long history of violence in Louisiana state penitentiary came to a head with 37 prisoners slashing their heel tendons as a protest against whippings (*New York Times*, 12 February 1953).

In May, 400 prisoners in the State Prison of Utah were involved in a riot, protesting against what they saw as unfair treatment (*New York Times*, 21 May 1951). A fresh riot was reported the following day (*New York Times*, 22 May 1951). It was mid-August before the rioting was reported as ending with the freeing of hostages (*New York Times*, 15 August 1951). In August, the second day of the strike by prisoners at Oregon State prison was reported, in a dispute over a guard (*New York Times*, 16 August 1951). Thirteen hundred prisoners from the State Prison, Moundsville, West Virginia, revolted over dirty cooking and inadequate clothing, after a committee had been appointed to examine their complaints of maltreatment (*New York Times*, 17 October 1951). The protest apparently ended when supplies of food were promised to the prisoners (*New York Times*, 18 October 1951).

More prison riots occurred in 1951–3 in the US than in the previous 25 years. MacCormick lists six incidents in 1951, 21 in 1952 and 12 in 1953 (MacCormick, 1954, p. 18). In the twelve months after March 1952, major riots occurred in at least 23 prisons in the US. They began in the summer of 1951 with riots in Colorado and Idaho prisons. A year later, the spread of riots escalated rapidly. In March 1952, there were incidents in three New Jersey prisons. The third of these, on 17 April, involved 231 men from the State Prison Farm at Rahway. On 20 April, a riot broke out at the State Prison of Southern Michigan, which continued for five days and involved 2000 prisoners. This institution contained nearly 6000 inmates and was the largest prison in the country, and one of the most overcrowded and unwieldy in administrative terms. They were followed by riots from Massachusetts to California, from Michigan to Louisiana. In May and June 1952, sit-down strikes occurred at Louisiana state penitentiary at Angola, which housed 2700 prisoners. A prison guard was killed by two prisoners in June in New Mexico state penitentiary. Brutality by prison guards was said to be responsible for a riot at Charlestown, the Massachusetts state prison, in July. In October, 1600 prisoners in Ohio Penitentiary set fire to prison buildings in incidents which lasted five days (*New York Times*, 12 February 1953).

Between 4 May and 1 August 1952, Montreal prison experienced three major riots, involving about 700 prisoners on each occasion. In January 1953, there were two riots in western Pennsylvania and in the first week of February there were three in Arizona State Prison.

The riots spread rapidly through North America. According to the Michigan Special Committee which, in particular, investigated the Jackson prison riot of 1952, the first disturbances were the prison riots of 1951 in Colorado and Idaho State Penitentiaries, followed by other incidents which 'should probably be considered forerunners of the 1952 series rather than as furnishing the impulse which set off the chain reaction. It seems more probable that it was actually set off in full violence by the riots in March and April, 1952, at the New Jersey

State prison at Trenton, followed immediately by the riots at Jackson Prison in Michigan' (Special Committee to Study the Michigan Department of Corrections, 1953, p. 1).

The Jackson prison riot was claimed to have been 'the most dangerous prison riot in American history' (ibid., p. 2). This was in view of the risk to hostages 'held in Cell Block 15 by the homicidal psychopaths who were the leaders of the riot there' (ibid.) and the unprecedented force of 275 officers and troopers of the state police, mobilized at the time of the riot in April 1952 and not withdrawn from the prison until August. By that time the prison authorities had organized their own riot squads. 'Never has a large prison population been, so long after a riot, in a state of ferment where violence may break out again at any moment' (ibid.). Jackson also involved more damage and more prisoners than any other prison riot to date (Heaps, 1966, p. 140).

This last comment says as much about the fears of the authorities, in the face of staffing difficulties, as it does about the objective risk of further disturbances. Poor employment conditions, training and prospects contributed to the very high turnover, for example, of basic correctional officers in Jackson prison. Following the April riot, 37 correctional officers left within a few days of the release of the hostages in Cell Block 15. In the period 1 July 1951 to 15 July 1952, 224 employees were hired and 185 were separated (i.e. suspended by order of the Warden for any suspected improper actions) from service, out of the total of 471 correction officers employed in the prison (Special Committee, 1953, p. 60).

Because of overcrowding in Michigan's state reformatory and mental hospital, Jackson prison had become an overcrowded dumping ground:

> It had 547 lifers, but it also had 307 men who could just as well have gone to a county jail, including thirty-five men convicted of nonsupport and one convicted of violating the game laws. One man was sent to Jackson for shooting a dog. There are men in Jackson serving life for rape and men serving five years for rape. The youngest man in Jackson prison was sixteen years old; the oldest was seventy-eight. One man had been in Jackson since 1907. Sixty per cent of the men sent to Jackson in 1951 had no previous prison records. But others had been in prison half a dozen times. There were blind men, one-legged men, tuberculous men, senile men, crippled men in wheel chairs, diabetics, asthmatics.
>
> (Martin, 1953, p. 19)

On 18 January 1953, prisoners seized six guards and set fire to the prison at Western state penitentiary, Pittsburgh. The following day, armed prisoners mutinied at Bellefonte prison for four days. On 9 February 1953, in Washington State penitentiary at Walla Walla, staff and prisoners were injured by a home-made bomb and a five-hour rebellion by prisoners in Oregan state penitentiary eventually ended peacefully. On 10 February, prisoners in Washington county jail held a sit-down strike in a demand pay for work done outside the prison (*New York Times*, 12 February 1953). It was noted in 1952 that the fact that only one of the riots at that time was in a federal prison pointed to the improved conditions in these institutions but that was poor solace to the institutions that had actually experienced riots (Wilson and Barnes, 1952, p. 138).

The question as to the true extent of these riots remains open. The *New York Times* records additional prison riots in 1953, some of them very large scale. In January, 110 prisoners in the Western state penitentiary, Pennsylvania, rioted (*New York Times*, 19 January 1953). In what was reported as a gesture of sympathy with this incident, the inmates of Allegheny county institution burned a factory and, in an apparently unrelated incident, 575 prisoners rioted at Rockview Penitentiary (*New York Times*, 21 January 1953).

The official investigation into the 1951–3 riots locates their causes mainly in maladministration, brought about and expressed by inadequate resourcing, substandard staff, lack of professional leadership, excessive size and overcrowding of prisons, unwise sentencing and parole policies and decisions, political domination and motivation of management, and enforced idleness of prisoners (American Correctional Association, 1953). Among these, MacCormick identifies enforced idleness as the most significant factor external to institutions and political domination as the most significant external factor. He instances the constantly changing staffing of prisons as a damaging consequence of this (MacCormick, 1954, p. 26). 'The fact that the vast majority of the 1952 riots took place in state prisons did not leave much room for complacency about conditions in federal prisons.' (Wilson and Barnes, 1952, p. 138)

The Special Committee set up in the wake of the Jackson riot, generally described as the most serious and significant of the 1952–3 riots, significantly was given the brief of studying the Michigan Department of Corrections. Its members included the mayors of Grand Rapids and Kalamazoo City, the president of the Detroit Fruit Action Company and the Secretary of Cunningham's Drug Stores in Detroit. It was chaired by the Chairman of the Board at the Detroit Edison

Company and its secretary was the assistant director of the Citizens Research Council of Michigan. Two attorneys and the President Emeritus of the University of Michigan completed the members. The four staff involved in carrying out the inquiry included professors of law and criminology from the University of California, the Commissioner of Public Welfare from the National Probation and Parole Association in Philadelphia and Donald Clemmer, Director of the Department of Corrections for the District of Columbia. The make-up of the Special Committee may have constrained its focus and shaped its conclusions. At any rate, in respect of the riot, the Special Committee identified two major causes and four contributory factors as follows:

Causes:

1. The excessive size of the prison and the combination of over-crowding and idleness existing there.
2. The heterogeneous nature of the inmate population.

Contributory factors:

1. Administrative weaknesses in the Department of Corrections at Jackson Prison.
2. The personnel situation at Jackson Prison.
3. The parole system and the prisoners' sense of grievance against it.
4. The penal and parole laws.
                    (Special Committee to Study the Michigan Department
                                      of Corrections, 1953, p. 5)

Significantly, this analysis of the origins of the Jackson Prison riot gave no explicit consideration to the actual regime, the heart of the institution, beyond the implied criticism in the commentary on lack of work for prisoners. Further, there is no evidence in the report of any direct views being fed in by prisoners about what they experienced. Neither is there any examination of social factors related to the riot: local political, social and economic factors in Michigan, the area from which a large proportion (47.6 per cent in 1951, ibid., p. 29) of the prisoners were drawn, social and criminal justice inequalities resulting in the disproportionately high percentage of black prisoners (40 per cent and growing, op cit. p. 27) and of first-timers in prison (60 per cent, ibid.).

In short, the inquiry report typifies a pattern of investigation into riots which expresses the values of the authorities in its composition, procedure, assumptions, analysis, conclusions and recommendations. In so doing, it implicitly defends the status quo and tends to examine how that may be 'improved', that is perpetuated, in the building of better and more prisons with better equipped and trained staff to deal with control and discipline on a preventive basis, rather than posing questions about the structure and administration of injustice and oppression in society as reflected throughout the criminal justice system, locating the prison in this context.

Typical of much retrospective analysis, Hartung and Floch characterize the 1952–3 riots as though they were the preconscious, spontaneous and unorganized, therefore non-politicized precursors of the 1970s riots (Hartung and Floch, 1956). Starting from the experience of the prisoners, and setting this against the institutional context of the 1950s, Berkman arrives at a more informed and critical view. He argues that at that time prisoners made their protests *within* the context of the prevailing authoritarian or totalitarian system of institutional management of prisons. 'Prisoners could only question the particular severity of certain sanctions and not the sanctions themselves. It is for this reason that the demands of the 1950s can be properly described as "housekeeping demands." What was at stake in the riots of the 1950s was not the architecture of the house, but the way it was kept' (Berkman, 1979, p. 39).

1953–60: When is a 'Wave of Riots' not a Wave of Riots?

The extent to which inmate solidarity produces 'waves of riots, spreading rapidly from one institution to another, has preoccupied those attempting to explain their origins. The fact remains that in 1954, when disturbances in prisons allegedly had declined, in reality disturbances in prisons continued to be reported. There were at least ten major prison riots in the US in 1954. The Pontiac state penitentiary riot in Illinois in June involved 450 prisoners, among whom one was killed when the guards crushed the riot (*New York Times*, 24 June 1954). There were repeated riots during 1954 at the state penitentiary in Missouri and in one incident alone four prisoners were killed and $5m of damage was done (*New York Times*, 24 September 1954). The Women's House of Detention in New York County also experienced repeated riots during September (*New York Times*, 25 and 28 September 1954).

A period of unrest in Washington state penitentiary at Walla Walla, which began in 1953, culminated in a violent riot in 1955. For two days, the prisoners ran the prison, hostages taken included the deputy warden, buildings were burned and $2–3m damage was done, but no lives were lost during the rioting (Stastny and Tyrnauer, 1982, p. 81).

Early in 1955, Attorney General Brownell warned that rioting would be a consequence of the overcrowding in federal prisons going unchecked. A campaign was fought to restore nearly $4m in cuts to the fiscal request for the Justice Department's budget for 1956 (*New York Times*, 30 January 1955). As if to fulfil this prophecy, the pattern of rioting continued throughout that year, most incidents being concentrated in the summer months, with notable exceptions in January and November. In August, riots took place in the state penitentiary, Nebraska, Bescar county jail, Walla Walla prison in Washington and in the Women's reformatory, Framingham, Massachusetts, where 50 women rioted (*New York Times*, 19 August 1955).

Reports of riots in 1956 were slightly less numerous, though no less dramatic. In Georgia state prison, four inmates broke the legs of, or injured, 36 prisoners in a protest against prison conditions (*New York Times*, 3 August 1956). A handful of leg injuries, including two broken legs, occurred in a similar incident later that year (*New York Times*, 14 November 1956). Being under sentence of death did not deter rioters. In the spring of 1955, nine prisoners under the death sentence rioted and started a fire in Chicago county jail, Illinois (*New York Times*, 17 March 1955).

Reportedly, mismanagement by politically appointed staff led to a riot at Montana prison in 1957 and a sit-down strike in 1958, when prisoners took hostages and threatened to burn them alive unless the use of buckets as lavatories was ended, young prisoners were no longer locked up with older men and the state parole commissioner was sacked (Hibbert, 1966, p. 420).

The treatment of prisoners in state prisons is typified by an incident at Canon City Penitentiary, Colorado, in 1951, described by a prisoner at the trial of the warden for brutality. This involved prisoners being stripped and forced to stand in the sun with their hands above their hands. Their feet blistered on the hot pavement. Then they were pushed into the gymnasium and whipped with a six inch leather strap. 'At intervals a wire noose was slipped around a convict's neck and he was dragged across the floor. When a convict fainted, he was revived with a bucket of water so none of the punishment would be wasted on him. After each had received about 45 lashes, the men were unchained, stretched out on the floor while a guard whipped the bare soles of their feet with the strap.' (Wilson and Barnes, 1952, p. 138)

In the mid-1950s, significant riots by prisoners and 'patients' in a number of quasi-penal institutions indicates the growing tendency for prisoners in different institutional settings to take collective action. In the spring of 1955, in the Rusk state hospital, Texas, there was a report of a riot by 'criminally insane inmates', who took hostages and did not surrender for six hours, when there were 13 people injured (*New York Times*, 17 April 1955). In the autumn of that year, a group of young inmates rioted in the St Louis workhouse (*New York Times*, 2 November 1955).

By the late 1950s, negotiation was already beginning to play a large part in the dealings between prisoners and the authorities after a riot. In the five-hour sit-down of 200 prisoners in Connecticut state prison, for example, the prisoners bargained to have a meeting with news reporters and made arrangements for further talks to take place (*New York Times*, 3 August 1956).

CONSCIOUSNESS-RAISING RIOTS: FROM ABOUT 1960 TO THE MID-1970s

Pallas and Barber suggest that consciousness-raising riots in the US divide into two periods: the organizing of black prisoners by the Nation of Islam up to 1971, and the 'broader revolutionary upheavals' of the late 1960s and early 1970s (Pallas and Barber, 1972, pp. 1–2).

The challenges presented by prison riots from about 1960 were not simply to particular prison regimes but were articulated increasingly in terms of a broader attack on social injustice and discrimination. The launching of activism was undertaken not by Marxist but by black prisoners. 'It was the Black Muslims, with their exclusionist and nationalist platform, who first coalesced organizationally in the 1950s, posing a basic challenge to the system' (Stastny and Tyrnauer, 1982, p. 153).

What Hartung and Floch describe as a shift from 'brutal' to 'collective' rioting in the 1950s, Stastny and Tyrnauer locate in the broader context of challenges to the legitimacy of custody and treatment prison regimes, and therefore to prisons themselves. Increasingly from the early 1950s, incapacitation through 'warehousing' and rehabilitation through 'remediation' were equally subjected to critical scrutiny and action by prisoners. 'Detotalization' is the term used by Stastny and Tyrnauer to denote this fundamental shift in the political culture of prisoners from that time. These broader challenges coincided with several distinct but intersecting perceived crises which affected penal policy and practice, namely in democracy, in crime and in the rehabilitative philosophy of imprisonment.

The crisis in democracy became visible when, during the 1960s, the US was shaken by protests against a number of aspects of its way of life which many respectable, well-off, white people had come to take for granted. Students, anti-Vietnam war campaigners and black people took to the streets to express their dissatisfaction with aspects of US society. Other groups also were represented in the disturbances, which took place in a number of settings, intercommunal and institutional.

Urban riots occurred in 1964 in New York, Chicago and five other cities. In 1965, there was a five-day riot in Los Angeles in which 34 people were killed. In 1967 there were 41 disturbances in other towns. On 6 February 1968, in a Gallup poll, the public for the first time rated lawlessness and crime as the most important domestic problem in the US (Useem and Kimball, 1989, p. 15).

The struggle of black people for their rights surfaced in the 1960s and marked the culmination of campaigns fought less visibly in a society rooted in the history of black slavery and segregation. Feminists and civil rights activists, and anti-war, anti-nuclear and conservation protesters, began to generate case law by their actions in the last quarter of the twentieth century, which revolved around civil liberties and freedom of speech. But many of these protests reached back to the Constitution of the US and its amendments. Friedman notes, for example, that the claim of black people for their rights was directly to the eighteenth-century Bill of Rights and to the Fourteenth Amendment to the Constitution of 1868 (Friedman, 1973, p. 576).

The crisis of crime in society was fuelled by the political right, using evidence such as the fact that between 1970 and 1975, reported crime in the US increased dramatically. Violent crimes increased 40.3 per cent from 731 402 to 1 026 284, a significant increase from 360.0 to 48.5 per 100 000 population and property crimes by 111.5 per cent from 4 836 795 to 10 230 282, an increase of 2380.5 to 4800.2 per 100 000 population (Federal Bureau of Investigation, 1971 and 1976). Such figures were used to justify calls for heavier prison sentences for offenders.

During the twentieth century, prisons became big business in the US. By the time of the Santa Fe riot in 1980, almost $15 000 per annum was being spent to house each prisoner in a state penitentiary (Morris, 1983, p. 33).

The philosophy of rehabilitation through imprisonment was fatally undermined by research, the implications of which were reinforced by the political left. It was also taken up by the rest of the political continuum, as justifying the position that since all penal measures are equally ineffective, the status quo is no worse than any alternatives. The justification for imprisonment on the grounds of rehabilitation collapsed in an increasingly visible way from the 1960s, not simply because conservatives were urging tougher responses to rising crime rates, but also because liberal and radical commentators and researchers were uniting to undermine the defence that penal institutions could turn criminals effectively away from crime (Cullen and Gendreau, 1989, p. 28).

Increases in incarceration rates in the US since the mid-nineteenth century, for a hundred years or so were accompanied by disproportionate increases in the prison populations of immigrant, non-English speaking and non-white people. Since the mid-twentieth century, relative declines in the over-representation of these groups in the prison population were accompanied by an increasing proportion of black and Spanish-speaking prisoners (Cahalan, 1979). Muslim prisoners achieved prominence in post-1945 prison activism.

Organized Muslim involvement in prisons in the US seems to date from 1942, when the leader of the young Nation of Islam, Elijah Muhammad, refused the military draft and was sent to the federal prison at Milan, Michigan. His statement that it suited Americans suddenly to regard black people as full citizens so as to get them to fight the Germans and the Japanese was supported by other Muslims, who followed him to prison (Butler, 1978, p. 56). In the mid-1970s, there were an estimated 12 000 Muslims in prison in the US, about a fifth of the black prison population (Butler, 1978, p. 56).

By the mid-1960s, other black organizations were displacing the Muslims as the leaders of activism among prisoners. The writings of radical activist prisoners such as Malcolm X, Eldridge Cleaver and George Jackson put revolutionary consciousness-raising at the top of the agenda for prison reformers. Berkman notes three factors which contributed to the scope and character of prisoner movements in the 1960s: the Civil Rights Movement, the Vietnam War and growing ethnic and national movements, especially the Black Muslims (Berkman, 1979, p. 40), the last group more activist after the death of Malcolm X in 1965. During the 1960s, a significant number of draft evaders came into prison, black activists began to campaign in prison and civil rights lawyers became more willing to take on the cases of prisoners (Berkman, 1979, p. 41).

Useem and Kimball locate prison disturbances after the mid-1960s in the context of broader social struggles. On one hand, there were changes resulting in gains for prisoners, including federal court decisions which extended to Muslims the right to practise their religion, established the right of prisoners to adequate medical care, the right to communicate with lawyers and courts, the right to express political beliefs and engage in political practices and abolishing arbitrary censorship of mail and publications (Useem and Kimball, 1989, p. 12). On the other hand, there was a defensive backlash against social unrest, the birth of the New Right, the curbing of young people's protests and the assassinations of the Kennedy brothers, Malcolm X and Martin Luther King (Useem and Kimball, 1989, p. 13).

Whether Bell is correct and the campaigns by many groups between the 1950s and the 1970s represents a revolution of rising entitlements (Bell, 1976, p. 232), the 1953 Supreme Court decision in *Brown* v. *Board of Education* against the doctrine of 'separate but equal', the end of racial segregation in the Civil Rights Act (1964), the 1966 ruling by a federal district judge that patients in mental hospitals have the right to treatment, the Age Discrimination in Employment Act (1973) and the Rehabilitation Act (1973), all contributed to the spread of militancy to more oppressed groups in US society (Useem and Kimball, 1989, p. 11).

The late 1960s to the early 1970s saw a period of increased inmate solidarity and political consciousness in prison riots. The riot in Attica prison is the high point of this feature, called 'wars of liberation' by some commentators (Johnson and Dorin, 1978, p. 32), in which organization among prisoners was notable (Colvin, 1982, p. 449).

There was increasing interchange between activist prisoners and activists in the community. New movements saw the prisoner as campaigning for all the rights and dignities of fellow citizens in the country. These included freedom of speech, a minimum standard of living, freedom of religious observance, freedom from punishment without a hearing with evidence and freedom to call on the court to protect one's rights.

Encouragement to prisoners to express their views collectively extended to 'administrative recognition of gangs, inmate councils, and political groups' (Useem and Kimball, 1989, p. 17). The classic example of this was the policy of management by prisoners developed at

Walla Walla prison in the early 1970s and charted in detail by Stastny and Tyrnauer (1982).

In the five years after 1967, the pace of prison rioting quickened. The 48 prison riots which occurred in 1972 totalled more than in any other year of the history of the US (Useem and Kimball, 1989, p. 18):

Date	Number of prison riots
1967	5
1968	15
1970	27
1971	37
1972	48

Soledad, 1967

In March 1967, prisoners in Soledad prison went on a general strike, described graphically by a prisoner of the time (Fillmore, 1971, pp. 68–80). Soledad was the first of six new men's prisons and one women's prison built in California in the 1950s. Soledad was named as 'California Training Facility' in keeping with the rehabilitative vogue for avoiding the word 'prison'. Irwin, then a prisoner in Soledad, describes the shift from the social order reflected in the prisoners' early acceptance of their definition as sick (Irwin, 1980, p. 60) to their critical stance gained through reading and learning. At first, only a few prisoners had been placed in the 'adjustment units' for recalcitrant men. Now, disillusionment with the rehabilitative ideal spread rapidly and contributed to its eventual dismantling. 'Racial conflict and the sense of injustice that followed this dismantling tore the correctional institution apart (Irwin, 1980, p. 65).

Undoubtedly, there were connections between the widespread communal protests which became more visible in the late 1960s and peaked in 1968 and prison riots, though their precise nature, particularly in retrospect, is difficult to ascertain. During the late 1960s and early 1970s, US government interventions in the Dominican Republic and Vietnam illustrated the imperialist and racist basis of foreign policy. 'Continued opposition to the state thus grew more radical and militant and was met with increased repression' (Johnson and Dorin, 1978, p. 34). There were revolts by people in ghettos, by students, Black Panther organizations and Third World liberation groups. The influx of people from these situations and groups into prisons meant that 'Black and Chicano prisoners, in particular, were quick to make the connection between the struggles of Third World peoples around the world and their own'. The Attica prison riot became seen by them, like George Jackson the prison revolutionary, as a symbol of 'the new prison revolution these forces had spawned' (Johnson and Dorin, 1978, p. 35).

In the wake of a wave of urban riots, the publication of *Soul on Ice* by Eldrige Cleaver in 1968 and George Jackson's *Letter from Soledad Prison* in 1970 evoked strong public reactions. Etheridge Knight prefaced a collection of writings of black prisoners with the statement that 'the whole experience of the black man in America can be summed up in one word: prison.' (Orland, 1975, p. 4). Martin Sostre wrote from Attica:

> Listen pig, are you really that naive to believe you can fool and pacify us with nightly bribes of ten-cent candy bars and cookie 'snacks' while caging us like human animals in your inhuman steel cages? . . . Every one of your prison camps has now become a revolutionary training camp feeding trained revolutionary cadres . . . The recruits are the thousands of Black militants and revolutionaries framed and kidnapped from the ghettos in your desperate effort to put down the Black Rebellion.
>
> (Ibid.: quoted)

Black prisoners spearheaded action arising from growing consciousness among prisoners in the US about their experiences of imprisonment. The bloody Attica, Rahway and Soledad prison riots raised public awareness of the grievances of prisoners about the conditions of their incarceration. Chief Justice Burger observed: 'It is a melancholy truth that it has taken the tragic prison riots of the past three years to focus widespread attention on the problems of prisons' (quoted in Orland, 1975, p. 6).

Two features of the riots of the decade after 1970 can be discerned. First, hostage-taking became an increasingly common adjunct to, and latterly central feature of, rioting. Hostage-taking, it should be noted, extends the principal roles of participants in the protest to include four people: the hostage-taker, the hostage, the responder and the commentator, and thereby increases the potential of the incident as a melodramatic demonstration with many stakeholders in its outcome. In this respect, prison riots shared a trend with international incidents, since between 1 January 1968 and 30 June 1975 there were 77 international hostage incidents, excluding airline hijackings or kidnappings of business executives (Jenkins, 1976, p. 1). Second, prison riots became increasingly associated in the public mind with violence and even organized terrorism.

The riots of the early 1970s publicized prison conditions but did not guarantee reforms. The official inquiry into Attica was viewed as admirable in its style and content.

> But eloquent reports on brutal prison conditions have become part of the mainstream of American thought and, as such, are routinely ignored. Neither the Attica riot nor the resultant report produced any fundamental change in America's prison system. Ultimately, Attica had as little real effect as the prison riots of prior decades . . . Despite riots and despite the proliferation of prison reform literature, prisons remained inflexible, inscrutable, and unjust.
>
> (Orland, 1975, p. 6)

The struggle between activist prisoners and the authorities, at any rate inside prisons, can be summarized as a campaign to replace the image of the sick prisoner by that of the prisoner as citizen with the same rights as other citizens. With increasing force and effectiveness, prisoners and their legal advocates have wielded the Eighth Amendment's ban on cruel and unusual punishment and the Fourteenth Amendment's guarantee of the due process of law since the mid-1950s. The first successful cases were fought for prisoners' rights to redress and protection against the most flagrant brutalities of prison life. The United States Supreme Court upheld in 1964 the claim of a prisoner of freedom to buy religious publications, and in 1968 pronounced the whole of Alabama's prison system unconstitutional on the grounds of its practice of racial segregation. It declared in favour of protecting the religious beliefs and practices of prisoners in 1972, condemned the censorship of prison mail in 1974 and, most significant, extended the principle of procedural fairness to the process by which prisoners were disciplined (Orland, 1975, pp. 9–10).

The decade heralded by the Folsom and New York disturbances and the prophecies of a bloodbath from the striking prisoners at San Quentin in 1970 was delimited, not to say dominated, by the two bloodiest prison riots of prison history in the US: Attica in 1971 and New Mexico state prison at Santa Fe in 1980.

Folsom, 1970

The general strike at San Quentin in 1968 was followed in November

1970 at Folsom prison by reputedly the longest and most militant strike in the history of the US (Berkman, 1979, p. 40). The Folsom riot involved almost all the 2400 prisoners refusing to leave their cells for nineteen days and producing a list of demands, headed 'Fascist Concentration Camp of Modern America' (Berkman, 1979, p. 62). These demands fall into three categories and show the changed character of riots since the 1950s: first, there were 'housekeeping' demands similar in character to those of the 1950s but more challenging; secondly, there were political demands, absent in the 1950s; thirdly, there were ten demands associated with the conditions of labour in the prison (Berkman, 1979, p. 62), the first time that prisoners in the US had openly challenged the authorities to offer them the civil right to sell their labour (Berkman, 1979, p. 70).

The New York Riots, 1970

In 1970, a further report of the 1953 Committee on Riots was prompted by a spate of riots and disturbances which began in 1968 (American Correctional Association, 1970), Colvin identifies 39 prison riots in the US between 1971 and 1980. He bases this on a search of the New York Times Index, using his own restricted definition of what constitutes a riot, referred to in Chapter 1 (Colvin, 1982, p. 450). The wave of prison riots experienced in New York City, from August to October 1970, began in the Manhattan house of detention and soon spread to other municipal jails. The immediate trigger for the riots seems to have been prisoners' complaints about bad conditions. In August, an uncensored questionnaire answered by 907 inmates of the Manhattan house of detention reported fear, violence, filth and degrading conditions there. Disturbances began on 9 August with the taking of two prisoner hostages. Two days later, prisoners were in control of four floors, burning bedding and smashing windows (*New York Times*, 12 August 1970). On 18 August, 94 prisoners refused to leave their cells and the tension was reduced slightly when the authorities announced plans to transfer 670 prisoners upstate to ease overcrowding. In mid-October, a further wave of riots began in the Queen's house of detention and spread to other jails. Soon, more than 1400 prisoners in three jails were in control of scores of cellblocks and between them held 23 hostages (*New York Times*, 13 October 1970). The following day, the riots spread to the Brooklyn house of detention and the next day the authorities stepped in with force to crush the riots in Brooklyn and Kew Gardens, quelling the Manhattan riot peaceably (*New York*

Times, 5 October 1970). The five-day revolt ended with the surrender of the last 41 prisoners barricaded on the top floor of the Manhattan institution (*New York Times*, 6 October 1970).

Wright's study of San Quentin prison in the early 1970s includes a useful portrait of the strike by prisoners in August 1970. This is based on his experiences as a 'student chaplain' and upwards of 150 interviews with prisoners. In his account, there is a notable gulf between the perceptions of prison administrators and the prisoners themselves.

He identifies the origins of the strike in the intention of Marion County Superior Court to hold court sessions concerning the three prisoners from Soledad known as the Soledad Brothers, inside San Quentin. About 800 prisoners held a sit-down in the prison yard in protest at this, stating that they feared the risk of manipulation of sessions by prison staff. The following manifesto of fourteen demands was written and submitted on behalf of the prisoners by Warren Wells, a Black Panther:

1. That all political prisoners be freed.
2. That the Soledad Three be freed.
3. That a black warden be hired.
4. That a black associate warden of custody be hired.
5. That a black associate warden of care and treatment be hired.
6. That a Mexican warden be hired.
7. That a Mexican associate warden of custody be hired.
8. That a Mexican associate warden of care and treatment be hired.
9. That nonwhite prisoners have proportional representation in all administrative, industrial, and vocational positions in the prison.
10. That B Section and A Section be closed until they are made to conform to sanitary and health standards.
11. That men in B Section, A Section, and the adjustment center be given one full hour of exercise a day and be given the rights that other prisoners have.
12. That all men presently condemned to death be given political asylum abroad.
13. That all forms of capital punishment and mass genocide on the people by the brutal hands of the American bureaucracies immediately cease by order of the Free World Solidarity Revolutionary Army for the People.

14. That all prisoners being tried by the Superior Court within the walls of San Quentin be tried by their peers.

(Wright, 1973, pp. 100–1)

Attempts by the warden and other staff to dissuade the prisoners from these demands, to ridicule the demands and to persuade them to leave the yard failed. The strike ended when tear gas was fired at the prisoners.

Most staff maintained that the demands were not serious grievances and that the strike was organized from outside the prison by the Panthers or the Communist Party (Wright, 1973, p. 101). Typically, the captain in charge of custodial officers said 'the sit-down was really led by about a dozen or so inmates who coerced the others into joining the strike . . . Ninety-eight per cent of the prisoners were on our side; it was only two per cent that kept everything messed up all the time. For people who haven't been so wonderful in life, these inmates are real critical of the officers' (Wright, 1973, p. 102). Wright adds:

> None of the officials I talked to saw the demands as reflecting the deep alienation and sense of injustice experienced by prisoners within the prison. They saw the demands for a black and Chicano warden as 'ridiculous', showing how racist the Panthers were, not as an attempt to make the power structure of the prison more responsive to the needs of nonwhite prisoners.
>
> (Wright, 1973, p. 102)

In contrast, the overwhelming majority of prisoners interviewed said they supported the strike, which in any case involved 25 per cent of the prison population, even though some thought some of the demands were 'unrealistic or inappropriate' (Wright, 1973, p. 104). This latter view was held of demands for the release of political prisoners and the abolition of capital punishment and not for demands prisoners generally saw as central. Only one prisoner felt that the strike was organized by outsiders (Wright, 1973, p. 105).

According to many prisoners:

> Black, brown and white, racism is a pervasive fact of prison life. Many of the prisoners interviewed felt that racism is systematically encouraged by the prison officials. A number of prisoners reported that the unity of the strike was broken basically through racist tactics by the prison administration . . . Racism, then, is seen by at least some prisoners as a strategy used by the prison administration

to keep the prisoners divided, to prevent the emergence of prisoner unity. This view was expressed not just by black prisoners, but by white and Chicano prisoners as well.

(Wright, 1987, pp. 106–7)

This example typifies widespread contrasts in prisons between staff and prisoner perceptions of imprisonment in general and the origins, nature and meaning of riots and other protests. It illustrates the difficulty of assessing the extent of prisoner support of riots. In San Quentin, many prisoners, for example, were hesitant about admitting openly their support for the Black Panthers. The fact that only 30 did so was used by staff as evidence for the view that only very few prisoners were militant. 'However, a far larger proportion of the prison population is sympathetic to the militant, radical position than are willing to openly express their views' (Wright, 1973, pp. 134–5).

These differences in perception lead to fundamentally different perspectives on the origins of riots. Whilst both staff and prisoners in San Quentin agreed that prisoners were likely to become more troublesome over time:

Where they differ is in their notions of the causes of this unrest and the implications it has for prison policies. The prisoners see the causes lying in the fundamental injustice and oppressiveness of the criminal justice system and the society at large. From the militant prisoners' perspective, the implication for policy is that the prison and the society must fundamentally change their priorities or else there will be, in the words of one black prisoner, 'a blood bath.' The prison officials, on the other hand, generally see the causes lying in the impulsiveness and irresponsibility of prisoners and in agitation from the outside. The implication for policy, in their eyes, is that prison discipline has to be tightened.

(Wright, 1987, p. 140)

Attica, 1971

The euphoric mood of prisoners organizing resistance to imprisonment at the start of the new decade was devasted by one short, lethal burst of fire from the guns of the state police at Attica on 13 September 1971. But even the carnage inflicted during the Attica riot interrupted rather than terminated disturbances at that prison. Bell, the chief assistant to the special state prosecutor, appointed to prosecute state police officials after the riot (see Chapter 6), comments:

Within three weeks after Scotti closed out the Attica investigation, 150 guards picketed to protest understaffing and overcrowding. Three stabbings of inmates and an unarmed attack on a correction officer in May . . . In July, eight guards and an inmate were hurt in a flare-up over a routine cell search . . . Attica then housed 2,000 inmates, 240 fewer than in 1971 when overcrowding was a major cause of the rebellion.

(Bell, 1985, pp. 367–8)

Prisoners began a general strike on 23 August which involved most of them refusing to leave their cells. After six days, it was settled non-violently, perhaps in the wake of the riot, with an agreement including:

> . . . a promise to reduce the population by 300, expansion of work-release and furlough programs, allowing inmates to touch, kiss, and hug their wives, children, and other visitors, showers daily instead of twice a week, fewer rectal searches, a greater effort to hire black and Hispanic guards, at least some of whom spoke Spanish, and greater efforts to house inmates close to their homes. About 60 per cent of Attica's inmates were from metropolitan New York, a trip of about 400 miles that was particularly hard for a family that did not have a car.

(Bell, 1985, p. 368)

The Attica prison riot itself left 43 men dead and more than 80 wounded. The Special Commission called to investigate it (often referred to as the McKay Commission, after Robert B. McKay who chaired it) called it 'the bloodiest one-day encounter between Americans since the Civil War' (New York State Special Commission, 1972, p. xi).

According to McKay, the Attica riot could have happened in any prison. The significance of Attica was its typicality and not the dramatic uniqueness of its violence, since 'the elements for replication are all around us. Attica is every prison; and every prison is Attica' (New York State Special Commission, 1972, p. xii). Fifteen years later, the dual significance of Attica could be discerned. First, it symbolized the appalling state of prisons in the US. 'Attica was just an archetype of the pathology of prisons at the time' (Burns, 1987, p. 6). Secondly, it represented the calculated injustices wrought by the authorities, in the defence of their brutal response to the rioting prisoners. It was noted that the significance of the word 'Attica' for many people is the:

... full-scale judicial assault that was mounted as a complement to the physical assault which had taken place in D-yard, when it became clear that the state had been responsible for all the deaths that occurred in the September 13th re-taking of the prison and that the stories of inmate atrocities had been gross fabrications, the prosecutions were a convenient and useful deflection of attention away from the State's culpability.

(Burns, 1987, p. 6)

The analysis of the McKay report is impressive in its critical awareness of the complexity of the factors predisposing prisoners to riot, and in particular in its emphasis on the significance for the prison of its location in wider society:

The problem of Attica will never be solved if we focus only upon the prisons themselves and ignore what the inmates have gone through before they arrive at Attica. The criminal justice system is at least as great a part of the problem of Attica as the correctional facility itself. The process of criminal justice will never fulfill either its promises or its obligations until the entire judicial system is purged of racism . . . If the criminal justice system fails to dispence justice and impose punishment fairly, equally and swiftly, there can be little hope of rehabilitating the offender after he is processed through that system . . . We cannot expect even the most dramatic changes inside the prison walls to cure the evils of our criminal justice system, nor of society at large.

(New York State Special Commission, 1972, p. xix)

Attica at least ensured that prisoners' rights began to figure as one of the issues respectable penal administrators could henceforth write about with impunity: 'If prisoners are to learn to bear the responsibilities of citizens, they must have all the rights of other citizens except those that have been specifically taken away by court order. In general, this means that prisoners should retain all rights except that of liberty of person' (New York State Special Commission, 1972, pp. xvi–xvii). In the wake of Attica, the National Prison Project of the American Civil Liberties Union was formed, with the support of prison reformers (Bernat, 1988, p. 12).

Unfortunately, the changes made in the light of the McKay report did not match its rhetoric. They were superficial and included such reforms as changing staff uniforms and titles and introducing impotent inmate advisory councils.

There were some initial attempts to improve officer training, recruit more minority staff, and improve some of the conditions of
imprisonment. Far more public energy, however, was devoted to
bringing to trial those Attica inmates accused of criminal acts in the
course of the uprising. At the same time, the prosecution of law
enforcement officers charged with illegal actions was sidestepped.
(Stastny and Tyrnauer, 1982, p. 1)

Did Attica demonstrate the growing influence of militant or revolutionary prisoners? The lack of research into this question has been
commented upon (Johnson and Dorin, 1978, p. 33), but two studies
cast light on the question. Glaser contrasts what he sees as a contrast
between the prisoners of the 1950s, who only sought to publicize their
complaints, and those of the 1970s, many of whom 'now address
themselves primarily to the so-called "Third World" of oppressed
peoples everywhere. They dream of joining forces in a global revolt
against alleged "imperialist domination"' (Glaser, 1971, p. 139). This
perception was sharpened by the division of prisons into staffs drawn
from the ethnic majority of largely white Anglo–Americans and
prisoners comprised substantially of ethnic minorities who were black.
Glaser saw the prospects for the prevention of riots as contingent on
giving prisoners opportunities to participate in managing prisons, to
develop alternatives to rioting (Glaser, 1971, pp. 144–5). Pallas and
Barber agree with Glaser. They contrast the 'traditional prison riots'
of the early 1950s with the 'revolutionary upheavals of the late 1960s
and early 1970s' (Pallas and Barber, 1973, p. 341). They chart the shift
from the unplanned, spontaneous early incidents which only challenged abuses of power and not their source of its legitimacy (Pallas
and Barber, 1973, p. 341).

The Attica prison riot occurred in a period of increasing unrest in
prisons in the US. In the wake of Attica, disturbances occurred at
Great Meadow correctional facility in New York State, where about 75
prisoners threw bottles and started fires in their cells in the early
hours of the morning of 15 September 1971. On the same day, a
planned rebellion at Clinton prison, also in New York State, was
reported to have been thwarted (*New York Times*, 16 September 1971).
Prisoners in Jackson state prison in Michigan went on strike for three
days, to support their claim for a minimum wage of $1 an hour. In
Sing Sing, near Ossining, New York, prisoners protested against 'lock-
step' discipline and the way profit-making activities such as the bake-
shop were claimed as rehabilitative by the authorities (*New York Times*,
19 September 1971).

At the beginning of October 1971, 300 inmates of the state prison, Norfolk, Massachusetts, demonstrated. Among other things, they demanded an end to the policy requiring prisoners to serve two-thirds of their sentence before becoming eligible for parole (*New York Times*, 3 October, 1971).

POST-REHABILITATION RIOTS: AFTER THE MID-1970s

'The modern American prison is a racist nightmare where racial hatred, inflamed by the guards and officials, is used to keep the prisoners fighting among themselves' (Franklin, 1982, p. xiii). This comment by a leading literary critic of prison-related literature, provides a critical vantage point from which to view the consensus politics of liberal political theory which has produced pluralist accounts of penal policies and practices in the US. In contrast, the reality of prison policy and practice since the 1970s is that the search, if there has been one, for common interests between and within staff and prisoner groupings has not led to visible outcomes, any more than that the struggle for penal reforms has led to the establishment of prison democracies. Even in Stastny and Tyrnauer's sympathetic case study of attempts by reforming wardens to move towards involving prisoners in government and self-government, they admit that by the late 1970s the move had been abandoned.

The Decline of the Rehabilitative Ideal

During the 1970s, prison reform had lost impetus. The rehabilitative ideal was under attack from both the Left and the Right. Budgets were under pressure from conservatives who opposed public spending on the scale prisons generated. By the end of the decade, prisons had shifted from the centre to the periphery of public attention (Stastny and Tyrnauer, 1982, p. 2).

The rehabilitative movement assumed 'that inmates were sick and could be cured with proper treatment; and that by giving inmates rights and privileges they would become productive and responsible' (Engel and Rothman, 1983, p. 104). But whilst administrators became more open and reformers attempted to reduce the social distance between staff and prisoners, 'the contradiction of roles – that of friend and guard, equal and superior – created both psychological and managerial problems for those involved' (Engel and Rothman, 1983, pp. 104–5). Thus, probably unintentionally, these changes led to increased violence, and, in the words of David Rothman, did 'less to upgrade dismal conditions than they did to create nightmares of their own' (Engel and Rothman, 1983, p. 105).

The extension of rehabilitative regimes brought about a relaxation of the authoritarianism which hitherto characterized many prisons (Engel and Rothman, 1983, p. 97). Consequently, although the power of the established prisoner elites was undermined, newly-arrived prisoners took the opportunity to engage in their own careers of 'exploitation and trouble-making' (Engel and Rothman, 1983, p. 97).

Prisoners More Litigious

One measure of this trend is the fact that in 1960, the total number of state and federal prisoner filings in federal district courts was 2177, whereas by 1984 it was 31 107 (Thomas, Keeler and Harris, 1986, p. 775). This may be viewed as an excess, a crisis or simply a sign that prisoners were wasting the time of the judiciary with 'frivolous suits', which were, as Judge Warren Burger put it, 'so minor that any well-run institution should be able to resolve them fairly without resorting to federal judges' (Thomas, Keeler and Harris, 1986, p. 778).

While the causes of the increase in litigation by federal and state prisoners remain complex and not easily explained, in part the explanation lies in the fact that, whilst significant, on the whole this increase has not kept pace with the 11 per cent annual average increase in US civilian litigation since 1966 (Thomas, Keeler and Harris, 1986, p. 787). But it also seems that prisoners use law suits 'as a form of social resistance to perceived problems in either the criminal justice system (trial or sentencing procedures, discretionary revocation of goodtime) or prison conditions (overcrowding, violence) . . . the deeper genesis of litigation lies in broader social acceptance of civil rights for a variety of 'unconventional' social groups' (Thomas, Keeler and Harris, 1986, p. 793).

So the fragmentation which is associated with penal policies and practices by staff and protests, including riots, by prisoners since the mid-1970s was associated not with superficial changes but with a philosophical vacuum left by the collapse of rehabilitationism. The consequent disintegration of what some would argue had always been an illusory institutional consensus centred on medico-treatment needs to be appreciated as a central feature of the situation and not interpreted as a sign of progress towards pluralism, Stastny and Tyrnauer admit: 'From the beginning, the larger prison polity – inmates, guards, treatment staff, administration – had been fragmented. Incompatible subcultures fed into conflicting interests and seemingly irreconcilable goals' (Stastny and Tyrnauer, 1982, p. 180). But they continue: 'Here the search for some basis of common interest was hampered by the breaks in continuity at higher government levels and the weakness of commitment to the reform program at all levels' (ibid.). This last sentence reveals the liberal optimism which fuels their perspective rather than pointing the way towards a critical appreciation of the nature and significance of the fragmentation which was occurring among staff and prisoners alike.

It is often asserted that social protest moved from revolutionary extremism in the late 1960s to realistic, and definitely more apathetic, conservatism a decade later. Undeniably, in society and in the prisons the revolutionary militancy of the early 1970s waned. There are two main views about this. The first, and more popular among liberals and the New Right perhaps, is that apathy about social protest, the decline of the Black Panthers and Eldridge Cleaver's repatriation are associated with the retrenchment of the Left and with people becoming more pragmatic and 'sensible' and concentrating on more positive and practical aspects of living. The second, more considered, view is represented by Johnson and Dorin's attempts to research the range of militancies of prisoners and produce a scholarly portrait of their variations and consequences. Their stratified random survey of 146 prisoners in maximum security in New York institutions between 1971 and 1973 reveals that while a high proportion of black prisoners display quasi-radical and militant views, 'full-blown political ideologies comparable to positions espoused by George Jackson or Eldridge Cleaver are virtually absent in this survey. In fact, only a handful of convicts (at most, three) described themselves in terms that even approximated the role of the revolutionary' (Johnson and Dorin, 1978, p. 41).

A pen-picture of San Quentin in 1972 reveals the potential for conflict between groups of prisoners, after the breaking-up of a fight:

Nothing has been resolved. The races are more estranged than ever. Weapons are stockpiled. Anyone who talks moderation is in danger of being killed as a 'Tom' or a 'nigger lover.' Men who were moderate are now filled with loathing and hate. Blacks are more certain that all whites are racists bent on genocide, and whites see all blacks as uncivilized brutes. Something will ignite another race war in a week, a month, or six months – and nobody can explain what either side will gain.

(Bunker, 1972, p. 47)

Two versions of the shift from centralized, authoritarian control of prisons, by staff and prisoners, to a more diffuse pattern of interaction, can be discerned. First, Stastny and Tyrnauer's case study of Walla Walla describes the replacement of the extreme rigidity of the former authoritarian pattern of staff-inmate relations by a pluralism of staff and prisoner groupings, many of the latter autonomous, such as ethnic clubs, status clubs, community and self-help groups, religious or semi-religious organizations and special interest clubs, reflecting a more open and interactive prison environment (Stastny and Tyrnauer, 1982, p. 157). They argue that Korn and McCorkle were mistaken to imply that handing over power to prisoners would simply generate 'patterns of internal group coercion more punitive, more rigid, and incomparably more discriminatory' (Korn and McCorkle, 1959, p. 525). On the contrary, they adopt Irwin's opinion that the view of prisons as run by corrupt oligarchies of staff and prisoners is unrealistic. Most prisoners 'bring their "pre-prison orientations" with them and are resistant to prisonization' (Stastny and Tyrnauer, 1982, p. 157).

Johnson and Dorin's research makes a significant contribution to an understanding of the shift which occurred between Attica in 1971 and Santa Fe in 1980. Focusing on the prison riot career of the minority of militant, radicalized prisoners identified in their 1971–3 survey, they propose how these prisoners may contribute to comparatively rare and violent incidents. Faced with what the prisoner perceives as a monolithic power structure:

> . . . purposely arranged to wreak damage on him as a helpless member of the underclass . . . the prospective militant must develop faith in an unimpressive group of peers, and must then gird himself for what may easily degenerate into a Pyrrhic victory – short-term ascendance following a bloody prison riot. And if our rebel is prisonwise, he may well fear the reign of inmates and the backlash from guards more than the disturbance itself. Yet there are forces that can make men desperate in prison, and desperate men are apt to defy the odds. The ghetto man, as we have seen, may be particularly susceptible to radicalization. In prison, where factors that spawn bitterness and resentment in the ghetto are magnified, the black convict group might plausibly contain a sizeable number of men who are ready to court danger to right longstanding wrongs and assert their autonomy. But comparatively few such

individuals populate prisons because the very factors that might predispose ghetto men to violent protest create a more conservative perspective – a focus on survival in an unpredictable and often arbitrary world.

(Johnson and Dorin, 1978, p. 45)

It is this fragmentation and individualization of the so-called extremist rioter which may contribute to an interpretation of the changes which took place between Attica in 1971 and Santa Fe in 1980. The solidarity which was a feature of the collective protests of the 1960s and early 1970s broke down into sub-collectivities of prisoners, negotiating the political struggles of their particularities and differences, invariably opposed to the authorities and sometimes even engaged in internecine conflicts with each other.

There is a high correlation between the incidence of protest and growing black consciousness in the 1960s. In the wake of Attica, there was a growing awareness of the impact of the growing movement for civil rights for black people in the 1960s on the nature of demands by prisoners in the 1970s. Many prisons held predominantly black prisoners. This was not because black people were more criminal than white people, but reflected the funnelling effect of social policies and the criminal justice system in a social environment which perpetuated widespread oppression and discrimination on racial grounds (Fraser, 1971, p. 49).

Most of the 1951–3 prison riots took place in the northern states, regarded generally as having made more progress towards humaneness. Yet, as is discussed further in Chapter 6, we can look critically behind this to ascertain whether other factors contributed to their outbreak. At one level it is puzzling, since after the 1970s it is arguable that the end of racial segregation in prisons, which particularly affected the southern states, actually contributed to increasing opportunities for racial conflict in prisons (Engel and Rothman, 1983, p. 95).

In the 1970s, in virtually all states of the US, committals to prison were rising, parole releases were falling and the general public were clamouring for tougher measures to be taken against criminals (Doleschal, 1977, p. 56). On the other hand, pressure for reform was building up in the early 1970s. The Board of Trustees of the National Council on Crime and Delinquency issued the following policy statement in April 1972: 'No new detention or penal institution should be built before alternatives to incarceration are fully achieved' (Nagel,

1977, p. 156). Similar statements were made soon afterwards by the American Assembly and the National Advisory Commissioner's Task Force (Nagel, 1977, p. 156).

Martin and Eckland-Olson's case study of Texas prisons highlights the one-sidedness of challenges of the structural power and sheer complacency and inertia of the penal authorities as late as the 1970s. They document the case of *Ruiz* v. *Estelle* in great detail, showing how the former – a prisoner, struggles against the latter, the Director of the Texas Department of Corrections, in a case which began with a petition and finished up as a *cause célèbre* for prison reform groups. Ruiz simply complained in his petition that his confinement was unconstitutional and the Texas Department of Corrections' total denial of his case actually contributed, by the late 1970s, to the massiveness of the judicial intervention which eventually occurred when the case went to court (Martin and Eckland-Olson, 1987, p. 82). The trial ran for an unprecedented 161 days and involved 349 witnesses testifying, and eventually the authorities were able to lean successfully on the allegations that prisoners are likely to lie and in any case nothing in the running of a prison can ever be perfect (Martin and Eckland-Olson, 1987, pp. 160–4). But around this archetypal trial numerous other court actions were fought as prisoners became more litigious and complaints by prisoners continued to come to court throughout the 1980s. Perhaps most significantly, even after the Santa Fe riot of 1980, when the judge in the *Ruiz* case issued, a year after the adjournment, a meticulous written memorandum detailing six aspects of prisons needing attention – overcrowding, security and supervision, health care, discipline, access to courts and related conditions – the authorities were unenthusiastic about embracing these (Martin and Eckland-Olson, 1987, p. 169).

Pressure for reform clashed head-on with established penal policy and practice. For instance, the dominance of the custodial approach in Texas was characteristic of the national trend, confirming 'existing beliefs and practices among Texas prison administrators' (Martin and Eckland-Olson, 1987, pp. 81–2). It confirmed also the view that 'resistance to misguided reformers, whether prisoners, citizens, legislators, or judicial personnel, was not only reasonable but positively required by an allegiance to a higher set of values' (ibid.). Thus, not only riots but all forms of protest by prisoners tended to be met not just with defensiveness by the authorities but, as incidents in Texas in the early and mid-1970s showed, violence 'even to the point of suggesting that prisoners should literally be beaten into submission' (ibid.).

But by 1 January 1976, the imprisonment rate in the US of 215 per 100 000 population was the highest in the world and still rising (Doleschal, 1977, p. 51). This rate of imprisonment was sixteen times greater than that in the Netherlands (Doleschal, 1977, p. 56).

At the same time, with the exception of the situation of some political prisoners in totalitarian states, prisoners in the US were serving sentences several times longer than anywhere else in the world. Only 2 per cent of prisoners in 1974 served less than one year, 24 per cent served sentences between one and 4.99 years and 74 per cent served five years to life. Seven hundred prisoners were awaiting execution (Doleschal, 1977, p. 52).

Walla Walla: A 'Typical' Penitentiary

Given this record of failure, therefore, it is unsurprising that some penitentiaries experienced problems from their opening. For instance, Washington state penitentiary at Walla Walla was opened in 1886 as a territorial prison (Tyrnauer, 1981, p. 37). Two years later Washington became a state and in 1901 a law was passed prohibiting counties from performing executions and designating the institution as Washington's maximum security prison. 'From its earliest years, the penitentiary was troubled by idleness, violence, and overcrowding' (McCoy, 1981, p. 4). Prisoners who set fire to the central cellblock in September 1926 were only repulsed with tear gas. In 1934, on Lincoln Day, a riot reputedly caused by bad food led to the deaths of nine prisoners and one guard and was quelled by the state police and prison guards using machine guns (McCoy, 1981, p. 4). In the riot of July 1955 involving a 72-hour siege, inmates 'set fires, tore apart prison buildings, and seized hostages, including the captain of the guards'. The warden later told the investigating state legislative committee that malcontents among the prisoners brought about the riot when they resisted his 'get-tough prison policy' (McCoy, 1981, p. 5).

For twenty years after the mid-1950s, Walla Walla prison was run by Warden Bobby J. Rhay, who worked with Dr William Conte, a psychiatrist who became director of institutions, to bring about a series of reforms. These began in the late 1960s and changed life in the prison radically. Censorship of mail stopped, phone calls were allowed, work was no longer compulsory, fair hearings had to precede punishment of inmates for disciplinary offences, inmates could dress as they pleased with no restrictions on their hair and beard length, contact with visitors was allowed instead of the customary glass partitions, outside work and home visits were allowed. Most significantly, an elected inmate council participated in running the prison.

Supporters of Rhay praised the vision of inmate self-government. Critics claimed that inmates used their freedom to intimidate each other in subversive gangs. Towards the end of the Rhay administration, prisoners rioted on Easter Sunday, 1977, 'burning the chapel and looting the prison store, and then suffered the consequences by being locked in their cells for a record time of forty-six days' (McCoy, 1981, p. 6).

Douglas Vinzant, a former minister in Mississippi, took over the warden's job in 1977. Vinzant maintained that huge nineteenth-century institutions were outdated and that small community-based prisons where prisoners could live close to their families and jobs were more likely to succeed. He continued the trend of Rhay's policies. For example, 'a dozen of the prison's toughest convicts formed an interracial committee that persuaded inmates to fight with words or fists instead of with knives' (McCoy, 1981, p. 6).

But some violent incidents produced the excuse some reactionaries needed. A changed management style meant the break-up of the participative committees and the reassertion of traditional means by which the staff imposed order. Thus, the upturn in violent disturbances could only be explained by referring back to the former stability enjoyed when a few powerful prisoner groups ruled the prison. Now, with power more dispersed among a much larger number of smaller groups of prisoners, there were more conflicts between them than ever before. The inquiry report into the riot at Joliet correctional centre on 22 April 1975 shows how significant as a foreground factor in the outbreak of rioting, disputes between gangs of prisoners had become by the mid-1970s (Rock, Philip J. and Joseph G. Sevcik, 1975, pp. 17–32).

Santa Fe, 1980

The violence of the prison riot at New Mexico penitentiary, Santa Fe, in February 1980 was shocking and surprising to commentators on penal affairs. The Santa Fe riot has been compared in ferocity with the more widely known Attica riot. Colvin's analysis, from his vantage point as principal investigator and researcher at the time, provides convincing evidence that the Santa Fe riot 'is without parallel in the penal history of the United States for its brutality, destruction, and disorganization among the rioters' (Colvin, 1982, p. 449). In the 36 hours before order was restored, 33 prisoners were killed and five staff injured (*New York Times*, 4 February 1980). Possibly as many as 200 prisoners were beaten and raped, 90 given drug overdoses and twelve staff beaten, stabbed or sodomized during the riot (Colvin, 1982, p. 449). The report of the investigation into the riot, by the Attorney General of New Mexico, was more restricted in its analysis than the McKay report, but adopted a similar reformist strategy.

In the Santa Fe riot, the repetitious nature of prison problems, including disturbances, over considerable periods of time can clearly be seen. Conditions for staff and prisoners at Santa Fe, typical of many state prisons, remained largely unchanged throughout the twentieth century. In 1912, guards at the prison, according to the warden, were 'the poorest paid lot in the service of the state' (Morris, 1983, p. 32). 'Forty years later prisoners would still be periodically beaten and brutalized by their fearful, low-paid keepers; would still be using chamber pots and open latrines; would still suffer regular bouts of dysentery' (ibid.). The post-1945 history of this prison is studded with incidents of disturbances by prisoners. There was a food riot at Santa Fe prison towards the end of 1948, another six months later and another in November 1952. A thwarted escape in June 1952 was followed by a general strike by prisoners. In June 1953, in a further disturbance, prisoners seized the decrepit hospital and took 21 staff hostage (Morris, 1983, p. 33). Minor riots in 1971, 1973 and 1976 reportedly were brutally suppressed (Morris, 1983, p. 47).

Although overcrowding was blamed at the time, three prisoners challenged more general prison conditions in a federal lawsuit. These included the fact that 1200 prisoners were kept in a prison designed for 900 and that there were deficiencies in the prison's mail policies, food service, visiting procedures and medical and psychological services (*New York Times*, 6 February 1980). It was the case also that a higher proportion of the prisoners than in many prisons were there for 'protective custody' (referred to in Britain as 'Rule 43' or as 'segregated for their own protection'), and in the riot these were among the first to be attacked. In addition, there had been five wardens running the prison in five consecutive years. The Attorney General's investigation said 'the movement of prisoners was not tightly controlled, there were too few guards for proper control and that the morale of guards was low'. Further, guards were difficult to hire because their starting pay was too low (*New York Times*, 6 February 1980).

But Colvin reviews several alternative explanations of the Santa Fe riot, including security lapses, poor food and basic services, over-crowding, alleged conspiracies by middle-level administrators and the increasing dominance of a 'new breed' of psychopathic, violent, disruptive prisoner. He uses a review of the decade leading up to the riot, during which there were five relatively orderly years without disturbances followed by five disorderly years, to demonstrate that none of these factors correlated with the growing incidence of disorder in the prison after 1975. His detailed analysis, based on many hundreds of interviews with those involved, as well as drawing on the extensive unpublished records of the Attorney General's investigation into the riot, points to changes in the way staff attempted to control the prison after 1975.

Apparently, until 1975 staff tacitly collaborated with the maintenance of social order by a number of inmate gangs, which relied for their power on drug-trafficking and the control of decisions affecting inmate programmes. After that date:

> In an attempt to wrest control of the prison from the inmates, the new administration removed all inmates from administrative positions in programs, tightened restrictions on inmate movement, stopped 'outside contact' programs, increased drug searches, and clamped down on possible conduits for drugs. The curtailment of drugs and many programs removed the major informal and formal incentive controls over inmates, removed important illegitimate and legitimate opportunity structures within the inmates' society and, thus, disrupted important sources of inmate power that had been connected to these incentives. The removal of incentive controls, necessitated by the exposure and public criticism of the former administration's practices, constituted a disruption of the previous accommodation between staff and inmates. Organized protests from inmates quickly erupted.
>
> (Colvin, 1982, p. 454)

Inevitably, perhaps, staff found they had to use more and more coercive means to control and discipline the increasingly disruptive prisoners (Colvin, 1982, p. 455). A spiral of violence among inmates developed, as they found that a propensity towards violence was their best protection against violence from others. Crucially, Colvin argues that fragmentation and self-interested individualistic violence by inmates was a feature of the riot, in contrast with Attica. It is easy to see how this changed inmate behaviour attracted the reputation of a 'new breed' of prisoner arriving in the prison. Around 1976, staff began to notice 'a "new breed" of violent and disruptive inmate emerging in the New Mexico prison. Clearly a sociological phenomenon, the "new breed" becomes inexplicable only when viewed primarily as a psychological or supposedly "genetic" aberration' (Colvin, 1982, p. 456). This mistake was based on a failure to identify how prisoners were acting differently in the light of changed circumstances (Colvin, 1982, p. 456).

Morris's account of the 1980 Santa Fe prison riot is based on official records of more than two hundred interviews with prisoners, their friends and relatives, officials and others involved and a great bulk of documentary evidence. In the course of the resulting detailed case study of the origins, process and outcomes of the riot, Part Four provides a horrific account of violence between prisoners, as those in Cellblock Four were battered, hacked and blowtorched to death (Morris, 1983, pp. 93–115).

The anarchic escalation of violence included the guards, who 'are savagely beaten, stabbed, reportedly forced to perform fellatio on their captors, and by inmate accounts brutally sodomized, now with an axe handle or a riot stick, now by prisoners. Naked and bound, they are under a hail of humiliation and threats, and in the process are dragged from place to place' (Morris, 1983, p. 80). Then the rioters began killing the prisoners in Cellblock Four, beginning with 'snitches' and extending to indiscriminate maiming and killing:

> Outside, a prison official hears a whistling sound from 4, scans the block with binoculars, stops on an incredible scene through a window, and watches in horror as four or five inmates hold a man down as another burns his head and face with a blowtorch. When his eyes explode out of the back of his head, the inmates burn his groin, then mutilate the body with shanks and torch him again. When they are through, one seared corpse, a man who weighed over 200 pounds, will weigh less than 50 pounds.
>
> (Morris, 1983, pp. 100–1)

A symptom of the divisions between prisoners demonstrated in the fragmented nature of the riot is the puzzling fact that twenty prisoners who were not informers, including five tough and respected prisoners from the segregation unit, were killed (Serrill and Katel, 1980, p. 13). Conditions in the prison at Santa Fe did not improve dramatically, even after the 1980 riot.

> [The guards] faced their own terrors and administrative neglect . . . In more than thirty internal prison memos . . . the corrections

officers, many of them new men hired after the riot, had documented numerous incidents of abuse, threats, and physical attacks by inmates . . . The maximum security inmates of cell block 3, the most unstable and dangerous in the pen – several of whom were about to be indicted for killings during the riot – had been stripping away a shoddy chain-link fence in the unit to make knives and picks. They had showered guards with urine and bleach, hit them with rocks and with their fists. They had roamed the cell block unhandcuffed, crawled under unanchored fences in the exercise yard, congregated by scores when there should have been no more than five outside at any one time . . . And the situation reached a climax at the end of October in a week of stabbings, inmate murders, and mounting terror . . . Security was lax throughout the penitentiary, said the protesting guards – no binoculars in watchtowers, patrol and pursuit vehicles with flat tires and dead batteries, riot-control grilles left open, as always, sally port gates that had not worked for a year, new electronic locking mechanisms carelessly placed so as to be vulnerable to hot-wiring by inmates, guards with faulty radios or none at all, and often only two officers assigned to supervise the 350 to 400 inmates of the entire south wing.

(Morris, 1983, pp. 201–2)

In the spring of 1981, despite a pay rise, 32 per cent of guards still left the job within a year (Morris, 1983, p. 202). Post-riot conditions reduce one sort of tensions, but raise other tensions to an unbearable pitch. 'Under the post-riot pressures, men killed each other and themselves as never before, save during the riot itself' (Morris, 1983, p. 209).

The Failure of the Authorities to Address the Significance of Prison Riots

The 1980s were marked by the failure of the authorities to deal adequately with the increasing scope, scale and diversity of violence and destructiveness which had been a feature of prison riots since Attica. The significance of shifts occurring in the 1970s in the character of prison riots was both intra- and extra-institutional. Inside the prison, Attica demonstrated strong prisoner leadership which reached an impasse in negotiations with Governor Nelson Rockefeller, who ordered the invasion of the prison by the military which led to most of the casualties. Santa Fe illustrated weak leadership by prisoners, with whom the authorities, partly mindful of the outcome of Attica, negotiated to the end, at which point the hostages were released and the prison restored to the staff without a single shot being fired.

Outside the prison, in society at large, at one level the legitimacy of prisons and their administration was increasingly questioned after the mid-1970s. Attica and Santa Fe 'were dramatic expressions of changes going on in the larger society, nationally and even internationally' (Stastny and Tyrnauer, 1982, p. 3). Silberman highlighted some of the changes in an address to the American Correctional Association shortly before the riot at Santa Fe.

> Contemporary prisoners – especially black prisoners – are unwilling to accept the kind of mutual accommodations and understandings between inmates and staff that, in the past, had kept the pressures towards anarchy and violence under some sort of control. In effect, inmates have withdrawn the consent on which prison government has always rested. Instead, they are protesting the conditions under which they live and are demanding a wide variety of changes; at times, they seem to be rejecting the legitimacy of prison government itself. The result has been a widespread breakdown in order and control.
>
> (Silberman, 1980, quoted in Stastny and Tyrnauer, 1982, p. 3)

Increasingly, since the 1960s, the legitimacy of the prison has been called into question, through the rioting of prisoners as dramatically as through the voices of researchers and prison reformers. During the 1960s and 1970s, there was increasing polarization between custodians and prisoners. The 1970s and 1980s saw a trend towards more groups and interests claiming a stake in the state of the prisons. At the same time, in the wake of the Santa Fe riot, there was growing pressure from the political Right against further prison reforms. Measures taken to tackle the alleged causes of the riot, namely to improve the pay and training of guards, decrease prison overcrowding by 50 per cent (leaving 650 out of 1150 prisoners to 200 guards), improve legal, food and medical services and extend activities for prisoners to five hours per day, still did not prevent nine prisoners and two guards being killed in the year following the riot (Engel and Rothman, 1983, p. 93).

One significance of Santa Fe was that in the decade after Attica, many prisoners continued to riot because they did not experience significant improvements in their circumstances. Accounts of riots in the 1980s focused mainly on deficiencies in their living conditions, rather than in the structural issues which had preoccupied the more radical rioting prisoners in the previous two decades.

In a five-day period of late May 1981, five riots erupted in three Michigan prisons, following a mutiny by guards in the largest prison in the continents of America and Europe. Detailed analysis suggests that they were the outcome of a five-year history of complex changes in the policies and practices of the prison system in Michigan, as a result of which shortages of resources, overcrowding and disorder in the prisons were worsened considerably (Useem and Kimball, 1989, pp. 114–60).

To what extend did prison riots since Santa Fe achieve improvements on behalf of prisoners? The evidence is patchy. Useem and Kimball conclude: 'The 1980 New Mexico riot had, by 1985, resulted in significant improvements in the Santa Fe Penitentiary; the Michigan riots had not. While we are writing too soon after the West Virginia riot to close the books, the developments in the first post-riot year have given no reason for optimism' (Useem and Kimball, 1989, p. 195).

In November 1984, the first of a series of riots involving the 3000 Marielitos prisoners confined in prisons across the US took place at the US Penitentiary in Atlanta. The Marielitos feared being deported to Cuba and rioted to draw attention to this fact, and also to the restrictions of being confined permanently in their calls.

> Two men usually share a cell designed for one. The food, generally cold, is brought to their cells. When the Cubans leave their cells, they are handcuffed, with the cuffs attached to a belt at their waists, there is nothing for them to do – no TV, nothing to read, no education, no activity except one hour (or less) a week walking in the prison yard. Lock-down is the Bureau of Prisons' (BOP) prescription for the Marielitos.
>
> (Keller, 1988, p. 24)

On 1 to 2 January 1986, prisoners at Moundsville penitentiary, West Virginia, rioted (Useem and Kimball, 1989, pp. 161–97). This was one of at least ten major prison riots since the autumn of 1985 in the District of Columbia and the states of Indiana, Michigan, Oklahoma, Tennessee, Virginia and West Virginia. 'The common theme has been that prisoners became tired of terrible living conditions, tired of unkept promises of change, and tired of being treated like animals. The fragile order that is maintained in most prisons explodes into a riot; an inexcusable yet understandable response to the frustration and anger caused by years of neglect' (Bronstein, 1986, p. 12).

In the late 1980s, litigation by rioting prisoners and their advocates centred round issues of human rights in relation to the responses of the authorities to these incidents. For example, prisoners at Cedar Junction maximum security prison in Massachusetts sued the State of Massachusetts for violating their civil rights by incarcerating them there (*New York Times*, 8 February 1987, I, p. 48, c. 1). In October 1989, riots, apparently exacerbated by overcrowding, occurred at Huntingdon prison and Camp Hill prison, Pennsylvania. At Camp Hill, when negotiations with staff broke down, the prisoners set light to most of the prison. An injunction was granted subsequently against the Department of Corrections, requiring them to release the shackled prisoners, held naked and without toilet paper and mattresses in triple-locked security for the previous fortnight, when the institution was put on lock-down (Presser, 1990, p. 3).

In a riot at Clinton correctional facility, Dannemora, New York, one prisoner was shot and four knifed (*New York Times*, 29 June 1987, II, p. 4, c. 6). But the uprisings in the autumn of 1987 by over a thousand Cuban detainees in Oakdale, Louisiana, and Atlanta, Georgia, federal prisons (*New York Times*, 6 December 1987, IV, p. 4, c. 1), have been claimed to have involved the largest number of hostages ever taken in a single series of incidents in US prison history (American Correctional Association, 1990, p. vi), with the families of hostages and prisoners keeping vigil outside these prisons (*New York Times*, 1 December 1987, II, p. 8, c. 3). This is a sobering reminder of the impossibility of segregating explanations of the origins of prison riots from the wider context of national and international politics. There was subsequent debate about whether the Justice Department had honoured the agreement for a full and fair review of the cases of immigrants.' (*New York Times*, 26 January 1988, I, p. 23, c. 1). At the same time, in parallel with such riots themselves, have been prisoners' continued attempts, not just in relation to immigrant status but wider struggles, to get redress for their grievances through the courts. The outcomes are not generally encouraging, from the prisoners' point of view. Several prisoners brought legal actions, quoting the Eighth Amendment, prohibiting 'cruel and unusual punishment'. But judgements illustrate how the criteria for assessing this shift according to the case in hand. In *Rhodes* v. *Chapman*, a complaint of overcrowded and deleterious conditions was judged to be upheld if the prisoner could show 'wanton and unnecessary infliction of pain', tested by the 'totality of conditions' (*Hutto* v. *Finney*). In 1986, the Supreme Court ruled in *Whitley* v. *Albers* that 'a prisoner injured while authorities are suppressing a prison riot can recover only if officials used force "maliciously and sadistically for the very purpose of causing harm,"' This judgement was against a prisoner claiming that his shooting during a prison riot violated the Eighth Amendment. The Supreme Court ruled that, 'obduracy and wantonness' in quelling the riot, rather than 'inadvertence or error in good faith', would have to be proved in order for the case to be found in favour of the prisoner. Subsequent cases brought by prisoners illustrated that the trajectory of this judgement was towards defending the authorities and undermining the power of the Eighth Amendment to speak to the interests of the prisoner (Lopez and Fathi, 1990, p. 3).

Prisoners continued to take more direct action. Riots occurred at Rikers Island prison in February (*New York Times*, 19 February 1988, II, p. 1, c. 5). Stringtown prison, Oklahoma in May (ibid., 15 May 1988, I, p. 212, c. 1), Trenton state prison in July (ibid., 9 July 1988, I, p. 29, c. 2), at Coxackee correctional facility in New York at the beginning of August (ibid., 2 August 1988, II, p. 12, c. 2) and Billerica prison and Lawrence county jail some fifteen miles away on 15 August 1988. In this last case, the destruction of one block of the prison at Billerica was attributed to serious overcrowding, the heat and the poor quality of the food (ibid., 16 August 1988, I, p. 24, c. 1). In November of 1988, guards at Salem prison in Oregon used high pressure hoses to suppress a riot by prisoners in support of gay rights (ibid., 2 November 1988, I, p. 18, c. 4), hundreds of prisoners rioted in 'gang war' at Puerto Rico penitentiary (ibid., 7 December 1988, I, p. 20, c. 5), more than 400 prisoners rioted at Guayana regional prison, Puerto Rico on the following day (ibid., 8 December 1988, I, p. 30, c. 1) and Christmas Day saw a riot at the prison in Hall County, Georgia (ibid., 26 December 1988, I, p. 19, c. 5). Seven prison buildings were burned in a riot at Banning Road camp rehabilitation centre, California (ibid., 11 January 1989, I, p. 13, c. 1), about 300 prisoners rioted reportedly in gang violence at the maximum security prison, Chester, Illinois, in late September (ibid., 27 September 1989, I, p. 14, c. 5) and tear gas was used by 200 correctional officers to deal with a riot at Rikers Island prison in early October (ibid., 7 October 1989, I, p. 26, c. 2). Within weeks Camp Hill medium security prison in Philadelphia experienced two riots on successive days, involving 1200 prisoners and leading to more than 130 prisoners and guards being injured (ibid., 29 October 1989, I, p. 28, c. 1). A night-time riot in Hudson county jail, Jersey City, in early December, led to one prisoner being shot and six guards injured (ibid., 8 December 1989, II, p. 2, c. 1). On

29 May 1991, prisoners at Southport correctional facility, Pine Heights, New York, took hostages when they rioted (Radio Four News, 29 May 1991). Southport was typical of many others – full to capacity and with emergency legislation invoked repeatedly, in response to recurrent small riots and violent incidents, including attacks by prisoners on other prisoners and on guards (Useem and Kimball, 1989, p. 160). By the mid-1980s, nearly three million men and women were under some form of correctional supervision in the US, or three in every hundred men, either in custody or on supervision (ibid., 2 January 1987, I, p. 17, c. 1).

Meanwhile, as the prison system continued to expand, plans were made for its even faster expansion in the 1990s, partly as a remedy for overcrowding (Quinlan, 1991, p. 3). Releases of prisoners, either in exchange for new arrivals or simply to reduce overcrowding, became more common (*New York Times*, 9 June, I, p. 27, c. 1). A hundred prisoners in Hudson County were transferred in the summer of 1989 to an encampment of tents in an attempt to reduce overcrowding in prisons (ibid., 17 August 1989, II, p. 4, c. 1). In a move reminiscent of British penal policy in the early nineteenth century, plans were made to move up to 800 prisoners from overcrowded prisons in New York to a prison barge in the city (ibid., 13 March 1989, II, p. 2, c. 1). In 1990, the Federal Bureau of Prisons noted as part of its commemorative publication concerning its 'proud tradition', plans to build new institutions and recruit staff for a federal prison population which was expected to double from 50 000 in 1989 to around 100 000 by 1995 (*Federal Prisons Journal*, Summer 1990, Vol. 1, No. 4).

4 Prison Riots in Britain

The analysis of the present trends of imprisonment in Britain and in the U.S.A. emphasize[s] that we must support the prisoners' struggle not only for their sakes, but for ours too. For the prison indeed oppresses not just those who are locked behind its bars; increasingly it reaches out to ensnare every one of us.

(Fitzgerald, 1977, p. 266)

INTRODUCTION

The history of prison riots in Britain divides into four periods comparable in duration to those in the US: traditional riots up to the early 1950s; riots against conditions from the early 1950s to the late 1960s; collective consciousness-raising riots after the late 1960s; and from the mid-1970s, riots of the post-rehabilitation period which were fragmented in character.

In contrast with the decentralized prison administration of the US, the century up to 1877 when the Prison Commission was established (40 and 40 Vict. c. 21, s. 4), saw prisons in England and Wales increasingly administered from London. The Prison Commission administered prisons and borstals after their introduction in 1908 in England and Wales. Central prisons were for those serving long sentences, overcrowding leading to many also occupying local prisons. Regional prisons were training institutions for selected prisoners serving more than twelve months. Corrective training prisons were for younger recidivists. Local prisons were the majority, and included most large, older prisons. The Criminal Justice Act of 1961 abolished the Prison Commission and absorbed the new Prison Board into the Home Office (Klare, 1962, p. 140).

A century after 1877, moving towards the millenium, the prison system in England, Wales, Northern Ireland and Scotland was run by a mixture of centralized and decentralized administrations, answerable to Parliament through some sixty divisions and subdivisions and the Director-General of Prisons, a senior civil servant. In England and Wales, prisons were the responsibility of the Home Office. In Scotland, both the National Health Service and the prisons were run by the Scottish Home and Health Department, one of the five departments in the Scottish Office. The prisons in Northern Ireland were run by the Northern Ireland Office, which operated like a Northern Ireland Home Office, whereas the medical services there were the responsibility of a principal medical officer in the Department of Health and Social Services, answerable to the Chief Medical Officer. The consequent separation of the medical service in Northern Ireland from accountability to the local Home Office department had practical consequences in terms of its autonomy in making professional decisions.

But centralization is not the end of the story of British penal policy and practice, which for almost two centuries was made and implemented in a complex matrix of statutory, voluntary and informal organizations and groups. Whilst the trend was towards centralization, the hub of which was the government of the day and the Home Office with its civil servants, Scotland and Northern Ireland had their own devolved powers, through ministers and, in the case of Scotland, the legal apparatus had a good deal of autonomy. The making of policy in the past owed as much to the activities of reformers such as Elizabeth Fry and John Howard as to the planning of professional custodians. During the twentieth century reforming groups such as the Howard League for Penal Reform and the National Association for the Care and Resettlement of Offenders developed powerful parliamentary lobbies and earned cross-party respect for their ability to deliver high quality information on penal affairs at crucial moments in public and parliamentary debates on criminal justice issues (Ryan, 1978). In riot history, the prisoners' rights organization, Preservation of the Rights of Prisoners (PROP), made dramatic if not always decisive contributions to these debates, most notably in its report after the Hull prison riot and in the wake of the official report (Home Office, 1977a).

TRADITIONAL RIOTS: UP TO THE EARLY 1950s

Prison riots can be regarded as traditional in the sense that the rioting prisoners resort to customary means of demonstrating resistance to the immediacy of imprisonment, with no wider implications. For example, traditional riots did not involve any statement of grievances by prisoners. They 'simply' rioted. Resistance to imprisonment was commonly expressed through invasions of prisons, escapes from prisons and mutinies, involving individuals and groups of prisoners rather than mass incidents involving entire institutions.

In the medieval period, prisons only existed at the margins of societal arrangements for curbing criminality and deviance. Prison, outside the incarceration by the Church in a monastery or similar institution under Canon Law, tended to be viewed as a temporary stopping place while a decision about the sentence was arrived at, rather than the outcome of that process of trial and sentencing. The earliest sentences to cellular confinement for long periods in Britain were probably those invoked in monasteries, under Canon Law. Additionally, unruly vagrants and paupers increasingly were confined in 'bridewells', or houses of correction, after the first was opened in London in 1557. Bridewells often housed people in large dormitories with no provision for separate accommodation for individuals.

Throughout the medieval period, considerable interplay concerning ideas about institutional responses to pauperism and criminality took place between Britain and other European countries. Workhouses for unruly poor people spread rapidly through Europe after the mid-sixteenth century. Initiatives by Roman Catholic humanitarians in Florence led to the establishment in 1650 of a small workhouse for vagrant boys and a prison for delinquent boys was opened as part of the Hospital of St Michael in Rome in 1704 by the Pope. A prison for women was built there in 1735. In 1773, the workhouse at Ghent, built in 1773, was reputedly the first to use cellular confinement and hard work as a means of reformation, in the manner of 'modern' prisons in the nineteenth century (US Bureau of Prisons, 1949, p. 18).

Invasions, Escapes and Rioting

Ditchfield's review of the literature leads to the conclusion that 'historically, riots have been uncommon in English prisons' (Ditchfield, 1990, p. 5). He quotes Thomas and Pooley (1980) in support of the view that 'before the 1850s, disorder in prisons was nearly always associated with particular individuals or groups of individuals' Ditchfield, 1990, p. 5). The feature of riots Thomas and Pooley were emphasizing was the general lack of 'anything approaching a wholesale uprising' (Thomas and Pooley, 1980, p. 5), which was more or less ruled out in the confined segregation of the silent and separate systems. But there is evidence of considerable collective disorder from time to time in some prisons and on transports and hulks, where prisoners could not so easily be segregated.

Even in medieval times, however, prisoners collectively resisted their imprisonment and sporadically this resistance surfaced in the form of riots. Whilst the historical record is patchy, incidents of 'escapes', which are really invasions of prisons by mobs attempting to release prisoners, can be found in Britain as early as 1268 when the Bishop of Lincoln's prison was attacked by armed men who released a prisoner (Pugh, 1968, p. 222). A similar break-in occurred in the London Tun a prison in the Cornhill district in 1298 and a combined break-out and break-in at the Tower in London in 1312 (Pugh, 1968, pp. 222–3). Other rescue riots have been noted at Ripon in 1337, at Lewes in 1382 or thereabouts and in 1421, 1450, 1470 and 1517 (Pugh, 1968, pp. 223–4). In 1381, Watt Tyler and others attacked Rochester, Canterbury, the Marshalsea and King's Bench prisons in Southwark and all the other prisons (Pugh, 1968, p. 223).

From 28 April 1768, the arrest of John Wilkes for producing allegedly seditious documents, notably *An Essay on Woman* and No. 45 of the *North Briton*, crowds rioted around King's Bench prison in London for several days (Wilkinson, 1991, p. 316).

In Newgate, the debtors' prison, all sorts of prisoners were thrown indiscriminately together. 'The days were passed in idleness, debauchery, riotous quarrelling, immoral conversation, gambling, instruction in all nefarious processes, lively discourse upon past criminal exploits, elaborate discussion of others to be perpetrated after release' (Griffiths, 1884, quoted in Hibbert, 1966, pp. 152–3).

Conditions in Newgate were an epitome of the state of prisons on which Howard reported in the 1770s. Twenty years later, in 1796, a riot was reported there (*The Times*, 23 November 1796). Reports emphasizing the appalling conditions in Newgate continued after Howard's visit well into the next century. Riots were still occurring there in 1819 (McConville, 1981, p. 230).

Millbank, a huge prison in the shape of a six-pointed star reminiscent of Bentham's Panopticon, opened in 1821 and accommodated convicts in separate cells where they worked alone for the first half of their sentences and in association thereafter. But this structure did not prevent disturbances. Soon a serious riot was only quelled when the Governor called in the Bow Street Runners (Hibbert, 1966, p. 178).

The dominant view in the nineteenth century was that prisoners were better fed than many free labourers (Tobias, 1967, p. 206). This helped to buttress the rationale for making the silent and separate systems in prisons less attractive and more deterrent than all other alternative ways of life. Nevertheless, the view of prisons as a training in crime was as credible then as now. Undoubtedly, prisoners' ingenuity at resisting the reformative ideology of imprisonment was 'able to triumph over all the apparatus of masks and individual stalls in chapels and on treadmills, over silence rules and separate confinement' (Tobias, 1967, p. 205). According to Tobias, the criminal culture was a source of support for offenders, in and out of prison (Tobias, 1967, p. 97). Today's participants in a food riot, Chartist demonstration or crop-burning were likely to be tomorrow's prison rioters.

The Prison Act of 1865 removed many of the local authorities' powers and that of 1877 took away the rest. The 1865 Act approved a return to a severe, deterrent prison regime and from 1877 this was implemented by Lieutenant-Colonel Edmund Du Cane, chairman of the Prison Commissioners, under whose unimaginative and rigid leadership the English prison system became 'a massive machine for the promotion of misery' (Howard, 1960, p. 103).

There was every reason for convicts to be discontented in mid-Victorian England. 'Because they were so badly fed, the convicts at Chatham were driven to eating live worms and frogs and rubbish and at Portland, Dartmoor, and other prisons they melted candles in their gruel to make it more satisfying' (Hibbert, 1966, p. 187).

By the turn of the twentieth century, the Act implementing many of the Gladstone Report's proposals may have been positive, but in 1906 a visitor to Dartmoor prison still recorded with horror:

> As I walked along the endless landings and corridors in the great cellular blocks, I saw something of the 1,500 men who were then immured in Dartmoor. Their drab uniforms were plastered with broad arrows, their heads were closely shaven . . . Not even a safety razor was allowed, so that in addition to the stubble on their heads, their faces were covered with a sort of dirty moss, representing the growth of hair that a pair of clippers could not remove . . . As they saw us coming each man turned to the nearest wall and put his face closely against it, remaining in this servile position until we had passed him. This was a strictly ordered procedure, to avoid assault or familiarity, the two great offences in prison conduct.
>
> (Quoted in Hibbert, 1966, p. 189)

Mutinies on Convict Ships

Prisons were scarcely used prior to 1800, save as a means of incarcerating debtors or people awaiting trial. Hitherto, the British system of transportation of criminals overseas was the only widespread method of dealing with them, apart from various forms of corporal punishment such as execution, flogging, branding, public degradation in the stocks, pillory and ducking stool, and bodily mutilations of various kinds.

Transportation appears to have been preferred by most convicts to remaining in the hulks (Tobias, 1967, p. 212). Although some transports may have set sail with an optimistic spirit (Tobias, 1967, p. 213), conditions on board were habitually so appalling that mutineers had little to lose. An eye-witness of prisoners arriving in Sydney commented that they presented 'a sight truly shocking to the feelings of humanity . . . some half and others entirely naked, unable to turn or help themselves . . . The smell was so offensive that I could hardly bear it' (Ives, 1914, p. 5, quoted in Orland, 1975, p. 19).

Transportation was justified on economic and pragmatic as well as humanitarian grounds. About 50 000 convicts were transported from Britain to the North American colonies between 1607 and 1776, and when the Declaration of Independence in 1776 put an end to this, in the subsequent 70 years more than 100 000 people were despatched for Australian, Tasmanian and Norfolk Island penal colonies, many dying en route and many more soon after arrival.

Undoubtedly, the appalling conditions under which sailors in the British mercantile marine and prisoners served, worked and lived during the many voyages of convict ships in the years between the sailing of the first fleet in 1787 and the landing of the last convict ship in Australia in 1868, contributed to the prevalent rumours of impending mutinies by sailors and convicts alike on the majority of ships (Bateson, 1985, pp. 216–17). The discovery by Rudé that a significant number of social protesters were transported to Australia during the late eighteenth and early nineteenth centuries may have contributed substantially to the predisposition of convict ships to mutiny (Rudé, 1978, pp. 242–52).

Bateson's authoritative history of convict transportation from England and Ireland to Australia, which comprises the core of the 'true' transportation system, is based on a reading of more than six hundred ships' surgeons' journals. From this, it is clear that compared with the massive loss of life from other causes, including shipwreck and diseases such as gaol fever, the number of prisoners injured in mutinies was small (Bateson, 1985, pp. 6–7), as was the handful executed (Bateson, 1985, p. 75). However, this does not mean that riots and similar disturbances did not occur regularly, but were somewhat un-der-reported. There would be little incentive for a ship's master to report an attempt to take over a ship, in a mutiny which cast a poor light on discipline on board. Nevertheless, enough records exist to point to mutinies as a significant feature of shipboard imprisonment. Attempted mutinies occurred on board the *Scarborough* in April 1787 (Bateson, 1985, p. 101) and in January 1790 (Bateson, 1985, p. 128), on the *Albermarle* in April 1781 (Bateson, 1985, pp. 133–4), on the *Sugar Cane* in May 1793 (Bateson, 1985, p. 146) and on the *Anne,* which sailed from Cork on 28 June 1800 for Port Jackson, and ex-perienced an abortive mutiny by about thirty convicts, one of whom was shot in the battle on deck (Bateson, 1985, pp. 177–9). On the voyage of the *Boddington* in 1793, there were 'frequent alarms of mutiny and conspiracy among the convicts and the guard of the New South Wales Corps, but no attempt to seize the ship actually occurred' (Bateson, 1985, p. 146). In those early years, the most noteworthy mutiny occurred on board the convict ship *Marquis Cornwallis,* a month out of Cork *en route* for Port Jackson in September 1795 (Bateson, 1985, pp. 148–50). A combined plot between convicts and soldiers to take over the *Barwell,* sailing from Portsmouth in Novem-ber 1797, was foiled (Bateson, 1985, pp. 165–7).

The attempt by convicts to take over the *Somersetshire* in 1810 was described as 'the most serious attempt at mutiny for a quarter of a century' (Bateson, 1985, p. 290). On the *Chapman,* an attempted mutiny in 1817 among 198 convicts who had embarked at Cork was quelled with three convicts dead and 22 wounded (Bateson, 1985, pp. 203–7). Attempted mutinies were also crushed on the *John Barry* in 1821, on the *Ocean* and the *Isabella* in 1823, on the *Mangles* in 1824, on the *Royal Charlotte* in 1825, on the *England* in 1826, the *Florentina* in 1830 and on the *John* in 1832 (Bateson, 1985, pp. 217–24).

The only successful mutiny in a convict ship seems to have oc-curred in 1797, when the *Lady Shore* was taken over, not by convicts but by guards and sailed to South America (Bateson, 1985, pp. 151–7). In 1820, the attempt by 28 convicts to take over the *Castle Forbes* on arrival at Port Jackson from Ireland seems to have been the only attempt to do this after the prisoners were disembarked (Bateson, 1985, pp. 211–12). The bloodiest recorded mutiny appears to have been on the 400-ton two squared-rigged two-decker *Hercules* which sailed from Cork on 29 November 1801, the rioting prisoners being quelled on 29 December with fourteen convicts killed, though it should be remembered that over the subsequent eight months of the voyage a further thirty, a fifth of the total on board, had died of disease (Bateson, 1985, pp. 179–82).

Riots on the Hulks

In 1777, Howard's report on the state of prisons described the unacceptable conditions in the filthy old prison ships which remained round English shores after shipment of prisoners to the United States was stopped. A number of mutinies and riots were reported in the hulks in the 1770s (McConville, 1981, pp. 106–7).

By 1850, transportation was becoming more difficult. Imprisonment in Britain followed by a ticket of leave in the colonies was increasingly common. The establishment in 1850 of a 'national' service for running convict prisons and the hulks and consequent attempts by staff to impose more discipline 'led to trouble on the hulks, which were old ships, where prisoners had more freedom and could therefore more easily combine to create trouble' (Pooley and Thomas, 1980, p. 5). Several uprisings on the hulks were reported. In April 1850, the *York* and the *Stirling Castle* both had riots. In 1851, a mutiny on the *Warrior* at Woolwich 'was suppressed only by calling in the Royal Artillery and the Royal Marines to support warders who, cutlasses drawn, went below to bring up 38 leaders, who were transferred' (Thomas, 1972, pp. 54–5).

Protests by prisoners in the late 1850s were attributable partly to the way convicts were transferred to the prisons as the hulks were closed. Following these transfers there was trouble in Chatham and Lewes prisons, the ringleaders from the latter being moved to Millbank and Pentonville (Thomas, 1972, pp. 55–6). The major riot in 1861 at Chatham convict prison illustrates the mood of the time.

Chatham was often in trouble and was nicknamed 'the slaughterhouse' by the prisoners. The governor blamed the officers for incompetence and worse. Some had given newspapers to the prisoners, and the latter apparently believed that the officers would support them against the administration. The convicts were controlled at bayonet point, an escape plan was thwarted and the leader of the riot removed.

(Thomas and Pooley, 1980, p. 5)

Rioting in Response to the Failure of Penitentiaries

Just as in the US, only half of Howard's principles for the penitentiary had been adopted, so in Britain, the penitentiary encountered immediate problems. Basically, in the US, the penitentiary system failed within half a century of its introduction because the inmates were subjected to tight discipline while the staff were a law unto themselves (Hawkins and Alpert, 1989, p. 46).

In Britain, the almost immediate breaching of the system of solitary isolation through overcrowding in prisons such as Gloucester, for example, led to the introduction of ever more punitive regimes to try to compensate for this. The treadwheel, the crank, bread and water, and repeated dousings with cold water in a dark cell were some of the measures used (Ignatieff, 1978, pp. 207–8). Threatened breaches of discipline by individuals or groups of prisoners led to a quadrupling of the punishment rate between 1825 and 1835 (Ignatieff, 1978, p. 178).

Despite Bentham's intention to eliminate disorder in prisons, collective resistance by prisoners, in some form, remains a feature of prisons in Britain throughout their history. Twenty years before Bentham published his plans for the Panopticon, Howard had identified among many other problems in prisons on and off shore the risks of criminality and disorder being transmitted between prisoners through the common incarceration of many different classes of prisoners, often irrespective of age, sex or the nature of the offence (Howard, 1977, pp. 15–16). However, he emphasized that the improvements he recommended were governed by what later advocates of the Poor Law Amendment Act of 1834 were to call the principle of 'less eligibility'. That is, conditions were not to be improved so as to raise prisoners above the level of other people in the community, but only so as to implement 'such strict regulations in preventing all dissipation and riotous amusement' (Howard, 1977, p. 77).

So the first great wave of prison building in Britain, in the mid-nineteenth century, created more than a score of three-, four- and five-storey complexes based on principles of cellular isolation of the individual prisoner, in the interests of reformation. In the 1990s, these buildings still formed the core of the local prison system in Britain. By the 1890s, however, criticisms of the prison system, which in 1894 precipitated the Gladstone Committee which reported in 1895 (Gladstone, 1895), pointed already to the manifest failure of these institutions. According to Dr Morrison, the Chaplain of Wandsworth Prison, whose article in the *Daily Chronicle* precipitated the Gladstone Inquiry, the cost of imprisonment was rising and warders were badly selected, underpaid, overworked and too military in character. Prisons were not so much instruments of reform as failing institutions. The silent and separate systems were 'torture not so much for the hardened sinner, who can in the end settle down to gaol life, as for the less guilty inmates.' Bentham's moralizing factory was running out of control. 'The great machine rolls obscurely on, cumbrous, pitiless, obsolete, unchanged. The silent world . . . goes on receiving new citizens and discharging old ones . . . ' In short, there was a 'complete and utter breakdown of our local prison system' (Rose, 1961, p. 59).

The Gladstone Report, whose major recommendations were reported in the *Daily Chronicle* as 'the inevitable end of a discredited system' (Rose, 1961, p. 64) and were enshrined in the Prison Act of 1898 may have been a milestone. But it did not prevent the quasimilitary machine of penal administration criticized by Morrison continuing for the following hundred years to incarcerate vast numbers of remand, mentally ill, alcoholic, homeless and minor offenders, alongside the small proportion of serious offenders, in the same increasingly decrepit and overcrowded Victorian prisons.

The convict service was administered separately from the rest of the penal system, even after 1877. Convicts were disaffected, throughout the mid-nineteenth century. Partly, trouble arose over the way the Penal Servitude Acts of 1853 and 1857 operated. The former Act allowed no remission but, under the latter, convicts sentenced after June 1857 received remission of more than a fifth and this created tensions. A strike at Portland in 1858 led to 230 convicts being transferred to Millbank and Pentonville. In February 1861, there was a riot at Chatham. In June one of the ringleaders tried to kill an officer with a shovel and in September 1862 a warder was murdered at Portland (Thomas, 1972, pp. 55–6).

Public concern about increasing crime led to the Act of 1864, which increased the minimum period of penal servitude, and to a mood of greater intransigence in the way prison regimes were operated. Reductions in the food rations followed complaints that the diet was too rich. Rioting followed. A mutiny at Portland was quelled when 'the civil guard, shooting at the ringleaders when they advanced armed with picks and shovels, dispersed and subdued the rioters' (Thomas, 1972, p. 59).

Corporal punishments and executions were the major punishments until the middle of the eighteenth century, when they began to be replaced by imprisonment, in the spirit of humanitarianism which accompanied the 'Enlightenment'.

In the 1870s, the ethos of punishment still dominated. The shift towards rehabilitation and the medicalization of the regime of some more specialized aspects of imprisonment occurred in the subsequent half century (Gunn *et al.*, 1978, p. 9). It was the 1920s before psychological and psychoanalytic theories about the treatment of offenders made a significant impact on some parts of the English penal system (Gunn *et al.*, 1978, p. 15).

The new era heralded by the Gladstone Report did not put an end to collective resistance by prisoners. In Maidstone, in 1906, the Royal West Kents were called to deal with trouble and a mutiny and escape occurred at Gloucester prison (Thomas, 1972, pp. 134–5).

The Prevention of Crime Act 1908 introduced preventive detention, only abolished by the Criminal Justice Act of 1967. This enabled the court to impose a sentence for the offence and another, of five to fifteen years, because the offender was a recidivist. It was announced that a prison would be located at Camp Hill on the Isle of Wight, where prisoners serving such sentences would be treated more leniently. Thomas comments that 'this relaxation inevitably brought a risk of loss of control' (Thomas, 1972, p. 133). In March 1912 the prison opened, and in August of the same year there was a mutiny.

Thomas accepts the 'commonsense' presumption that riots follow a degree of relaxation in the discipline of the prison regime. Thus, Thomas correlates the relaxation of the silence rule with the increasing incidence of collective unrest in prison. 'Evidence of the structural function of silence, and the relationship between communication and loss of control, is furnished by crises which arose as a result of the presence of some political groups during the 1914–18 War' (Thomas, 1972, p. 130). Apparently, such prisoners were allowed to associate and talk during exercise periods under the 'Churchill Rule', and this led to 'considerable disorder' at Wandsworth amongst conscientious objectors . . . and at Lewes which housed Irish prisoners' (Thomas, 1972, pp. 130–1). The end of the war did not see the end of prison riots. In 1926, the year of the General Strike, prisoners at Pentonville Prison, London, rioted and in the process tried to mob the governor, allegedly in response to the suicide of a prisoner (*New York Times*, 26 January 1926, p. 2:5).

On the whole, in the early years of the twentieth century, there was slow amelioration of the unremitting harshness for many prisoners of the conditions of imprisonment. Dietary punishment and flogging (Hobhouse and Brockway, 1922, p. 240) and the rule of silence (ibid., p. 355) continued into the 1920s. Reading punishment borstal, which as Reading Gaol had incarcerated Oscar Wilde, in 1967 was still enforcing the strict rule of silence during working hours on pain of further punishment (author's observation during visit).

Dartmoor Prison Mutiny, 1932

The Dartmoor mutiny of 1932 was the incident in British prisons which, prior to the 1960s, attracted the most attention (Thomas, 1972, pp. 157–62). It actually consisted of a series of riots, beginning with the incident on 24 January in which the main building was damaged by fire and smaller riots on 29 January and 20 February (Fox, 1956, p. 23). It probably attracted more attention than any prison riot since the Chatham disturbance of 1861 (Priestley, 1989, p. 180).

It is possible to interpret the Dartmoor riot as, in Priestley's words, 'a rehearsal for later *émeutes*' (Priestley, 1989, p. 180). But its character as an isolated incident associated with an escape attempt which went wrong, in which the grievances of prisoners were to be inferred rather than spelt out and communicated to non-rioters either inside or outside the prison, meant it had more in common with traditional riots. It occurred, as Priestley notes, following 'an attempt to reintroduce an older notion of discipline after the relatively liberal governorship of Gerald Fancourt Clayton' (ibid.).

> For a brief period the whole of Dartmoor was left in the hands of the mutineers. Shots were fired at prisoners who got up on the walls and order had to be restored by squads of policemen brought in from Plymouth. The fact that it had happened at all was a considerable shock to a system that had hitherto thought of itself in more or less reformist terms. Long prison sentences were subsequently handed out to the ring-leaders of the mutiny and many of them were transferred to Parkhurst to serve their additional years. It is from the Dartmoor and the Parkhurst of the 1930s that there first emerge in the published biographies of prisoners and ex-prisoners signs of a truly articulated inmate society, one that speaks in the authentic tones of the criminal classes.
>
> (Priestley, 1989, p. 180)

Du Parcq notes in 1932 that in the convict prison for recidivists such as Dartmoor, since communication became possible between prisoners, the possibility of escape or mutiny depended on the strength and reliability of staff and the site and character of the prison building. There is no mention of any other factors such as penal policy or the regimes of the prison (Du Parcq, 1932). A postscript to general fears at the time comes from the decision to ban American crime films in many US prisons after the Du Parcq Report, on the grounds that they may have fuelled the disorder in Dartmoor and therefore might infect other institutions (Fox, 1956, p. 48).

Riots increased in frequency during the Second World War. This was partially a reflection of some major disturbances in prisoner of war camps in 1942 (*The Times*, 25 March 1942, p. 2:5) and 1945, the latter associated with a mass escape. In one of the 1945 incidents, at an unspecified location in North West England, one prisoner was killed and another injured (*The Times*, 12 February 1945, p. 2b). The mass escape involved 70 prisoners, in Bridgend (*The Times*, 12 March 1945, p. 4e).

The Irish potato famine of the 1840s, accelerated the flight of starving Irish people to England, Wales and Scotland, where the racialist stereotype of the male – unreliable, drink-sodden, crime-prone Irish*man* – was built on the paradox of the exploitation of these often homeless and starving people. They became the railway navvies of the nineteenth century and cannon fodder for the armed services in the First World War.

Overcrowding was a prominent, though not the only, theme of the perceived crisis of imprisonment in the second half of the twentieth century. The impact of the principles of less eligibility established by the mid-nineteenth century, was still felt towards the end of the twentieth century. But by then the problems of disciplining and regulating the increasing numbers of prisoners in increasingly over-crowded and inadequate conditions were exacerbated by the problems of maintaining order in institutions where the prospect and the fact of dissent, in the form of public and dramatic rioting, grew ever greater.

The factors influencing penal policies and practices often are highlighted more in international comparative studies. A comparison of English and Polish criminal justice systems produced the following list of relevant factors: the role of central government including electoral strength, the (admittedly limited) role of parliament, the Home Office (with its network of influential advisers, pressure groups and academics), criminologists, public opinion, the mass media and advertising (Bright, 1987, pp. 24–5). Clearly, these factors interact in a complex fashion. Additionally, the context in which this takes place has itself changed since the Second World War. Some of the key changes include reorganizations of social services, health services and in the penal and criminal justice system itself. Ideological shifts in policies such as increasingly powerful lobbies for a return to 'law and order' have paralleled economic changes, such as rising unemployment since the 1970s. Moral panics have followed the invention of words such as 'mugging' in 1972 and a succession of youth cultures, beginning with the Teds, through mods and rockers and skinheads.

RIOTS AGAINST CONDITIONS: FROM EARLY 1950s TO LATE 1960s

Though they went largely unremarked in official reports, prison riots continued to feature in the 1950s and 1960s as they had done in previous decades.

The Second World War marked a shift away from the liberalism of the late 1930s towards the more rigorous approach to penal policy and practice demonstrated in the 1948 Criminal Justice Act. This led to the introduction of new detention centres and attendance centres for young offenders. It also marked the end of a long period of relative stability and even, latterly, decline in the size of the prison population. For the next forty years, the prison population was set to rise dramatically. Although the prison building programme expanded, the core of the accommodation remained the old, relatively over-crowded and decrepit Victorian prisons which on the whole now served as local 'catch-all' prisons for a wide variety of prisoners.

The system of penal institutions in Britain grew enormously in the generation after the Second World War. Between 1950 and 1969, the number of people in custody rose from 20 000 to 35 000, the number of staff from 5500 to 15 000 and the number of establishments from 57 to 111. At the same time, the range of alternatives to custody increased and the variety of institutions, from top security prisons to open prisons and prison hostels, also grew (Jepson, 1975, p. 17). Three associated changes in the organization of penal institutions took place: firstly, in the early 1960s the centralized Prison Commission, responsible for the prison service, was abolished and the Home Secretary took over; secondly, the Prison Service was divided in England and Wales into four regions, each with its own Directorate; thirdly, the 1970s saw a convergence between the operation of penal institutions and headquarters on the one hand, and establishment staff and civil servants on the other. 'In the face of growth, diversification, and increased problems of security and control, regionalization emphasized not the independence of establishments and their governors but rather their interdependence' (Jepson, 1975, p. 18).

In 1976, of the 24 local prisons in England and Wales, with a total Certified Normal Accommodation of 9999 prisoners, or a quarter of the prison system, 23 were built before 1900. Of the remaining establishments for adults, half the 16 closed prisons for men, with a Certified Normal Accommodation of 5476, were also constructed before 1900. But assertions that conditions in local prisons are worse than those in higher-security prisons, where more riots have occurred, need to be treated with caution. King and McDermott have shown that in British prisons, in spite of major improvements in, for example, staff: prisoner ratios, in aspects such as access to sanitary facilities the higher security prisons in the late 1980s were experiencing similar conditions to the local prisons in the early 1970s (King and McDermott, 1989).

In the postwar decades, 'security', 'rehabilitation through therapy' and 'productive work' were all aspects of penal policy and practice which found expression in local prison regimes. It was 1967 before the Mountbatten Report on prison security led to the introduction of maximum security units and prisons. Grendon prison was created in the vogue for psychiatric approaches to rehabilitation and half a dozen prisons, including Pentonville in London, became involved in the 1960s in group counselling for prisoners. Prisons such as Coldingley developed an emphasis on involving prisoners in productive work.

From the early 1950s to the late 1960s, a succession of widely dispersed but fairly regular prison riots occurred. Though mostly reported in *The Times*, they largely escaped more widespread media attention or recording in reports of the Prison Commissioners of the day. They included a number of riots between 1953 and 1955 and a more concerted series of incidents from 1961 to 1962.

Between 1945 and the late 1960s the Home Office, in effect, denied the existence of prison riots. For example, there are no entries concerning riots in prisons in Home Office reports of the work of prisons during this period. This was not a departure from official policy. The postwar years, until at least the mid-1970s were marked by the extreme defensiveness and secretiveness on the part of the Home Office about what went on in British prisons. After that time, there was a gradual relaxation of censorship of staff comment and more invitations to the media to have access to prisons to find out about conditions in them. Critics such as Peter Evans, Home Affairs Correspondent of *The Times* for more than a decade, attacked the senior managers of the Prison Department for 'bureaucratic inertia' in 'the reluctance of the Prison Department to acknowledge [that] the seriousness of the crisis had contributed to the feelings of frustration of prisoners and staff . . . The general sense of frustration has helped to fuel outbreaks of trouble' (Evans, 1980, p. 84).

In 1950, there were disturbances at Portland borstal (*The Times*, 6 January 1951). The incidents in 1954 were apparently unrelated. In May, five prisoners and fifteen prison officers were reportedly injured in a riot by fifty prisoners at Wandsworth prison in London (*New York Times*, 7 May 1954). Two prisoners were sentenced to the 'cat' for 'incitement to mutiny' after a disturbance at a football match at HM Prison, Parkhurst (*The Times*, 24 April 1954, p. 6:b). A month later, a riot at Wandsworth prison involving 260 prisoners armed with scissors and hammers barricading themselves in a workshop, was quelled by prison officers. At that time, it was noted that the prison held 1640 men, of whom 500 were living three to a cell (*The Times*, 27 May 1954, p. 3). In July, an incident involving twenty prisoners 'mobbing' staff led to an officer having boiling water poured over him in a mailbag shop at Strangeways prison, Manchester (*The Times*, 15 July 1954, p. 8:g). In early August, prisoners in Nottingham prison threw shoes and tools in a disturbance which led to an officer being injured (*The Times*, 1 September 1954, p. 2:g).

In 1955, fourteen convicts went on hunger strike in Dartmoor prison, in a protest over food ((*New York Times*, 23 January 1955). In 1959, The Department did admit that there were strikes in both Birmingham and Cardiff prisons (Annual Report, 1959, p. 24). In that year, disturbances at Wakefield prison centred around the hunger strike by Fuchs, the 'atom spy', who was protesting at atomic tests (*New York Times*, 11 May 1959).

Wave of Riots, 1961

In 1961, there was a series of more obviously related incidents in more than half a dozen English prisons, notably Brixton, Lincoln, Maidstone, Pentonville, Shrewsbury, Stafford and Walton. These were notable for their peaceful nature although they were generally responded to with disciplinary charges rather than with attention to any ex-pressed grievances about prison conditions. On 13 April, 40 men at Brixton prison refused lunch by putting down their trays after collect-ing the food and returning to their cells. On the same day, 40 men at Maidstone and 30 at Shrewsbury refused work (*The Times*, 17 April 1961, p. 10:d). Three incidents at Liverpool led to 157 prisoners facing disciplinary charges: seven men in the canvas shop stopped stitching and broke windows; a sit-down by 150 prisoners occurred in an exercise yard an hour later; in the evening, a demonstration of 'shouting, singing and jeering' was quelled by staff (*The Times*, 18 April 1961, p. 12:e). At Wandsworth prison, one of at least four demonstrations involved 140 prisoners refusing to return to their cells after exercise (*The Times*, 11 April 1961, p. 10:a). The Home Office apparently believed that the incidents at Maidstone and Shrews-bury were protests by prisoners at the poor quality of the food (*The Times*, 15 April 1961, p. 8:f). It is doubtful whether this single cause was responsible for all the incidents. Several dozen prisoners at Staf-ford prison refused work on 21 and 22 April (*The Times*, 24 April 1961, p. 8:d). There were demonstrations at Pentonville prison and on 18 April, six prisoners at Lincoln prison staged a sit-down on the exercise yard (*The Times*, 20 April 1961, p. 5:c). It was said at the time that there were fears of nationwide mutinies among British prisoners ((*New York Times*, 16 April 1961). At about that time, the Home Secretary announced plans to set up a wing at HM Prison, Brixton for up to 20 'violent' prisoners, for whom 'although discipline will be strict, every attempt will be made to give the regime a diagnostic and therapeutic bias' (*The Times*, 21 April 1961, p. 18:f). It was emphasized that this unit, for 'chronically violent prisoners' had 'no direct rela-tionship with recent incidents' (*The Times*, 17 April 1961, p. 10:d)

In 1959, the White paper, *Penal Practice in a Changing Society*, set out an ambitious re-examination of penal methods, which was somewhat forestalled by the resignation within two years of its setting up of a third of the six members of the Royal Commission on the Penal System in 1964, on the grounds that it was unrealistic to attempt to produce a general set of principles of penal practice. In 1969, the Home Office publication *People in Prison* signalled the end of treat-ment and training as the rationale for penal policy and practice and proposed as the main function of prisons the protection of society through 'humane containment' of prisoners. But the structure of classification, allocation and training prisons did not change in keep-ing with this shift (Wallace, 1981, p. 23).

Postwar prison riots occurred in the context of increasing manifestations of collective protest in other aspects of postwar society. Civil
disorder was noteworthy in many parts of Britain. For example, four
major manifestations of civil disorder which were evident in London
since the mid-1950s, all reflecting wider social problems: labour conflict; civil disobedience exemplified in the 'ban the bomb' movement,
paralleled by the anti-Vietnam war movement in the US which hardly
affected Britain; ethnic conflict in the form of many small-scale attacks on non-white Commonwealth immigrants and more recent attacks by non-whites on the police; in the 1970s, increasing protest and
sometimes terrorism related to Irish nationalism (Gurr, 1976, p. 71).

CONSCIOUSNESS-RAISING RIOTS: FROM THE LATE 1960s

The 1970s were noteworthy for the birth and rapid growth in Britain
of Preservation of the Rights of Prisoners (PROP), a union claiming
to represent the interests of prisoners, whose history was recorded in
detail as a PhD thesis by its press officer at the time (Fitzgerald, 1977).

In contrast with press accounts in the US of riots earlier in the
1960s, official reticence in Britain, including the virtual denial of the
existence of PROP, was noteworthy. The 1969 riot at Parkhurst prison
on the Isle of Wight in Southern England 'was blandly dismissed in a
six-line paragraph in the Prison Department's annual report for 1969.
It was considered to warrant no more space than an account, also in
the annual report, of the chaplain's annual retreat and conference'
(Evans, 1980, p. 83).

The Parkhurst prison riot of 24 October 1969 was perceived by the
Prison Department as requiring a medical rather than simply a security response. Following the report of the riot, it was noted that 'the
special problems posed by the concentration of disturbed and difficult prisoners at Parkhurst are the subject of a continuing study as a
result of which it has been decided, among other measures, to establish a medically-oriented unit in the prison' (Home Office, 1970,
p. 15). The following year, it was noted that 'the serious disturbance
at Parkhurst in October 1969 underlined the need for measures to
cope with the special problems arising from the concentration of
disturbed and difficult prisoners there. One of the wings was therefore set aside as a medically-oriented unit to provide, in conditions of
closer control, individual care and support to emotionally disturbed
prisoners' (Home Office, 1971, pp. 19–20).

An account written by a prisoner at the time of the circumstances leading to the riot illustrates the gulf between the above perception by the authorities and prisoners' perceptions that their longstanding grievances about injustice, intimidation and violence by staff in the prison were not attended or addressed by the Home Office (Stratton, 1970).

The internal report by George Gale, a senior official in the Prison Department, into allegations of staff assaults on prisoners at Parkhurst in 1968–9, was suppressed by the Home Office. PROP called attention to the lack of public accountability of the prison and the failure of the Board of Visitors to maintain a critical, independent stance on the prison (PROP, 1979, p. 11).

The struggle between prisoners and the authorities from the late 1960s can be viewed in terms of the perceptual gap between the commitment of the former to raising critical awareness of defective precepts and practices and the efforts of the latter to medicalize riots. Or at least there were attempts to explain them in terms of the pathology of their participants, in groups or as individuals, and thereby deny their critical implications for the way prisons were run.

During the 1970s, the prison system continued to expand. The daily average population of people in prison in 1980 was 42 109 (Home Office, 1981, p. 15) and the total number of staff, excluding administrative staff at headquarters, had risen to 24 081 (Home Office, 1981, p. 22).

Discipline, management, control and security were keywords which found a place increasingly in the postwar Prison Service. The Fulton Report (1967) led to the firm location of the administration of prisons in the British Civil Service. 'Treatment' as a philosophy for imprisonment was increasingly supplanted by 'custody'. The Mountbatten Report on prison security led to the introduction of maximum security units and heightened emphasis on security at some prisons. By the late 1970s 80 per cent of establishments were closed (Jepson, 1975, p. 19). The mood of penal policy was more punitive than it had been just before the outbreak of war in 1939. The 1948 Criminal Justice Act led to the introduction of new detention centres. Yet rehabilitation was to linger on at the margins of the penal system until into the 1990s.

From Treatment and Training to Humane Containment

The Prison Rules (1949) expressed the purpose of imprisonment as oriented towards rehabilitation, through treatment and training intended to equip prisoners to lead useful lives after discharge. In the following 25 years, this philosophy reached its peak and was then discredited and discarded by the Home Office, in response to the narrower lobbies of researchers and penal reformers and the broader societal pressures away from medico-treatment models and towards justice models of processing offenders.

The Criminal Justice Act 1948 demonstrated a more vigorous and punitive response to crime, particularly in relation to young offenders, through the new detention centres, than had been reflected in debates about penal policy in the late 1930s. The abolition of capital punishment was counterbalanced by the trend towards longer sentences of more serious offenders and repeated minor offenders, and through measures such as corrective training (CT) and preventive detention (PD).

In the late 1960s, there were two prisons in Northern Ireland catering for 600 prisoners. By the mid-1980s, this number had increased to three men's prisons, one women's prison and a young offenders centre.

One of the major tensions in the Prison Service in England, Wales and Scotland, as the industrial action by prison officers in 1980 showed, was the longstanding tensions between the Home Office and Scottish Office administrators, regional staff and local staff, and between governor grades, uniformed staff and administrative staff.

A much criticized aspect of the Prison Service has been its over-centralization and bureaucratic impersonality, its lack of accountability to the public and its secrecy (Fitzgerald and Sim, 1982, p. 30). Du Parcq notes in the wake of the Dartmoor prison riot (1932, p. 14) that the Prison Commissioners could overrule any action of the governor in dealing with the riot.

The Fulton Report (1967) symbolized the transition from the traditional role of the Prison Commissioners, which entailed providing prisoners with a disciplined environment, to the managerial style of the Civil Service in the Home Office in London, which replaced it. This was combined with the growing strength of the macho, militaristic tradition of the uniformed prison officers, through their union, the Prison Officers' Association (POA) and their quasi-military culture. According to Thomas, the priority role of controlling prisoners accounts for the enduring militaristic structure and organizational culture of prison staff in the century since 1877 (Thomas, 1972, p. 6). From the 1960s, the historical reasons for the nature of the culture of prison officers were less significant than the increasing tendency for the POA to reflect a reactive and reactionary approach to penal policy changes and aggressively controlling responses to collective incidents, including rioting, by prisoners.

The problems of the prison system can be described best in terms of a series of growing crises, in overcrowding, dilapidation of buildings, management, public order and in the philosophy of imprisonment. Together these crises increasingly called into question the basis for the legitimacy of the prison system as it stood. Yet, the ostrich-like mentality of the senior managers of the Prison Department at the Home Office and the defensiveness of the POA combined to ensure that the realities of the situation were not subjected to rigorous scrutiny by those staff best placed to undertake it. In short, most of the critical insights came from elsewhere, from researchers, academic commentators, penal reform groups and, ironically, from protesting prisoners themselves.

Crisis of overcrowding

After being static for many years, between 1913 and 1948 (in 1913, 14 892 male and 2335 female, and in 1948 15 736 male and 923 female), the prison population rose steadily over the next forty years to around 50 000 by the late 1980s.

This was a matter for official inquiry by the late 1960s, when evidence to the Eleventh Report from the Estimates Committee noted that by December 1966, 1494 men were accommodated two to a cell and 7206 three to a cell (House of Commons, 1967, p. xii). Barlinnie prison, Glasgow, was said to be the most overcrowded prison in Scotland, holding 1530 prisoners in accommodation for 950 (House of Commons, 1967, p. lxxv). Ten years later, despite constant increases in the prison building programme, the same concerns about overcrowding of prisoners were being expressed. Far from prisons being 'holiday camps', the Expenditure Committee maintained that 'the true harshness of prison life does not stem solely from the deprivation of liberty and limited choice, not from the actual physical conditions, but from the daily or hourly pressure which prisoners inflict upon each other' (House of Commons, 1978, p. xxviii).

By June 1980, the Home Office announced plans to deal with overcrowding, partly by extending the prison building programme, including expanding the number of special wings like C Wing in Parkhurst prison, which it noted was being used as normal accommodation following the riot earlier in 1980 (Home Office, June 1980,

p. 7), to cope with the fact that the prison population rose from 32 500 in 1968 to 44 800 early in 1980, nearly 18 000 of whom (40 per cent of all those held in custody in England and Wales) were sharing in twos and threes cells designed for one (Home Office, June 1980, p. 2). In the same month, a report by the Parliamentary All-Party Penal Affairs Group argued that more radical ways of reducing the prison population needed to be found, including reserving custody as a last resort for people who, whether pre- or post-trial represented a real danger to society (Parliamentary All-Party Penal Affairs Group, June 1980, p. 51).

Crisis of dilapidation
The British prison system was increasingly feeling the consequences of the fact that the greater proportion of its accommodation dated from the last great period of prison building, in the latter half of the nineteenth century. A century later, the Fifteenth Report from the Expenditure Committee noted the adverse effects on the quality of life in prisons of cell-sharing, inadequate and communal toilets, baths, showers, laundries and kitchen, working and visiting facilities (House of Commons Fifteenth Report, 1980, p. xvii). The May Committee drew attention to the fact that the Home Office's assessment that a third of prisons were physically 'good' and only one-fifth 'poor' was 'heavily influenced by long and now ingrained habits of tolerating low physical standards' (May 1979, p. 123). By the early 1980s, the view of the House of Commons Home Affairs Committee was that the crisis of dilapidation in the physical stock of prison buildings fuelled the crisis of overcrowding (House of Commons, July 1981, p. vi).

Crisis of management
The Fifteenth Expenditure Committee report (House of Commons, 1978) was followed by the appointment by the government of an independent Committee of Inquiry, chaired by Mr Justice May, which reported in October 1979 (May, 1979). Following the May Committee Report, the government instituted changes, intended 'to place management of the prison service of England and Wales on a more effective footing, by enhancing the status and capability of the central administration, by strengthening the operational role of regional headquarters, and by increasing public accountability of the prison service through independent inspection' (Home Office, June 1980, p. 1). But a decade later, the concerted view of informed commentators was that this had not been achieved. In terms of its impact on the

problems of the prison system, the May Report was a non-event. A decade later, managerial failure continued to be explicitly blamed for the crisis in administration and management (Stern, 1989, p. 35).

Crisis of public order

Between 1968 and 1979, prison riots tended not to be seen as a crisis arising from the collectively negative experiences of prisoners. They were seen by the Prison Department in terms of their relationship with other security and control problems rather than as happenings which necessitated addressing in their own right.

From the prisoners' points of view, the most common grievances associated with riots were allegations of staff violence against prisoners, lack of justice in the ways prisoners were dealt with and a lack of public accountability and excessive secrecy in the way rules governing the regime were used to control prisoners. In 1968, a protest by prisoners was set in the context of escape attempts and, rather than its significance being examined, was simply used to justify the case for increased staff vigilance, even in conditions of apparently good physical security.

> Early in the year, prisoners in the security wing at Durham barricaded themselves in a suite of rooms and used the telephone there to inform the outside world of their achievement. In August some of the prisoners in the special security wing at Leicester made a determined and ingenious attempt to escape and came very close to success. In October, three prisoners succeeded in getting out of the special security wing at Durham and, despite being surprised in the act of climbing the perimeter wall, one of them made good his escape.
>
> (Home Office, 1969, p. 5)

The public order crisis in prisons was part of a wider crisis. Since the late 1960s, problems of public order in various parts of Britain became increasingly apparent. In practice, the most serious manifestations of what were perceived as threats to public order as maintained by the police in society took place in urban England and Northern Ireland. With hindsight it is possible to see that Northern Ireland was very much used by the British authorities as the testing ground from the late 1960s for many of the techniques which were later to be used to curb both prison and intercommunal rioting. In the industrial disputes between the Home Office and prison officers in the late 1970s, it was military police from the British forces which had served in Northern Ireland who were among those drafted into the camps and half-built prisons, such as Frankland, which were now rushed into use as overspill establishments.

The Home Office's reticence about reporting prison rioting from the early 1950s to the mid-1970s was consistent with the denial that there was any significance in the incidents. It went hand in hand with a reluctance to submit to the rigours of public investigation. Despite the fact that the Parkhurst riot was admitted by the Home Office in the annual report to be serious enough to have caused staff injuries and twelve prisoners to be subsequently tried and seven sentenced to further imprisonment, the report of the inquiry into it was never published.

> Nor has it been properly circulated so that prison staff could ben-
> efit from lessons drawn. Astonishingly, the section on publicity
> given in the 1969 annual report did not even mention coverage
> given to the riot, but instead chided press, radio and television for
> 'a tendency for greater prominence to be given to stories about
> individual prisoners, particularly those who have achieved some
> notoriety, than to developments in penal treatment.'
>
> (Evans, 1980, p. 84)

Crisis in the philosophy of imprisonment

> Some of the elements of 'crisis' within the contemporary prison
> system arise from internal tensions within the prison service: as
> regards the role of the staff (simply control, or also more positive
> 'therapeutic' tasks in relation to prisoners?); as between the train-
> ing and outlook of prison officer and governor grades; and as
> between staff in the prisons and what is often perceived by the latter
> as a remote centre of administration in the Prison Department.
>
> (Harding and Koffman, 1988, p. 151)

In 1971, a series of demonstrations by prisoners at Albany prison was reported as 'successfully contained by staff'. Such incidents were perceived as 'intensified problems of security and control, insepara-ble from the containment of long sentence prisoners' (Home Office, 1972, p. 40).

It was during 1972 that prison staff first became aware in a wide-spread sense of the existence and importance of PROP as a body advocating the interests of prisoners (Fitzgerald, 1977). It was also the first year in which the Prison Department's annual reports elevated prisoners's protests to the separate heading of 'demonstrations', in the chapter on 'security and control'. The account, running to nearly three pages, is framed by the introductory understatement that 'the potential of unrest is inherent in an organization which has the complex aims of both containing and rehabilitating prisoners' (Home Office, 1973, p. 43). The first part of the year's events reportedly began with a series of demonstrations at Brixton prison in early May, continued with a minimum of one incident per week in at least 41 prisons, and concluded with 'a cluster of demonstrations at 29 prisons at the end of August' (Home Office, 1973, p. 43). 'On 4 August about 22 per cent of the total adult male population in closed prisons demonstrated at one time: 5500 prisoners in twenty-eight prisons' (Evans, 1980, p. 86). 'Most of the demonstrations were passive, and the pattern of the Department's policy was to seek to contain them without needless confrontation or provocation. This aim was generally achieved: personal violence was largely avoided; and most of the demonstrations were orderly and good-natured' (Home Office, 1973, p. 43).

At the end of the summer of 1972, disturbances in prisons became more violent. Even the Prison Department admitted that the Albany prison incident from 25 to 28 August 1972 marked a change, 'away from the previous pattern of passive and mostly orderly demonstrations. There was damage to property; there was overt indiscipline; there were prisoners on roofs; missiles were thrown about' (Home Office, 1973, p. 44). Further incidents occurred at Parkhurst, where prisoners stayed on the roof for a week, Camp Hill, Albany, Chelmsford, Dartmoor, Maidstone, Cardiff, Liverpool and Peterhead. There was evidence that most or all of these incidents were protests linked with support for the Albany rioters (King and Elliott, 1978, p. 297) and Gartree (Home Office, 1973, p. 44). From the prisoners' point of view, though, they were being locked up for a prolonged period while staff, themselves engaged in a work-to-rule, searched the prison, cell by cell. It was not simply the fact that prisoners were confined, but the provocative attitudes of many staff during this period. When the riot exploded, it was the most serious incident in the life of Albany. (ibid., p. 296)

Explanations of the origins of riots tended to locate them in immediate or 'trigger' factors rather than attending to structural features of imprisonment. Rather than admitting the possibility that critical attention to issues of prison administration and management, such as emerged from some media coverage, might have been fruitful, there was a tendency in official reports simply to hint that media coverage produced further riots. Thus, the annual report of the Prison Department for 1972 referred to 'a substratum of unrest, the encouragement provided by the interest of the media, and the attraction of the relatively untried but currently popular form of a sit-down demonstration, [which] tended to sustain something of a chain reaction over a considerable period' (Home Office, 1973).

In contrast, King and Elliott present a telling case study of Albany prison from the late 1960s to the early 1970s, which clearly demonstrates how the quality of life in a dispersal prison was deteriorating (King and Elliott, 1977).

Responding to Riots by Increasing Sanctions and Targeting 'Troublemakers'

In a survey of disturbances in Gartree prison, Zeeman (Zeeman *et al.*, 1975, p. 19) identifies twenty 'more serious incidents' during 1972. These included five major incidents:

> 29th March: a hunger strike by all 370 prisoners, for one meal only; 13th June: 350 men refused lunch and further complaints about food, together with a work strike of 350 about rates of pay, both ending on 15th June; 26th July: 378 men involved in a work strike; Complaints about the food also, which ended the same day; 1st September: 350 men in a work strike; Complaints regarding an adjudication; 211 sat down on the exercise yard and 30 climbed onto the roof. These incidents ended on 4th September; a disturbance in D Wing, Wormwood Scrubs on Friday 31st August 1979, led to a number of prison officers and prisoners being injured.
>
> (Home Office, 1982)

Despite the growing number of incidents, the Prison Department viewed continuing protests by prisoners in 1973 as having no pattern of interrelated or coordinated incidents (Home Office, 1974, p. 45). The view of the authorities was that a low-key response had been adopted and that this had largely avoided incidents escalating. 'In those few cases where violence did develop, it was successfully contained' (Home Office, 1974, p. 45). This description of tactics underemphasizes strategic shifts associated with the policy responses of the Prison Department to those prisoners perceived as threatening good order and discipline. Notable among these were three reviews:

(a) The review of rewards and punishments initiated in the autumn of 1972 in response to the prison disturbances that year. This was completed early in 1973 and involved abolishing dietary punishments whilst extending privileges and the levels of other disciplinary awards (Home Office, 1974, p. 17).

(b) The review of the use of Prison Rule 43, which provides for the segregation of prisoners, either for their own protection or for the preservation of good order and discipline.

(c) The review of dispersal policies, following the Gartree disturbances of November 1972, in which the Home Secretary confirmed the policy of dispersing high security risk prisoners in a small group of prisons with high perimeter security, in order to avoid concentrating the risk of disruption (Home Office, 1974, p. 45). At the same time, the Home Secretary intended to tighten security in several ways in selected prisons (Home Office, 1974, p. 46) and to set up two new control units within two dispersal prisons 'to provide a deliberately spare – though not spartan – régime for the hard core of intractable trouble makers whose behaviour had been found seriously and persistently to disrupt the prisons which had to contain them' (Home Office, 1974, p. 45).

Lack of Accountability

One consequence of the secrecy surrounding British prisons is their lack of accountability, recognized explicitly by William Whitelaw, who wrote: 'When I became Home Secretary in 1979 I set myself four objectives in prison policy. First, to open up the prisons to the media and so stimulate public interest and debate as the essential background to remedial action' (Whitelaw, 1983, p. 12).

By 1974, the wave of prison riots had receded. Referring to the prison protests, the view of the Prison Department was that 'the prison service was emerging into a period of steady recovery and consolidation after the anxieties of 1972 and 1973.'

The Department's view that demonstrations by prisoners had declined proved to be wishful thinking. The following year, 1975, a fresh wave of incidents was acknowledged:

> Demonstrations by prisoners have become more frequent in recent times, and there have been a considerable number involving from two to three to a maximum of 268 prisoners in any one establish-

ment. There has in general been no discernable pattern, the underlying reasons concerning such diverse topics as the quality of food, rates of pay for industrial work, visiting arrangements for top security prisoners and changes in prison routine. Perhaps the most concerted campaign was that against the alleged shortcomings in the parole system resulting in demonstrations at a number of prisons. All the demonstrations were passive and involved no personal violence; by and large they were resolved without lasting deterioration in relationships between prisoners and staff.

(Home Office, 1976, p. 27)

The fact that the immediate trigger for incidents was assumed to be the underlying cause precluded the need to look further into their significance.

In November 1975, prisoners at Wormwood Scrubs attracted media attention by climbing onto the roof (Home Office, 1976, p. 27). Despite measures taken to curb it (Home Office, 1977, p. 27), this pattern of activity was to be repeated in later disturbances to great effect, notably in the Hull prison riot of 1976 and the Strangeways prison riot of 1990.

The Prison Department reported that the number of incidents, about 30, occurring during 1976, was the same as in the previous year (Home Office, 1977, p. 27). Hostage-taking of staff by prisoners was a feature of four of these incidents (Home Office, 1977, p. 28).

An unpublished paper analysed the number of collective disturbances in British prisons, between 13 May and 6 September 1976. It found that of 42 prisons only eleven had no disturbances in this period. The establishments with the greatest number of incidents included Camp Hill, Gartree, Albany, Maidstone and Stafford, followed by Hull, Chelmsford, Liverpool, Wandsworth, Manchester and Haverigg. Significantly, the old local prisons were by no means at the top of the list, or isolated from other institutions in their proneness to disturbances (Anon., 1976).

In a survey of the characteristics of convicted adult males serving sentences in 42 local and training prisons in Britain, it was found that prisons holding younger offenders serving longer than average sentences were most likely to experience collective disturbances. That is, riots and protests tended to occur where there were 'up and coming' rather than 'established' higher status prisoners (Anon., 1976).

Undoubtedly, by the turn of the 1980s William Whitelaw had largely achieved his aim of opening up prisons to public scrutiny, reducing Home Office censorship of press releases and the curbing of free speech by governors. But it is doubtful whether this increased the public accountability of prisons, although it represented a dramatic attempt to reverse a long tradition of Home Office secrecy and defensiveness.

Ironically, the expansion of the penal system in the 1970s was accompanied by the collapse of its positive rationale for imprisoning people. In Britain by the early 1970s, the medico-treatment model which fuelled the rehabilitative philosophy of imprisonment was severely under attack. By the end of the 1970s it had been fatally undermined. In 1971, Lady Megan Bull, medical officer, was persuaded to become governor of Holloway prison and in her eleven years as governor the ghost of the belief in prisons' power to reform people was laid to rest in Britain.

In the late 1970s, many of the organizational and administrative problems which had beset the prison system for years were coming to a head. Prisons were overcrowded. Prison officers were becoming militant about their conditions of work, and payment for mealtime supervisory duties through continuous duty credits in particular. There was growing disillusionment among many grades of staff with the running of the prison system. There were queries about the effectiveness of custody, and particularly imprisonment as the most problematic part of the continuum of custody to justify in treatment terms. Prison governors were concerned to ascertain whether the historic militaristic command structure of the Prison Service was to be replaced, in keeping with the growing emphasis on modern management and industrial relations, as 'treatment and training' declined. Prison officers wanted to find out whether the decline of treatment and training of prisoners meant that in the future their role was to contract to 'turnkey' activities, or whether in the future they would be expected to act in a prisoner welfare capacity. It was in this context of uncertainty that the 'May Inquiry' into the prison system was ordered by the Home Secretary in 1978.

The 'May Inquiry' into the prison system was ordered by the Home Secretary in 1978, partly to counter the growing militancy of the Prison Officers' Association (POA) and partly over the payment of officers for meal-time supervisory duties (continuous duty credits). In the context of growing disillusionment of many grades of staff with the running of the prison system, officers were concerned about whether they were to be mere turnkeys, or were expected in future to take on more responsibilities, such as a welfare role. Governors were concerned to ascertain whether the historic militaristic command structure of the Prison Service was to be replaced, in keeping with the growing emphasis on modern management and industrial relations, as 'treatment and training' declined.

The May Report proposed a number of strategies to tackle difficulties arising from increasing pressures on the prison system in the face of resource constraints. Rather than proposing political action to reduce the prison population, the May Report recommended organizational and managerial improvements and improvements in regimes, security and control, and industrial relations, alongside an expansion in the prison building programme (May, Vol. 2, pp. 258–9).

However, it was the early 1980s before HM Chief Inspector of Prisons reluctantly acknowledged the consequence of Brody's review of English and American research into the effectiveness of sentencing (Brody, 1976), in terms of undermining the validity of attaching the reformative rationale to imprisonment:

> We believe that it is important not only to understand the limitations of the research and its findings, but also to recognize that real benefits have followed in the train of the treatment philosophy. Never-theless, the main thrust of the conclusions that treatment and training regimes have not shown systematic reformative effects seems to remain without serious challenge . . . If the treatment philosophy were to be jettisoned it is not clear what would replace it. However, one concept which was put forward for debate by Prison Department [sic] last year is known as the 'justice' model. Compulsory treatment and training form no part of it. There is a general assumption that the deprivation of liberty is punishment enough in itself, and that efforts should be concentrated on what an inmate may do rather than what he may need, it being understood that he would surrender only those rights and freedoms necessarily and inevitably lost by virtue of his imprisonment. In this scenario staff would not be engaged in a systematic attempt to reform inmates but would instead become neutral custodians with a duty to act with high standards of propriety and equity. The May Committee rejected a similar concept on the grounds that it presented 'a means without an end' and was 'not a fit rule for hopeful life or responsible management'. We, too, would have some reservations about accepting this concept if it meant the loss of many of the more positive elements of prison life.
>
> (Chief Inspector, 1983, pp. 22–3)

POST-REHABILITATION RIOTS: FROM MID-1970S

One feature of the post-rehabilitation period was the tendency for prison riots to be identified very clearly with specific categories of prisoner, who saw themselves and their circumstances as sharply defined as different from those of other prisoners. Precisely how and when this shift from the euphoric mood of the late 1960s and early 1970s, when a strong cohort of prison literature seemed to be optimistic about identifying the universal aspects of the experience of imprisonment, is not clear. But its consequences can be seen in the nature of incidents.

The second feature of this period seemed to take the Home Office and academic commentators by surprise, namely the tendency for riots to spread from the dispersal prisons, known widely as the traditional locations of dissent, to Northern Irish, Scottish, Category 'C', remand and local prisons. In effect, the explanation of riots could no longer be contained within the category of 'dangerous' prisoners. Other voices were clamouring to be heard.

This final section of this chapter details aspects of the emerging fragmentation of prison riots in these different aspects of the British prison system. As a prelude to this, the most visible signs of the shift were events in Hull prison in 1976.

Hull, 1976
The most significant riot of the 1970s, at Hull prison between 31 August and 3 September 1976, may mark the end of the period of the brief phase of collective organization by prisoners in Britain. Hitherto, especially through the activities of PROP, prisoners had managed to convey the impression of coordinated activities, in ways which overrode divisions between them. If there was no sharp historical break between collective consciousness-raising and the highlighting of the differences between different categories of prisoners, at any rate the general debate about whether the small group of Irish republican terrorists in HM Prison, Hull was responsible for the riot brought this issue to the fore.

The three inquiry reports into the Hull riot – the Fowler, Prescott and PROP reports (Fowler, 1977; Prescott, undated; and PROP, 1978), illustrate contrasts between the standpoints of the authorities and the prisoners. Whereas the Fowler Report portrays staff perceptions of relaxation in the progressive regime, that of PROP notes 'the Hull Riot did not just happen out of the blue. It was preceded by years of petitioning by prisoners, and public appeals that action be taken to investigate the rapidly deteriorating conditions and increasingly harsh regime' (PROP, 1976, Introduction). The PROP report predicted a riot on the scale of Attica if reforms were not introduced (ibid.).

Paul Hill, one of the 'Guildford Four' convicted of the Guildford and Woolwich pub bombings in 1974 and released in 1990 when their sentences were quashed on appeal, describes graphically his participation in the riot:

> Most prisoners prefer to avoid riots; the penalties are just too grave. It was a measure of how bad things were in Hull that men so quickly, instinctively, did what they did. The deterioration in conditions, the bitterness caused by the enforcement of petty restrictions, the arbitrary 'nickings', the beatings, the bad visits, the squalor, the dread and tension, the appalling working conditions – all of these led to a spontaneous eruption of fury. The riot had not been planned; it did not have to be. When it broke out prisoners had acted as one man with one aim: to wreck the jail, to avenge themselves by fighting back. I was an unrepentant rioter. The feeling of euphoria that being on the roof gave me was matchless. I felt that by fighting back I had regained some kind of control over my life. The riot meant that I could stay up late, to wander freely around in the darkness, chat to whoever I liked, smoke as much as I wanted, look out into the night. I was going to suffer, but it was worth it.
>
> (Hill, 1991, p. 172)

Ironically, most of the staff disciplined and prosecuted were involved in offences against prisoners committed *after* the riot ended. But, meanwhile, Fowler's priorities were primarily the control rather than the betterment of prisoners. The account by the Prison Department of the action to be taken following the Hull prison riot refers solely to the 'official' Fowler Report and concentrates mainly on the implementation of its recommendations regarding administration and security (Home Office, 1978, p. 23). Fowler did not roundly condemn dispersal prisons *per se*. But he recommended a review of dispersal policy. One result of the recommendations of the Fowler Report was the setting up of a Dispersal Prisons Steering Group, to facilitate the oversight of dispersal prisons without bypassing Regional Offices and bringing them completely under the direct control of Prison Department Headquarters (Home Office, 1979, p. 26).

From the early 1970s in Northern Ireland and a decade later in England, Wales and Scotland, the 'problem of disturbances', which many prison officials in Britain had either denied altogether, or tended to compartmentalize as simply a feature of the dispersal prisons, became increasingly visible and embarrassing to the authorities. Despite efforts to play down the widespread incidence of prison riots, they spread to different parts of the UK and began to occur, apparently at random, in parts of the penal system outside the dispersal prisons. In some cases, these incidents seemed to be expressive in character, in others specific grievances were stated by the prisoners.

According to a Prison Department official, until October 1990 incidents in establishments were monitored by regional offices. Before that date, there was no coordinated incident monitoring from headquarters in London. One characteristic of riots in this period is their apparent lack of a generic rationale. That is, collectivities of rioters appeared to act often in isolation from, and sometimes actually in conflict with, other prisoners. There is a sense also in which rioting emphasized the fragmentation of different groups and interests in prisons, rather than reinforcing the unity shared hitherto by many staff and prisoners who had to work, and grumble, day by day in the same inadequate conditions.

To some extent, the division of this section into a Scottish, Northern Irish and English and Welsh narrative reflects an inescapable feature of the divisions within penal arrangements in the UK, namely the tendency either for Irish and Scottish issues, for instance, to be elided and ignored or for them to be simply set outside the discussion as raising issues which would require their own exegesis and, therefore, are too complex to take on board. A summary of events in Scotland and Northern Ireland is included at this point, to increase the possibility of making necessary links between these different arenas of penal policy and practice. At the risk of offending advocates for Wales, it should be said that insufficient data has emerged during the research for this book to enable a separate account to be written here. But that is a comment on the difficulty of excavating the narrative concerning prison riots in Cardiff, Swansea and other prisons where Welsh issues may be identifiably associated with riots, rather than on the lack of authenticity of such a narrative. The point is to cultivate the awareness that the generation of an account of prison riots from a particular vantage point should be accompanied by a critical review of other silences in the text.

Identifying disorder as a problem of the disruptive prisoner rather than of the prison system

In England and Wales, Scotland and Ireland, distinctive prison regimes emerged in the postwar period to attempt to identify and contain what the government saw as the minority of prisoners whose disruptive attitudes were capable of posing control problems as individuals and inducing collective disturbances, especially riots.

Whether the problem was viewed as the Irish Republican Army (IRA) or the 'disruptive prisoner', the theory proceeded from the same origin, namely that the individual prisoner presented the control problems and not the prison system.

> By individualizing the problem attention is distracted from the idea that it is the prison system, by its very nature, that generates the 'problems' itself. By definition new 'problems' will always arise – it is inherent in the repressive, authoritarian structure of the prison system. At an extreme level the rhetoric becomes, as it did in Inverness and in the isolation cells in Peterhead: 'if you treat a man like an animal, then he'll respond like an animal.'
>
> (MacDonald and Sim, 1978, p. 11)

Scotland

Conditions in prisons in Scotland and Northern Ireland reflected the above problems, compounded by their own societies, histories and penal policies and practices.

There are indications that the regimes in Scottish prisons were harsher than those in English prisons in the first half of the twentieth century. At Peterhead prison prisoners are not recorded as behaving unusually violently, in fact less so than elsewhere, yet the punitive style of the warden's job was emphasized by the carrying of cutlasses before 1939, the carrying of rifles until 1959 and by the use of the whip well into the 1940s' (Independent Committee of Inquiry, 1987, p. 25).

The Scottish Office Prison Report for 1946 notes a food riot at Peterhead prison. In 1955, prisoners went on hunger strike. In 1959, the protest by prisoners about a shooting incident was followed by the decision to end the policy of staff carrying firearms (ibid., p. 24).

As in England and Wales, the postwar trajectory of policies in Scotland affecting the regimes of prisons was determined by government responses to the perceived problems of housing long-term prisoners. Following Radzinowicz's rebuttal of Mountbatten's recommendation of concentration, the dispersal system was established by 1970. In Scotland, a new system of classification of prisoners, introduced on 1 July 1966, was seen as the means of locating prisoners in appropriate institutional regimes. Classification, applying to male prisoners only, had operated for more than a century, to identify two types of prisoner: 'the majority, who recognize the legitimacy of the system, and the deviant, subversive minority, who manipulate the first group to further their own ends' (ibid., p. 26). The post-Mountbatten refinement of classification in Scotland involved, first, dividing prisoners according to their security risk, A being the highest risk and D being the lowest risk. Second, prisoners were classified according to age and 'aptitude for training'. Those who seemed to oppose imprisonment could be placed either in the segregation unit at Inverness Prison or in the solitary confinement unit at Peterhead Prison.

By labelling a minority of the prisoner population as potentially disruptive, classification intensified the problems of control that the system was partly intended to solve. The effect was compounded by the reduction of the quality of life of prisoners experiencing segregation and isolation in Inverness and Peterhead. Predictably, 'in the 6 years between 1966 and 1972 there were a series of confrontations at both Peterhead and Inverness. Conflict was endemic in both institutions' (ibid., p. 28). This culminated in the riot in Inverness in December 1972, during which several prisoners and officers were injured. This contributed to the plans of the Scottish Office to develop a new Special Unit at Barlinnie, the Glasgow prison, with a more positive regime.

Riots in Scottish prisons, 1975–87
The series of major confrontations between prisoners and the authorities which occurred at a number of Scottish prisons between December 1985 and January 1987 have been described as 'the worst and most violent confrontations in recent penal history' (Independent Committee of Inquiry, 1987, p. 37).

Low Moss Prison experienced disturbances in December 1985; there were rooftop protests at Saughton and Barlinnie in June and July 1986 and again in Perth and Barlinnie in January 1987. A 'dirty protest' took place in the segregation unit of Inverness Prison in November 1986 and, in March 1987 when prison officers were taking industrial action at poor conditions and overcrowing, a hunger strike at Barlinnie involving 300 prisoners (ibid., p. 11).

The disturbances at Peterhead between Sunday 9 November and Friday 14 November 1986, which culminated in a rooftop protest, were the largest in scale of these incidents.

The independent committee of inquiry recalled that statistics from the Council of Europe showed Scotland's rate of commital in December 1986 as higher per 100 000 than any other member state and for 1986 as a whole, second only to Northern Ireland (ibid., p. 103). There was an increase of 50 per cent between 1984 and 1985 in the number of adults sentenced to three years or more and by 1985 27 per cent of the prison population was serving sentences of more than three years (ibid., p. 104).

Nearly a decade earlier, conditions in Peterhead, built in 1888 and for two decades Scotland's only maximum security prison, had been described as extreme. It was situated on a bleak part of the north-east coast of Scotland, thirty miles north of Aberdeen. Protests against conditions were repeated through the period. In May 1975, five prisoners went on hunger strike and in 1977 more than eighty prisoners twice refused food. In October 1978, seven prisoners barricaded themselves in for 24 hours. In August 1979, ten prisoners took to the roof in a four-day protest at the news that legal aid had been refused to prisoners wishing to petition the European Court of Human Rights over conditions (ibid., pp. 31–2). In the late 1970s, A Hall housed the category 'A' and long-term prisoners, where there was 'no fixed sanitation, no separate recreation, no separate dining facilities, so that it is possible for a man doing 20 years to spend the whole of his sentence, apart from his working hours, within the confines of the hall. The cells are cold, badly lit and badly ventilated' (Anon., 1978–9, p. 10). The general response of the prison authorities and the Scottish Office to these protests was to punish the prisoners and ignore their grievances (ibid., p. 32). On 5 May 1982, a riot followed allegations by prisoners of staff brutality (ibid., p. 35). A significant disturbance in October 1983 in which fifteen officers were injured was followed by the major eighteen-hour riot of January 1984, which ended when officers in riot gear attacked the barricades (ibid., p. 35). Tension remained high in the prison throughout 1984 and 1985. A month after the Scottish Office Industry and Home Affairs Minister had visited Peterhead Prison in October 1986 and stated that conditions were 'extremely good', riots occurred there and in several other Scottish prisons. At Peterhead on that occasion, the riot lasted four days (ibid., p. 37).

After the Peterhead incidents, the official announcement of an inquiry by HM Chief Inspector of Prisons was followed by demands for an independent inquiry, among others from local Members of Parliament, the Scottish Association for the Care and Resettlement of Offenders (SACRO), the Scottish Council for Civil Liberties (SCCL), the Scottish Churches Council and, significantly, the Scottish Prison

Officers' Association (SPOA). A public meeting was called on 4 December 1986 at the Gateway Exchange in Edinburgh, representing prisoners and their families as well as the above interests, which decided unanimously to set up an independent committee of inquiry.

The case for an independent inquiry was argued forcefully in the subsequent report of the Independent Committee of Inquiry, on the grounds that official inquiries 'are often inadequate in developing a full, comprehensive and impartial investigation of events and issues' and often tend to be '"views from above" rather than "views from below". This is particularly evident in those inquiries into penal establishments and their regimes. Prisoners are rarely, if ever, provided with an opportunity to put a case from within the prisons' (Independent Committee of Inquiry, 1987, p. 13).

The independent committee of inquiry recommended the closure of Peterhead and the reduction in the use and length of prison sentences (ibid., p. 104). It concluded that in Peterhead 'the treatment of long-term prisoners is lacking in direction. In short there is a policy vacuum. The regime itself is hard, brutal and lacking in compassion. Prisoners and staff alike are entrenched in a prison culture incomprehensible to outsiders' (ibid., p. 101):

> It is a matter of grave concern that 71% of the respondents to the questionnaire issued to prisoners stated that they have experienced brutality by prison staff and 62% stated that they have witnessed acts of brutality. Prison officers carry out such acts in circumstances (e.g. solitary confinement cells or isolated corridors) which make allegations difficult to substantiate. This, combined with the lack of proper and effective complaints procedure, makes it virtually impossible for prisoners to seek redress . . . Symbolically, Peterhead stands in the minds of staff, prisoners and the public alike for confrontation, boredom, despair and violence.
>
> (Ibid., pp. 101–2)

The independent inquiry deplored the plans of the Prison Department to move the Barlinnie Special Unit from its Glasgow prison base, with its reputation for dealing with long-term prisoners in a relatively humane way, the philosophy of which 'stands in direct contrast to the current thrust of penal policy which is dominated by security, control, segregation and isolation' (ibid., p. 101). The concentration of long-term prisoners in a single site 'creates penal apartheid in Scotland's prisons by once more establishing a dustbin prison in which those regarded as difficult can be isolated, segregated and brutalized' (ibid.).

A further half dozen incidents occurred in Scottish prisons in 1987, including Peterhead and Perth in October, the latter bring 'further evidence that a fundamental review of Scottish penal policy, including sentencing, should be undertaken (ibid., p. 101). New institutions continued to attract incidents. Prisoners at Shotts prison in Lanarkshire, a four-year-old £15m purpose-built prison, took over two floors in April 1990 and rioted again in September 1991. In the latter case, prison officers in riot gear eventually broke through a barricade on the top floor of 'B' hall and 53 prisoners surrendered (*Guardian*, 3 September 1991).

Ireland

It would be a simplification to suggest that Irish prisoners have occupied a comparable position in Britain to some black prisoners in prisons in the US. Nevertheless, although Irish prisoners in Northern Ireland were clearly in a different situation to those in a mainland prison, there is some basis for locating riots involving Irish prisoners in the same framework of divisions which can be argued to have increasingly outflanked and undermined rehabilitationism in the 1970s.

The linked themes of imperialism, division, concentration and invisibility have held together official responses to the perceived risk of collective disruption and its effective control in prisons. These themes have become increasingly manifest since the mid-1970s. In the context of the general tendency to sustain the marginality of 'problem' categories of prisoner in the face of the high priority given to them in practice, it is not surprising that the circumstances of Irish republican, remand, women, short-term and black prisoners, for instance, have remained largely invisible. It is to some of these categories of prisoners, though by no means all as yet, that prison riots have spread since the mid-1970s. The situation of black prisoners is of particular note. Despite the tendency for officialdom in Britain to ignore the presence of a considerable proportion of black prisoners in the penal system, black issues have been neglected in British prisons until comparatively late in the twentieth century. Yet, HM Chief Inspector of Prisons has drawn attention to the fact that in 1989, in Cookham Wood prison, the population of ethnic minority prisoners had varied between 42 per cent and 60 per cent in the recent past (HM Chief Inspector of Prisons, 1990, p. 24).

Imperialism and Invisibility

Irish republican prisoners are commonly excised from debates about British penal policy and practice. This gives a clue to the insidious lack of self-awareness which meshes with racism at all levels from policy formation through to institutional management and practice. Some categories of prisoner, such as black and Irish prisoners, tend to have their circumstances ignored. As far as Irish prisoners are concerned, it would be possible, but misleading and inadequate, to present conditions in northern and southern Irish prisons simply as an example of the difficulties perceived by British governments since 1970 of maintaining public order in Britain. Such problems more accurately should be viewed in the context of a much longer tradition of responses by the British authorities to disorder in colonies in various parts of the world. The history of the most recent of these – Malaya (1948–58), Kenya (1954–9), Cyprus (1957), British Cameroons (1960–1), Brunei (1963), British Guiana (1964), Aden (1964–7), Borneo/Malaysia (1965–6), Persian Gulf including Oman (1970–1) – directly fuelled responses by British governments to social unrest.

Imprisonment on a large scale formed a central feature of the British response to disorder in each of the above settings. Emergency powers tended to be granted to the local police and military forces. These were used in Malaya to herd people into concentration camps so as to deprive guerrillas of sources of food and shelter. In Kenya, 'Operation Anvil' on 24 April 1954 involved screening the entire African population of Nairobi and removing about 16 500 people to concentration camps, as well as more than 100 000 people in Kikuyuland being sealed off from the rest of Kenya in fortified villages. Starvation and torture were features of these camps which led to many deaths and injuries. Similar accusations against the British were made of policies in Cyprus and Aden.

In Northern Ireland, the British authorities were able to refer to this colonial history in different conditions where the dissident people were white and, though they retained their own language and culture, spoke the same language as the British. Furthermore, the history of conflict between the British and the Irish extended over several centuries. Events in the 1970s need locating in the broader context of activism by republican prisoners in the twentieth century.

Republican unrest in prisons

At the turn of the twentieth century, the campaigns to free Ireland from British rule brought together the twin themes of nationalism and republicanism. Over and above the cause of the IRA, the Countess de Markievicz, who played a leading role in the 1916 uprising, added a concern for women's suffrage. The Countess campaigned beyond the aims of the Sligo Women's Suffrage Society and the Irish Women's Franchise League (Van Voris, 1967, p. 64), for 'a free Ireland with no sex disabilities in her constitution' (Van Voris, 1967, p. 63). It has been said that without the Fianna na hEireann, which she founded, the Easter Rising would have been impossible (Van Voris, 1967, p. 66).

Lady Lytton's account of her force-feeding when on hunger strike highlights the unpleasantness of this response, adopted by the prison authorities faced with Irish hunger strikers in the early 1920s as well as fifty years later in the early 1970s:

I offered no resistance to being placed in position, but lay down voluntarily on the plank bed. Two of the wardresses took hold of my arms, one held my head and one my feet. One wardress helped to pour the food. The doctor leant on my knees as he stooped over my chest to get at my mouth. . . . The doctor offered me the choice of a wooden or steel gag; he explained elaborately, as he did on most subsequent occasions, that the steel gag would hurt and the wooden one not, and he urged me not to force him to use the steel gag. But I did not speak nor open my mouth, so that after playing about for a moment or two with the wooden one he finally had recourse to the steel. . . . He said if I resisted so much with my teeth, he would have to feed me through the nose. The pain of it was intense and at last I must have given way for he got the gag between my teeth, when he proceeded to turn it much more than necessary until my jaws were fastened wide apart, far more than they could go naturally. Then he put down my throat a tube which seemed to me much too wide and was something like four feet in length. The irritation of the tube was excessive. I choked the moment it touched my throat until it had got down. Then the food was poured in quickly; it made me sick a few seconds after it was down and the action of the sickness made my body and legs double up, but the wardresses instantly pressed back my head and the doctor leant on my knees. The horror of it was more than I can describe. I was sick all over the doctor and wardresses, and it seemed a long time before they took the tube out. As the doctor left he gave me a slap on the cheek, not violently, but, as it were, to express his contemptuous disapproval, and he seemed to take for granted that my distress was assumed . . .

When the ghastly process was over and all quiet, I tapped on the wall and called out at the top of my voice, which wasn't much just then, "No surrender," and there came the answer past any doubt in Elsie's voice, "No surrender."

(Lytton, 1976, pp. 268–71)

It was a period in which the practice of passive resistance by conscientious objectors in the First World War and by the suffragettes was soon transferred to the Irish prisoners. In April 1920, after over 5000 raids and 500 arrests, dozens of prisoners in Mountjoy went on hunger strike. This ended successfully after eleven days, when, assisted by a general strike in Dublin, they were released (Van Voris, 1967, pp. 279–80).

Mountjoy, 1923

On 13 October 1923, 400 prisoners in Mountjoy started a hunger strike, in pursuit of the recognition of Ireland's independence. This soon spread to nearly 8000 prisoners in several prisons and camps (Van Voris, 1967, p. 331). On 20 November 1923, Dennis Barry was the first hunger striker to die under the regime of the Irish Free State. On 23 November, the strike was called off (Van Voris, 1967, p. 332). Hunger striking was by no means confined to male prisoners, women playing a distinctive part by mounting their own hunger strikes in Mountjoy and Kilmainham prisons in the early 1920s, as Margaret Buckley's memoirs of her imprisonment show (Buckley, 1939, Foreword and pp. 30–1). There was not unanimity over tactics among prisoners. At one point, prisoners in Mountjoy met to discuss their differences and 'all in favour of "state of war" methods lived on the top landing; the others occupied the first floor' (Buckley, 1938, p. 19).

The conditions for further unrest were still being created. During December 1923, 3481 political prisoners were freed. But in January 1924, the Free State government issued a fresh Public Safety Act, under which the authorities again began filling the prisons with people without trials (Van Voris, 1967, p. 333).

Campaigns against internment in southern Ireland

Under the Defence of the Realm Act of 1918, the number of Irish prisoners interned in mainland prisons such as Dartmoor, Stafford, Usk, Lincoln and Lewes reached 7000 by 1921 and these prisons quickly became hotbeds of dissidence (McGuffin, 1973, pp. 27–8). A riot at Lewes was followed by threatened disturbances in other prisons and a mass escape from Usk. (McGuffin, 1973, p. 30). Among other Irish prisoners interned in Ireland, escape attempts and hunger strikes were the order of the day, About 50 women of the 250 interned joined men on hunger strike during the Civil War. (McGuffin, 1973, p. 80). A mass hunger strike involving more than 8000 prisoners in Mountjoy, Kilmainham, Curragh and Newbridge prisons began in October 1923, around 200 of whom remained on strike for 41 days, before two men died and prisoners called the protest off. (McGuffin, 1973, p. 45)

The 1930s were a period of mass hunger strikes and escape attempts, used by prisoners in their campaigns for political status. (McGuffin, 1973, pp. 53–4). During the Second World War, censorship restricted public knowledge of conditions in the internment camps, many people believing they were glorified holiday camps. In fact, 'huts were damp, cold and draughty. The men had no privacy and were crammed 60 to a hut. Dysentery was common and lice endemic. The total number interned varied, but in all about 800 men were resident in the 'Curragh Holiday Camp'. (McGuffin, 1973, p. 53) The worst riot in Curragh during the war occurred on 14 December 1940, when a protest over the reduced butter ration led to a hut being burned down and an escape tunnel discovered. Prisoners were 'savagely beaten before being put in solitary confinement for ten weeks.' (McGuffin, 1973, p. 54). Eighteen women interned in the old jail of Armagh during the Second World War suffered particular hardships. They had only one visit a month, practically nothing sent in to them and the cells in which they were locked up, singly, for twenty hours a day were bitterly cold. Their twenty-two-day hunger strike in protest at conditions was ignored by the authorities. (McGuffin, 1973, p. 82)

The short-lived lifting of internment in Southern Ireland in 1957 and its reintroduction there in July of that year was followed the following year by a mass breakout of prisoners on 2 December 1958. (McGuffin, 1973, p. 58). Internment ended in Southern Ireland 15 March 1959, as the republican border campaigns lost their impetus. (McGuffin, 1973, p. 77)

Campaigns against internment in Northern Ireland
The setting up of the State of Northern Ireland in June 1921 left intact the existing internment camp at Ballykinlar, County Down. (McGuffin, 1973, p. 62). Conditions were bad, but there was only one organized attempt at mass revolt through escape before internment

ended on 6 December 1921. (McGuffin, 1973, p. 63) After renewed agitation, internment was in effect reintroduced with the passing in 1922 of the Civil Authorities (Special Powers) Act, known as the 'flogging bill'. (McGuffin, 1973, p. 64) Internees were soon moved to the *Argenta*, a boat moored off Carrickfergus, where conditions for the prisoners were described as atrocious. (McGuffin, 1973, p. 65) Disturbances including a hunger strike in 1922 in sympathy with hunger strikes in prisons in southern Ireland led to 200 men being moved to Derry prison (McGuffin, 1973, p. 67).

The years between 1924 and 1938 when internment was lifted, saw riots on the streets of Northern Ireland, largely directed against poverty and unemployment. (McGuffin, 1973, p. 68) The reintroduction of internment on 22 December 1938 followed the discovery of a Republican plot. Derry prison, Crumlin Road prison and a hulk, the *Al Rawdah*, were used for internees. Conditions in the latter were described by survivors as 'abominable', only one incident, associated with an abortive escape attempt, being recorded before the hulk was closed and prisoners transferred away. The most significant riot of the period was the Derry mutiny on Christmas Day of 1940, when 120 prisoners took over a wing and barricaded themselves in with supplies. Eventually, prison officers with fire hoses and acetylene torches attacked.

All the prisoners retreated into a double cell and, jammed in there, were no match for the guards who smashed in the door and turned on the hoses. On and off, this lasted for almost half an hour and the men were very badly buffeted by the powerful jets and almost drowned. They were then dragged out individually and forced to run the gauntlet between two rows of B men [special constables of the Royal Ulster Constabulary] who batoned them on the head . . . No medical treatment was given for almost a week.'

(McGuffin, 1973, p. 71)

The last internees were released on 30 July 1945 (McGuffin, 1973, p. 75).

Internment was reintroduced on 21 December 1956 and lasted until 1961. During this period, although there was only one recorded instance of brutality by the authorities, in the beating up of attempted escapers by special riot police on 15 March 1958, the right to reasonable and decent treatment fought for by prisoners in the riots and hunger strikes of 1938–45 had by and large to be struggled for all over again (McGuffin, 1973, pp. 76–7).

By August 1971, when the political temperature of Irish–British relations had risen so as to alarm the British authorities, the British government again introduced internment without trial. After the hunger strike by prisoners in 1972, the British government had to concede political status to sentenced prisoners in Northern Ireland. 'Bloody Sunday' in 1972, when thirteen civilian marchers in Derry were killed by members of a British paratroop regiment, revived memories of martyrdom from 1916 and 1923 and raised the political profile of republican protests.

The Special Powers Act, originally introduced in 1922, the year Ireland was partitioned, was replaced by the Emergency Powers Act of 1973. The Prevention of Terrorism Act was introduced in 1974. Since 1969, republican prisoners in Ireland had protested about internment without trial, courts without judges, force-feeding of hunger strikers, alleged mental tortures and the denial of political status for detainees and prisoners. Republicans protested at what they described as a conveyor belt criminalization of people, using powers of arrest and interrogation without rights, for three days, under the Emergency Powers Act, and seven days under the Prevention of Terrorism Act. Allegations of physical and sexual abuse and torture of men and women were common (London Armagh Group, 1984, p. 12).

The search by the British government for a more acceptable form of imprisonment began. The Emergency Powers Act led to the setting up of Diplock courts, which empowered a single judge without a jury to sentence for scheduled offences. Lord Diplock led a commission to examine appropriate legal procedures to deal with terrorists in Norther Ireland. The changes Diplock recommended were incorporated in the Northern Ireland Emergency Provisions Act 1973 which replaced the Special Powers Act 1972. Internment ended when the new form of imprisonment was introduced late in 1975. But at the same time, the government announced that after 1 March 1976, prisoners convicted of what were called 'terrorist' crimes would not have political status. The use of imprisonment increased rapidly. Between 1969 and 1978, the number of prisoners in Northern Ireland increased from 600 to 3000. Many of these prisoners, campaigning for political status, rejected their criminal status and became involved in various protests. So, increasingly in the 1970s and 1980s, their protests took the form of campaigns against the Prison Rules and involved ideological and political conflict over their status. Following the example of Kieran Nugent on 14 September 1976, many became known as the 'blanket men'. At one point, as many as 400 Irish Republican prisoners in the

H Blocks of Long Kesh prison, 40 women in Armagh jail and 150 remand prisoners in Crumlin Road jail, were wearing blankets rather than prison clothes. (Anon., 1979). A committee of inquiry headed by Lord Gardiner visited Long Kesh to report back on conditions there and head off possible international criticism and political embarrassment. It was a token gesture. Despite efforts by the authorities to maintain secrecy, in January 1978 the European Court of Human Rights found Britain guilty of 'inhuman and degrading treatment'.

In 1979, of 80 convicted republican prisoners in England and Wales, 28 were serving life sentences with recommendations of a minimum of 30 years, and thirteen with recommendations of a minimum of fourteen years (Fitzgerald and Sim, 1982, p. 47). All republican prisoners were categorized as security category A. All save four had not been allowed transfers to Irish prisons, despite the fact that the families of 55 of them lived in Ireland. Between 1972 and 1975, 22 civilians and 26 servicemen were transferred from Northern Ireland to England to continue serving their sentences (Fitzgerald and Sim, 1982, p. 48).

Conditions of imprisonment in prisons in Northern Ireland were reportedly harsh throughout the postwar years. Strip-searching of women, for example, had gone on since 1949, but gathered pace in 1982. Some measure of the intensity and nature of strip-searching can be gathered by the report that between November 1982 and 11 March 1983 there were 772 strip searches carried out on an average of 24 women by groups of up to ten officers at a time (London Armagh Group, 1984, p. 12).

The way in which repeated strip searching of protesting women prisoners was alleged to be carried in the early 1980s, reinforces the dehumanizing impact of imprisonment: "We are told to go into the cubicles and strip. A curtain is fastened across the cubicle about waist-high to the floor. You are always in view of the prison staff who sometimes number as many as ten . . . While you are naked you are asked if you have a period. If you have, you are forced to remove your sanitary protection. A paper bag is provided for your tampon or towel. The bag is then opened and the contents examined. Your body is then inspected. You are told to turn completely round so no part of your body is left unseen.'" (London Armagh Group, 1984, p. 5)

Irish issues linked with incidents in mainland prisons
There were many protests in British mainland prisons against prison conditions in Northern Ireland. The interconnections between the

Irish republican issue and incidents in English prisons in particular during the 1970s were reinforced by the policy of transferring 'IRA' prisoners to a number of mainland dispersal prisons. In November 1975, for instance, Irish prisoners staged a rooftop protest at Wormwood Scrubs prison in London. Other similar protests were made 'against enforced solitary confinement, extensive censorship of newspapers and books which Irish prisoners are permitted, and the refusal of the Home Office to permit some Irish prisoners to write to solicitors about possible legal action over physical injuries allegedly received while being held before trial' (Fitzgerald and Sim, 1982, p. 48).

It would be easy to fall into the trap of attributing disturbances in mainland prisons, such as the 1976 Hull riot, to the agitations of the relatively small numbers of Irish republican prisoners concentrated in them. Nevertheless, there is little doubt that many of these Irish prisoners experienced their sentences as putting them in triple, or even quadruple, jeopardy – labelled as Irish, as republican, as non-political and therefore criminal, as disruptive and therefore dangerous – and thereby justifying their collective resistance to imprisonment as an oppressed minority.

Dirty protests and hunger strikes

Since the 1970s, prison-based protests in Ireland based upon an intensification of one or more aspects of the deprivations of imprisonment – clothing, food and sanitary conditions – increased. Thus, blanket protests, hunger-strikes and dirty protests became the characteristic vehicle for the campaign for political status, rather than rioting with violence.

In 1976, Relatives Action Committees were formed to support Irish prisoners claiming political status. In May 1978, disturbances among remand prisoners in Armagh led to a squad of male prison officers in riot gear confining the women in their cells for several weeks (London Armagh Group, 1984, p. 9). Women prisoners alleged assaults by prison officers on 7 February 1980. These incidents apparently contributed to the women being confined in their cells without sanitary facilities for three days. They began emptying their excreta through the spyholes and windows and when these were blocked, smeared it on the walls. They refused to stop their no-work protest, in support of the granting of political status in exchange for a return to normal conditions. 'As their own excrement was almost the only part of their lives over which they could exercise control, they used it as another form of protesting the political nature of their imprisonment' (London Armagh Group, 1984, p. 9).

All prisoners involved in the H Block dirty protest were tried and convicted by the Diplock courts. Police methods of interrogation used to obtain confessions were subject both to official inquiries and criticism from pressure groups such as Amnesty International.

In March 1979, Women Against Imperialism 'held the first of repeated annual demonstrations in Northern Ireland, supporting the claims of prisoners in Armagh jail for political status. Prisoners in the H Blocks of Long Kesh began a hunger strike for political status in October 1979 and were joined by three women prisoners in Armagh jail. In 1980, the dirty protest and blanket protest were stopped to draw attention to the hunger strike, which led to ten prisoners dying, including Bobby Sands. The 1980 hunger strikes caused the largest street demonstrations for nearly a decade (Holland, 1980, p. 8).

A decade later, efforts by politicians to address the protracted problems of Northern Ireland were no nearer a solution. Increased numbers of disturbances, some involving fights between loyalist and republican prisoners, were reported in Crumlin Road prison, Belfast, in the early 1990s (*Guardian*, 30 August 1991). A two-hour riot involving fifty prisoners at this prison on 22 September 1991 was reported, involving injuries to four prison officers (*Guardian*, 23 September 1991). After an escalation in deaths arising from both Irish republican and loyalist activity in the Autumn of 1991, there was increasing pressure on ministers to introduce internment again (*Independent*, 17 November 1991, p. 1)

The day before the publication of the Government's White Paper on prison policy and practice, partly in response to the Woolf Report, disturbances involving about seventy prisoners in Mountjoy prison, Dublin, pointed up the continued marginalization of issues affecting other prisoners in the UK, outside the narrow confines of England and Wales. It continued to be policy and practice in England and Wales which preoccupied the Government.

England and Wales

Since 1945, when there were 15 800 people in British prisons, the problem of overcrowding had been regarded as serious (Evans, 1980, p. 16), although this was mainly viewed as a crisis of English prisons. In the 1970s, prison governors wrote to Merlin-Rees, Home Secretary, linking overcrowding with the wave of prison disturbances: 'If the present trend continues there will be a serious loss of control' (Evans, 1980, p. 105). But at that time, it was not the prison population as a whole which was meant, but those among them who were seen as disruptive and possibly capable of influencing others towards collective violence. Despite the seriousness of the riots of the early and mid-1970s in terms of their number, financial cost and destruction of accommodation and their consequent impact on the running of prisons in Britain, the Home Secretary stated in the House of Commons on 22 February 1979 that in the light of reports he had received he was satisfied that the Gartree prison riot 'was not a planned concerted action by prisoners with genuine grievances, and that no further inquiry was needed' (Home Office, 1979, p. 24). This continued in the following year, when the Prison Department was concerned to point out that rioting prisoners were quickly brought under control by staff.

Since the 1960s, British prisons shifted towards designating a small proportion of prisoners as risks to security and/or good order and segregating them in units, variously named, but fulfilling the function of prisons within prisons. Whether this trend caused or resulted from prison riots is more debatable than the observation that these units were associated with public and professional controversy and, at the same time, numerous disturbances involving prisoners.

The possible introduction of special security wings into British prisons was first discussed at the time of the trial of the 'Great Train Robbers' in 1963. E-Wing in Durham prison had been set up as a security and punishment block, after a number of escapes in 1961. Conditions there were rumoured to be brutal. Prisoners from E-Wing contributed to the inquiry into allegations of ill-treatment of prisoners in Durham (Home Office, Cmnd 2068, 1963).

The Mounbatten Report (Home Office, 1966), which followed the escape of the spy George Blake, led to prisoners being categorized according to their security risk. By 1970, British prisons held 225 men serving ten years and 218 serving more than ten years, including 159 serving 'life'. Most of these prisoners, along with those otherwise considered to be high security risks, were categorized as 'A' class and, among these, a number of previous and potential escapers were given the status of 'E men' and required to wear appropriately bright prison clothing. Many of these prisoners found their way into the security wings, modelled on Durham, which were phased out in the early 1970s, but not before a spectacular series of well-publicized incidents in many of them. For example, in the Durham security wing 'there were hunger strikes, escape bids, secret transfers, disturbances, protests and a dramatic escape at the end of 1968' (Cohen and Taylor, 1972, p. 18). There were also two major incidents – a mass protest on 9 February 1967, known as the 'football mutiny', by prisoners who were playing football and were refused permission to retrieve a ball from a security area, and a protest on 3 March 1968 over related grievances, during which 21 prisoners barricaded themselves into the chapel for just over 24 hours (Cohen and Taylor, 1972, pp. 18–29).

The identification of a category of 'dangerous' prisoners as a minority with disruptive potential provided the rationale for the birth of control units after Mountbatten, their demise in 1974 and replacement by more sophisticated attempts to prevent riots. A comprehensive review of policy and practice concerning the management of prisoners considered difficult is contained elsewhere (Bottoms and Light, 1987; Bottomley and Hay, 1991) and is not attempted here. It is clear that the strategies adopted, from the introduction of segregation units in the late 1960s to the development of special units in the 1980s in Lincoln, Parkhurst and Hull, reflected an assumption that the problems of maintaining order in prisons were generally more due to the maladaptation of individual prisoners than an indication that the system for their control itself was in need of fundamental change (Bottomley, 1991, p. 111).

Since the late 1960s, there was a tendency to see both problems of, and possible solutions to, disturbances in terms of the characteristics of that section of the inmate population presumed to be a management problem. This is associated with theories of riots, discussed in Chapter 6, which locate their origins in the activities of a small group of 'disruptive' prisoners.

Typical of research which illustrates and reinforces such thinking is Pope's study carried out in 1973. This surveyed two maximum security prisons in the north of England and two in the south, analysed what were seen by prison staff as the characteristics of male prisoners who were management problems and considered some responses by staff to them (Pope, 1976, pp. 2–5). As compared with the general prison population, prisoners viewed as a management problem were found to be generally younger and serving either less than three years or more than ten year sentences. But the prisoners in these groups together made up no more than half of the total group considered to be a problem. Further, only 12.2 per cent of the total were in prison for offences against the person. The number in this group in prison for burglary and theft constituted a further 22.9 per cent. Those serving sentences for robbery formed the largest proportion, at 25 per cent. Listings by staff of the kinds of problems each man represented, led to five groups being identified:

> *Anti-authority and subversive:* 148 prisoners, 59.7% of prisoners presenting management problems and 8.3% of prison population;
> *Problem personality:* 65 prisoners, 26.2% of prisoners presenting management problems and 3.7% of prison population;
> *Prisoners needing protection:* 7 prisoners, 2.8% of prisoners presenting management problems and 0.4% of prison population;
> *Escapers:* 8 prisoners, 3.2% of prisoners presenting management problems and 0.5% of prison population;
> *Others:* 20 prisoners, 8.1% of prisoners presenting management problems and 1.1% of prison population.
>
> (Pope, 1976, p. 4)

Those in the first category included:

> Those men who have been involved to a greater or lesser degree with activities in the prisons designed to confront or undermine the authority of the staff. The motivation behind such activities can range from being part of concerted attempts to derive greater power for the prisoner community to individual efforts pursued as part of institutional cultural prescriptions . . . while their activities varied from roof climbing and passive sit-down demonstrations to 'walking at snails pace to and from labour to aggravate escorting officers'.
>
> (Pope, 1976, pp. 3–4)

One consequence of this perspective may be simply to increase the labelling effect of 'disruptive' prisoners.

After the prisoner disturbances of the early 1970s in British prisons, control units were introduced to handle disruptive prisoners in harsh, punitive regimes which were 'intentionally austere' (Stern, 1989, p. 34). The much-criticized control units were later abandoned and in their place a variety of segregation, security and special units were developed, all one way and another attempting to curb disruption by individual, and groups of, prisoners.

Criticisms of the operation of the measures taken by the Department to curb rioting prisoners continued. The two units, opened at Wakefield and Wormwood Scrubs prisons in 1973, came under fire

from professional, media and academic commentators from the outset. The Prison Department responded by emphasizing that they were
not for prisoners 'with personality disorder or mental illness', or for
'the merely troublesome prisoner'. 'Control units are for the small
hard core of really persistent and serious troublemakers who are
reckoned to be capable of mending their ways, and the regime has
been framed on that basis' (Home Office, 1975, p. 35).

The recommendations of the most significant official report concerning the treatment of long-term prisoners, the Control Review
Committee (Home Office, 1984), were not taken up and implemented fully. The conceptual tension it identified between a perspective which focused on the individual prisoner viewed as difficult and
the need to examine the prison regime for features which may contribute to that difficulty (Home Office, 1984, para 44), remained
unaddressed subsequently in policy-making. The Special Security Units
set up on C Wing at Parkhurst and in Lincoln and Hull prisons
specifically to be used for disruptive prisoners, including rioters, were
not used for this purpose, but attracted a range of other prisoners
considered to need this accommodation.

Meanwhile, in 1980, there had been widespread industrial action
taken by the Prison Officers' Association in the latter part of the year
in pursuance of their meal-break claims (Home Office, 1981, p. 23).
The publication of the May Report was viewed by the Prison Department as partly an organizational response to the discontents of both
prison officers and prisoners. On the staff side, an Industrial Relations Section was set up in the Prison Department, with the brief of
improving industrial relations (Home Office, 1981, p. 24). The Dispersal Prison Steering Group produced a statement of aims for dispersal prisons, consistent with the idea of 'positive custody' proposed
in the May Report (Home Office, 1981, p. 29).

The 32 incidents of 'concerted indiscipline' by groups of prisoners
occurring in 1980, reported on by the Prison Department, were presented as not significantly different from those in previous years.
Again, as in previous years, no attempt was made in the Department's
report to assess the significance of these incidents in terms of critical
reflection on the prison system itself.

In the mid-1980s, the eight dispersal prisons in Britain were associated with a relatively low incidence of escaping, but had been the
scenes of at least nine major collective disturbances in the previous
ten years (Rutherford, 1985, p. 408). During the mid-1980s, 'new
generation' thinking about prison architecture and regimes was im-

ported from the US into Britain, partly to reduce such problems. New generation thinking is viewed by the Home Office as a means of intensifying the control of prisoners, without the negative connotations of other forms of segregation and concentration, thereby lessening the risk of outbreaks of indiscipline such as rioting.

Throughout the 1970s and 1980s, 'ghosting', or the practice of transferring prisoners from one prison to another, was used increasingly as a means of control. Initially, transfers tended to be used mainly in the wake of disturbances to split up the participants. By 1990, a television documentary revealed the extent to which ghosting had become official policy. In the 'ghost train' system of such transfers, authorized by Home Office Circular 37/90, a governor was allowed to move to a local prison for 28 days any prisoner suspected of causing disruption, a practice condemned by the National Association of Probation Officers (NAPO) (Campbell, 1991, p. 4).

Throughout the mid-1970s, the view of the Prison Department was that dispersal prisons were especially vulnerable to riots and other disturbances, since 'their population contains both dangerous and violent men, some of them sophisticated professional criminals including many with previous experience of prison. A proportion feel they have little to lose by resorting to violence in order to challenge the regime. Others use their experience and knowledge of the prison system to challenge many of the rules and procedures . . .' (Home Office, 1976, p. 29). There was evidence to support this, since the most prominent disturbances up to the mid-1980s had occurred in the dispersal prisons. Parkhurst: 24 October 1969; Albany: 8 September 1971, 26–8 August 1972; Gartree: 26 November 1972; Hull: 31 August – 3 September 1976; Gartree: 5 October 1978; Parkhurst: 22 March 1979; Hull: 11 April 1979; and Wormwood Scrubs: 31 August 1979 (Ditchfield, 1990, p. 3).

Playing down significance of incidents as protests
The Prison Department's annual report for 1978 noted that incidents of 'concerted indiscipline' numbered 30 in a range of penal establishments during each of the years 1976, 1977 and 1978. These included five in dispersal prisons, five in training prisons, seven in local prisons, two in remand centres and two in borstals. The numbers involved were normally between 30 and 60 prisoners but in two cases over 100 prisoners took part. In ten incidents, prisoners climbed onto the roofs. Some idea of the scale of damage caused by these incidents can be gained by the report that in one such incident involving five

prisoners over three days at Parkhurst prison the following year, 1979, the bill for damage was £50 000 and two entire wings were made unfit for habitation (Home Office, 1980, p. 20).

The large-scale riot occurred at Gartree prison between 5 and 6 October 1978. It spread rapidly through the prison and continued overnight.

> During the course of the night groups of staff made several at- tempts to enter A, B and D Wings to regain control, but they were thwarted by massive barricades and by boiling water and missiles thrown by the rioters. Attempts by the rioters to break through the fabric of the building into the prison grounds or onto the roof were, however, prevented. The rioters continued to smash up furni- ture and fittings until, at about 7.30 am on 6 October, the first indications came that they were willing to end the action.
>
> (Home Office, 1979, p. 24)

One result of the Gartree prison riot was that three out of four of its wings (242 places) were made uninhabitable (Home Office, 1979, p. 21).

In February 1979, thirteen organizations associated with prisons and penal reform, including the Howard League for Penal Reform, NACRO and the Prison Reform Trust, published a joint manifesto for penal reform. This proposed measures to reduce the prison popula- tion including maximum penalties. It also proposed that a code of minimum standards be introduced to improve prison conditions, attention to prisoners' rights through abolishing censorship of mail, improved visiting and access to telephones, the establishments of a Prisons Ombudsman and the replacement of the prison disciplinary system and Boards of Visitors by independent Prison Disciplinary Tribunals.

Between 21 and 25 August about ten prisoners took to the roof at Peterhead prison in Scotland and shouted to watching journalists that conditions in the observation block of punishment cells was the main target of their protest.

Introduction of riot control squads: from 'demonstrations' to 'concerted indiscipline'
In 1979, it was reported by the Prison Department that 'the number of incidents of concerted indiscipline by groups of prisoners has remained at about the same level for the last 5 years, the number of

26 for 1979 not being significantly different from the average of about 30'. (Home Office, 1980, p. 19) The most notable reported incident was 'an act of concerted indiscipline by prisoners in D Wing of Wormwood Scrubs prison on 31 August which was quickly brought under control by staff from Wormwood Scrubs and other establishments' (Home Office, 1980, p. 19). New 'MUFTI' squads were responsible for this action.

The redefinition of collective demonstrations as concerted indiscipline was accompanied by the introduction of new methods of curbing protests by prisoners. These were used by 'minimum use of force – tactical intervention' or MUFTI teams, comprising prison officers wearing protective equipment, who were trained to charge at protesters and break up protests forcibly. The Prison Department admitted that they were used before 31 August 1979, although it was criticism about the handling by 'MUFTI squads' of that particular incident which led the Home Secretary to ask the Regional Director of the South-East Region of the Prison Department to Investigate.

In D wing of Wormwood Scrubs prison in London on 31 August 1979, in the account given by PROP, a peaceful sit-in by prisoners in pursuit of claims for privileges was broken up violently by up to 300 prison officers armed with sticks and staves (PROP, 1979, p. 9). This seems to have been the first time Special Groups or 'MUFTI' squads of riot-trained and protected prison officers were used since their formation in February 1978 after the Hull riot, although as noted above, staff in riot gear had been used in at least one prison in Norther Ireland in 1978.

It is arguable that the riots of the 1970s were drawing the attention of the Home Office to problems whose solution required prison officers rather than prisoners to be disciplined and controlled. By the mid-1970s, the control of prisons had already passed largely into the hands of the Prison Officers' Association, without whose consent little was possible (Rutherford, 1985, p. 410):

One instance of this shift of power was evident in the aftermath of the disturbance on the dispersal wing at Wormwood Scrubs in August 1979. The local branch of the Prison Officers' Association barred probation officers, psychologists, chaplains and teachers from certain parts of the institution and on occasion from the prison as a whole. The official inquiry found: 'There are strong indications that the governor came under pressure from the POA so severe that some of the policy decisions affecting the wing that he made at the time were against his own better judgement and the advice of his most senior advisers.'

(Rutherford, 1985, p. 410)

Criticisms of MUFTI, and the lessons being learnt by the police following the Scarman Report (1981) after the Brixton urban riot, and the other riots which followed in 1981, led to 'Control and Restraint' (C and R) teams of prison staff being introduced by the mid-1980s, to restore order after a disturbance. C and R worked at three different levels, from the control of one prisoner to curbing incidents involving large groups, and training was more sophisticated than for the crude violence of MUFTI. Throughout, an attempt was made to separate officers carrying out the C and R work from those commanding such operations.

'No discernible pattern'

The Home Office continued to deny that the succession of prison disturbances in 1980 had any significance. In 1981, the Home Office reported in the same vein as precious years that the 32 incidents of:

Concerted indiscipline by groups of inmates in 1980, including rooftop demonstrations by five or more inmates, was in line with the average for the previous five years. As before, the incidents conformed to no discernible pattern. All types of establishment were affected and, when inmates gave reasons for their behaviour, those covered a wide range, including complaints about the quality of food, cell conditions, visits procedures, delays in the delivery of clean clothing and, in a few, minor instances, restrictions imposed on the regime because of industrial action by staff. 10 of the incidents were over in no more than half an hour but 4 lasted for about 24 hours and one – a refusal by four prisoners to take food or to 'slop-out' – spanned 3 days. The average number of participants was about 60, ranging from 5 incidents involving fewer than 10 inmates to 4 involving more than 100. Most of the incidents took the form of sit-down demonstrations, refusals to work or mass rejections of food and were entirely peaceful. There were, however, two incidents during the course of which an officer was assaulted and a third following which two officers required hospital treatment. That incident was at Nottingham prison on 6 November, when officers had to bring under control a violent demonstration by 11 inmates, some armed with bricks and other weapons, who had barricaded themselves in a television room. 4 of the inmates sustained minor injuries.

(Home Office, 1981, p. 35)

Rooftop demonstrations were reported separately:

There were 22 incidents in which inmates succeeded in getting on to roofs in 1980, compared with 10 in each of the two previous years. Whilst this increase gives cause for concern because roof climbings have a potential for serious injury, damage and disruption, the number of violent or destructive roof-top demonstrations has been much the same in each of the last three years. The increase in 1980 was in short lived and passive attempts by individuals to draw attention to grievances; and all roof climbers in 1980 were resolved without the use of force and without serious injury.

(Home Office, 1981, p. 35)

In two cases, Wormwood Scrubs on 24 June and Risley Remand Centre on 15 December, considerable damage was reported. In the former instance, five prisoners caused £20 000 of damage. In the latter case, 38 young prisoners caused £2000 of damage and by flooding from a water tank in the roof made a wing uninhabitable for almost a month (Home Office, 1981, p. 35).

Calls for the reduction of overcrowding in prisons in England and Wales came in the summer of 1980 from the Parliamentary All-Party Penal Affairs Group and in 1981 from the Home Secretary of the conservative government, William Whitelaw, using the threat of legislation to reduce the prison population (Cavadino, 1981, p. 91).

If overcrowding was one of the principal causes of rioting, one would have expected riots to have occurred mainly in local prisons, since, as the Inspectorate noted in its report for 1981, 'overcrowding is almost entirely restricted to local prisons' (HM Chief Inspector of Prisons, 1982, p. 7).

The Chief Inspector's report for 1982 noted that measures such as the Criminal Justice Act of 1982, which extended suspended sentences and abolished imprisonment for vagrancy and soliciting offences, plus the building programme of £40m per year plus £20m for refurbishing, would still not guarantee to reduce overcrowding (HM Chief Inspector of Prisons, 1983, p. 6). Further, many prisoners were locked up for most of the day, without work, and numbers more worked only for a few hours per day (Chief Inspector, 1983, p. 9).

In many ways, disturbances at Albany prison on the Isle of Wight, since its opening in the late 1960s, and the way they were perceived and responded to by the Home Office, stand as an epitome of the history of rioting by prisoners in the quarter-century after 1967. Collective complaints by prisoners during the period between 1967 and 1983 were persistently misrepresented by the media and misunderstood and over-reacted to by the authorities. Each of the two major series of incidents occurring in 1971–2, referred to earlier in this chapter, was distinctive. The first involved responses by long-term prisoners to the policy of dispersing them. The second, for instance the sit-down demonstrations of 2 June and 4 August, involved a series of largely peaceful demonstrations organized by PROP, on the basis of principles of civil disobedience (King and Elliott, 1977, pp. 305–6). Despite the peacefulness of the PROP-led protests of June 1972, subsequent POA reaction, picked up by the mass media, led to a security clampdown, searches and intimidation by staff. Predictably, prisoners responded by rioting in their cells for two days and nights, causing much damage. On 28 August the *Daily Mirror* headline was 'Siege at the Jail of Fear'. 'Albany had become the most notorious prison in the country.' (King and Elliott, 1977, p. 31) In May 1973, prisoners responded to a strengthening of dispersal policy by fresh disturbances in which they demanded the isolation of those deemed to require more security (ibid., p. 32). The trajectory of dispersal policy, and of alienation from it by a minority of rioting prisoners, was set for the following decade.

The Inspectorate of Prisons spent three days at Albany prison in 1983 and reported on the major disturbance there earlier that year, that:

At the time of our visit, there were still signs of the extensive damage which had been caused to the workshops and inmate accommodation. After discussions with staff and prisoners it became clear to us that one of the major causes of the discontent which had led to the disturbance was the employment of prisoners on the sewing of mailbags – an occupation many consider to be unsuitable for long-term prisoners. We were glad to learn that the intention to continue with this form of employment at Albany had been abandoned.

(HM Chief Inspector of Prisons, 1984, p. 1)

Fresh Start

One attempt by management at solving the problems of running prisons economically and effectively was the 'Fresh Start' scheme. This was introduced in the guise of employing prison officers as far as possible in adequate numbers to work straight shifts on enhanced pay, rather than allowing excessive overtime to continue. Behind Fresh Start lay a longstanding power struggle between management and prison officers for control of the Prison Service and hence of prisons. The situation was exacerbated by the relative strength of the Prison Officers' Association, which tended to ride roughshod over the sensitiveness of prison managements about prisoners' grievances and to block many significant reforms in the organization and operation of prisons.

'Fresh Start', as an attempt by the Prison Department to reduce staff overtime, was not effective at solving the political problems of the overuse of prisons. The roots of prison riots lay less in understaffing and overcrowding of prisons than in the continued inhumanity and injustice of imprisonment. Far from bringing order to prisons, Fresh Start and changes in the regional and local arrangements for managing prisons, such as the introduction of area management, were followed in the second half of the decade by several waves of rioting, culminating in the series of riots in 1990, which began in Strangeways.

Overcrowding continued to dominate the prison statistics. Between 1986 and 1988, the total number of people in prison in England and Wales, including police cells, on 30 June each year rose from 46 816 to 50 302 (Prison Statistics England and Wales, 1986, 188).

The 1986 riots

Between 29 April and 2 May in 1986, widespread disturbances in 46 prisons in England were described by the inquiry report as 'the worst night of violence the English prison system has ever known' (Hennessey, 1987, p. 101). In that period, riots occurred in at least 22 prisons in England, beginning with Gloucester. In the process, 45 prisoners escaped, many more were injured although there were no lives lost, and there was much damage, including the virtual destruction of Northeye Category C prison.

The Hennessey Report into these riots, by the then Chief Inspector of Prisons, drew attention to shortcomings in the quality of life of prisoners, partly through reduced activities and partly through deteriorating relationships between staff and prisoners in the atmosphere of industrial unrest involving prison officers and their managers

(Hennessey, 1987). There was widespread concern among penal reform organizations about the lack of implementation of Hennessey's recommendations. 'His report was subject to blatant (but highly effective) news manipulation by the Home Office which severely limited press coverage of his findings. Remarkably his report was never debated in Parliament' (Prison Reform Trust, 1990, p. 1).

The Prison Reform Trust produced a report and commentary based on accounts of the riots by six prisoners. This attracted controversy. It locates the causes of the riots as lying beyond the industrial action by the Prison Officers' Association (POA) in response to budgetary constraints imposed by the Home Office. It identifies the need for improved communication between prisoners and staff to help to defuse the acute anxiety and anger caused by the industrial action. It argues for increased participation by prisoners in the day-to-day decisions affecting their lives in prison through the establishment of staff/prisoner committees. 'If prisoners had a peaceful and realistic method of contributing to the organization of meal rotas, a way of voicing their dislike of, for example, the tannoy system is Wymott prison, they may be less liable to use direct and destructive action' (Prison Reform Trust, 1986, p. 21).

Notably, this report by the Prison Reform Trust refers to more fundamental causes of the 1986 riots, yet only implicates communication and participation in day-to-day decision-making as factors contributing to them. Another Trust report details further problems.

In the mid-1980s, there was evidence of the continuing use of the medieval-style body belt to restrain prisoners judged to be creating a disturbance in the terms of Prison Rule 46, in 41 cases in 1981 and 107 cases since 1982 (Prison Reform Trust, 1984, p. 8): 'The body belt is a legacy of the Middle Ages . . . it is a thick leather belt which is fastened round the prisoner's waist and which has handcuffs (iron for men, in leather for women) attached to a ring on either side. The prisoner's feet may also be tethered with thick leather straps. According to prisoners with personal experience, when restrained in a body belt a person's arms cannot be extended to their full length. The prisoner's body becomes hunched and cramp is likely to set in.' (Prison Reform Trust, 1984, p. 1)

The 1988 riots: more Category 'C' prisons erupt

Major riots occurred in the summer of 1988 at Haverigg and Lindholme Category C (low security) training prisons. No staff or prisoners were killed or seriously injured, although there was much damage and the loss of 239 prison places (*The Times*, 17 July A: p. 5:g).

Risley, 1989: remand prisoners riot

During the spring of 1989, a serious riot at Risley Remand Centre involved the loss of 156 prison places and was followed by an internal inquiry by Ian Dunbar, South West Regional Director of the Prison Service, a summary of which was later published.

The Chief Inspector noted in the 1989 report that prison regimes had received comparatively little research attention and that this would be remedied in a forthcoming study (Inspector, 1990, p. 61). This, however, was too late materializing to head off the major riot at Strangeways which occurred in April 1990, within weeks of the publication of this report.

Strangeways, 1990

The significance of 1990 was not simply the virtual destruction of one of the Victorian dinosaurs of prison buildings by a group of prisoners, but also the involvement of a range of other local, young and remand category prisoners in the wave of riots which followed.

On Sunday 1 April, the day following large-scale violence which had occurred during the police quelling of poll tax riots in Trafalgar Square, London, prisoners at Strangeways prison, Manchester, rioted. Nearly sixty years earlier, the inquiry into the Dartmoor prison riot had noted that 'it is a matter of common knowledge among prison officials that if there is to be disorder Sunday is the day on which it is most likely to occur' (Du Parcq, 1932, p. 14).

The Chief Inspector of Prisons had only published his report on Strangeways three days before the riot of 1 April 1990. Whilst upbeat in recognizing recent improvements in the regime, it stated that the prison still had 'some awful buildings, particularly the visits areas and reception for remands, both [were] quite unsuitable for continued use' and 'overall, in spite of improvements, the treatment of prisoners at Manchester still left much to be desired' (HM Chief Inspector of Prisons, 1990, p. 85).

The Strangeways riot was the most major of what according to Woolf Inquiry were six further disturbances which occurred in April 1990 at Glen Parva, Dartmoor, Cardiff, Bristol and Pucklechurch. The disturbances at Strangeways continued for 25 days. Subsequently, incidents occurred at almost a score of other penal institutions in Britain. In June, prisoners in York Magistrates' Court cells were reported by other former prisoners as likely to riot if conditions did not improve (*Yorkshire Evening Press*, 16 June 1990). But by then a wave of riots had taken place which were more or less associated with the Strangeways riot.

On 6 April, about sixty remand prisoners in the young offender remand centre and young offender institution at Glen Parva got loose when a prisoner overpowered an officer and took his keys in an escape attempt. The prisoners barricaded themselves on the first floor and began spraying the officers with fire hoses, but following negotiations with staff they had all surrendered within four hours, with five staff injured (Woolf and Tumin, 1991, 1.61–67, p. 8).

On 7 April at Dartmoor, an inadequate, damp building erected in 1809 with a regime regarded by prisoners as rigid and illiberal (Woolf and Tumin, 1991, 1.71, p. 9), a number of prisoners began to throw dustbins down from the landings, instead of returning to their cells after watching the Grand National horse race on television, and then broke through onto the roof of D Wing wearing hoods and masks which had probably been prepared in advance. Fires were lit in a number of areas, all but one prisoner surrendering by 18.00 hours on 8 April. Three days later, this prisoner, with three others who had joined him, surrendered (Woolf and Tumin, 1991, 1.70–91, pp. 10–12).

> The prisoners who were interviewed and gave evidence made it clear that their major complaints were about slopping out, the inadequacy of the recesses [lavatories and wash areas], the fact that they had to eat food in their cells and that there was trouble with infestation by vermin. There was also a suggestion that prisoners were not treated like human-beings or adults. A frequent complaint was the pettiness of some rules and the way they were enforced.
> (Woolf and Tumin, 1991, p. 11)

The Cardiff disturbance began on Sunday 8 April when prisoners on one wing rioted in that dilapidated Victorian local prison. Prisoners involved in the riot knew about the Strangeways and Dartmoor incidents and some of the 203 prisoners accommodated in A Wing were involved in this riot, which lasted half a day (Woolf and Tumin, 1991, 1.97–109, pp. 11–13). On the same day, prisoners transferred from C Wing of Dartmoor were involved in a day-long disturbance which spread to three wings of the institution and led to prisoners getting onto the roof and causing £3.5m of damage (Woolf, 1991, 1.113–28, pp. 13–15) to buildings which had been recommended by the Prison Commissioners for demolition as unfit for prisoners fifty years previously.

The last of the April 1990 disturbances, the riot by young prisoners at Pucklechurch remand centre which began on Sunday 22 April, was quelled in two assaults by Control and Restraint (C&R) units on the following day. Of the 103 male prisoners in the institution, 35 were injured in its retaking. Also injured were 47 staff.

Lord Justice Woolf began his inquiry into the Strangeways riot on 14 May 1990. The Woolf Report was the most far-reaching prison riot inquiry in British penal history and possibly the most influential report since the Gladstone Report, and was published on 26 February 1991. But whereas it took a chaplain's complaint to trigger the reforms of the Gladstone Report, it took twenty years of repeated riots before the Home Office would command an inquiry of Woolf's scope. A brief which strayed so far beyond the immediate riot to its wider implications for penal policy and practice was published on 26 February 1991. In its extensive pages of evidence, analysis and recommendations it steered a moderate reforming path between the defensiveness of the Fowler Report after the Hull riot in 1976 and the radicalism of the evidence of the Prison Reform Trust to the Woolf inquiry. Woolf's recommendations were as pragmatic as its description of the riots of 1990 was broad in scope. In its conduct, Woolf examined the immediate circumstances of the Strangeways riot between June and August, was joined by Judge Stephen Tumin, HM Chief Inspector of Prisons, for the second part of the inquiry concerned with the wider issues underlying the riot, and had the benefit of three assessors: Gordon Lakes, former Deputy Director General of the Prison Service, Rod Morgan, Professor of Criminal Justice at Bristol University, and Mary Tuck, former Head of the Home Office Research and Planning Unit. Thus it departed somewhat from the tradition, since the Mountbatten Report and the appointment of Brigadier Maunsell as HM Chief Inspector of Prisons, of bringing in 'outsiders' who had no formal involvement in the criminal justice system to head up inquiries and inspections.

Woolf identifies the need to maintain a balance between security, control and justice in the running of prisons. 'The April riots occurred because these three elements were out of balance. There were failures in the maintenance of control. There were failures to achieve the necessary standards of justice. There could easily have been a collapse in security' (Woolf and Tumin, 1991, p. 17). Woolf sees the maintenance of justice as contingent on the maintenance of control (Woolf and Tumin, 1991, p. 17).

Security, control and justice will not be set at the right level, and will not be held in balance, unless there are changes in the way the Prison Service structures its relations, both between management and staff, and between staff and prisoners. There is a fundamental lack of respect and a failure to give and require responsibility at all levels in the prison system. These shortcomings must be tackled if the Prison Service is to maintain a stable system.

(Woolf and Tumin, 1991, 1.153, pp. 17–18)

To this end, Woolf makes twelve central recommendations:

(a) Closer cooperation between different parts of the criminal justice system through a national forum and local committees.
(b) More visible day-to-day leadership of the Prison Service by the Director General through a published contract with Ministers.
(c) Increased delegation of responsibilities to governors of prisons.
(d) An enhanced role for prison officers.
(e) A contract for each prisoner setting out expectations and responsibilities wherever he or she is held.
(f) A national, eventually binding, system of Accredited Standards in prisons.
(g) A Prison Rule that no establishment should exceed its certified normal accommodation and that Parliament should be informed if, exceptionally, it does.
(h) A public commitment from Ministers to provide access to sanitation for all prisoners by February 1996.
(i) For prisoners to be located in community prisons near their homes wherever possible and to have more visits and home leaves thereby improving their links with families and the community.
(j) A division of establishments into small and more manageable and secure units.
(k) A separate statement of purpose, separate conditions and generally lower security categorization for remand prisoners.
(l) Improved judicial procedures in prisons, including relieving Boards of Visitors of their adjudicatory responsibilities, introducing a grievance procedure and disciplinary proceedings to be dealt with by the Governor and an independent Complaints Adjudicator.

Some indication that, despite the strenuous efforts of penal reform groups to use Woolf to bring about prison reforms, a new era of penal policy was not about to be ushered in came when Kenneth Baker, Home Secretary, announced an independent inquiry into the escape ten days previously of two IRA suspects from Brixton prison in London (*Guardian*, 17 July 1991). At the same time, a 'secret riot', unreported by the Home Office, at Frankland prison near Durham was revealed by the newspaper, during which 'IRA and Palestinian terrorists and a group of Mafia and London gangsters' destroyed a landing and caused £200 000 of damage, apparently in protest at being 'ghosted' round the prison system (*Guardian*, 17 July 1991).

The Home Secretary responded to the Woolf Report by bringing forward the end of 'slopping out' by prisoners from the end of 1997 to 1994. But this was not the end of the story. One contradictory consequence of converting cells to integral sanitation was that, following one common approach to conversion, in the process one cell in three became two toilets for two other adjoining cells. This increased overcrowding in the very prisons where pressure on sanitation was greatest. This led the government to halt progress on these reforms in the autumn of 1991 (*Guardian*, 27 September 1991). For by the autumn of 1991, more than 1800 prisoners were being held in police cells and the number was reported to be rising by a hundred each week. Against Home Office predictions and normal trends for the time of year, the prison population had risen in six months by nearly 2000, from 45 106 on 31 March 1991 (NACRO Briefing No. 28) to 47 017 (*Guardian*, 27 September 1991). In October 1990, the Home Secretary also announced that a new offence of prison mutiny would be introduced as soon as possible, which would carry a maximum penalty of ten years' imprisonment, to run consecutively with the sentence the prisoner was already serving.

Meanwhile, riots continued. Early on 21 August 1991, police in riot gear surrounded Lindholme Category C prison near Doncaster and control and restraint teams moved in, with reported injuries to four prison officers and seven prisoners, to quell the fifth disturbance there in three years (7 a.m. news, Radio Four, 21 August 1991). 'At the height of the battle, some 250 inmates, armed with dustbin lids and chair legs, rampaged through the jail while firemen from Doncaster were stoned' (*Guardian*, 22 August 1991). The National Association for Care and Resettlement of Offenders (NACRO) pointed out that reports on previous incidents recommending better earnings for prisoners had been ignored. The Chairman of the POA at the prison called it under-resourced and short-staffed (*Guardian*, 22 August 1991).

On Sunday night 25 August 1991, about seventy prisoners rioted for six hours in H Block of Moorland Prison, a newly-opened purpose-built £56m 'showpiece' prison for remand prisoners under twenty-one, a few hundred yards from Lindholme prison. The Moorland riot heightened debate about the causes of prison riots. The most plausible immediate explanation was that prisoners' longstanding collective grievances surfaced in their new surroundings, which were relaxed enough to allow them a good deal of free association, and hence permitted this form of expression. Eleven prisoners had been transferred briefly from Lindholme to Moorland after the riot in Lindholme (27 August 1991). In the three months since opening, Moorland had decanted more than eighty prisoners into H Block, from police cells and Armley Prison in Leeds. Conditions in some police cells had been described by the Board of Visitors Co-ordinating Committee as 'disgraceful'. Armley Prison, Leeds, was an overcrowded Victorian local prison, general conditions in which, and conditions for remand prisoners especially, had been repeatedly condemned.

A riot at Everthorpe Prison on 2 September, while it was being emptied for conversion to a low security prison (*Guardian*, 3 September 1991), pointed to the possibility that it was the disruption to the daily life of the prison which produced such riots.

But a week later, Cardiff, Oxford, Tyneside and Handsworth in Birmingham were disturbed by a series of urban riots, in the very downtown localities from which many prisoners tended to be drawn. These riots took a variety of forms, generally perceived as small in scale when compared with those of 1981, but not in their impact on public fears (*Observer*, 15 September 1991). It was noted that in Cardiff, the 'Wreck Boys', the 'Square Boys' and the 'Michael Stone Boys' were among groups of residents involved in internecine battles focused on a local shopkeeper (*Guardian*, 3 September 1991). Two commentators on the Tyneside disturbances noted that unlike the mass riots of 1981 and the Broadwater Farm uprisings of 1985, 'the Tyneside disorders are small beer – the rioters come in clumps, not mobs'. (Hugill and Rose, 1991, p. 23). In the process, the rioters acted as though at odds with each other and with other bystanders, rather than attracting waves of popular local support. They were condemned by the Government as inexcusable and assumed by the 'liberal' press to arise from unemployment and poverty (*Guardian*, 3, 4, 11 September 1991).

Whatever their origins, the urban and prison riots of late summer 1991 expressed in a seemingly random and dispersed way similar intense anger on the part of the rioters. However, these were not mass protests against the authorities. Their origins and character were more fragmented and diverse.

Government concern about maintaining public confidence in the police and the curbing of lawlessness in the community was reflected in the Criminal Justice Act (1991) which received the Royal Assent on 24 July 1991. This progressed the Conservative Government's will towards the availability of harsher sentencing options as alternatives to imprisonment and longer sentences for more serious offenders. It also advanced the delegation of key functions of remand prisons and bail support services to the voluntary and private sectors. Prison mutiny was to be a criminal offence, carrying further imprisonment as its penalty.

One stated purpose of the Criminal Justice Act 1991 was to reduce the size of the prison population. But for more than a decade, the post-rehabilitation era had been marked by the failure of prison managements to address urgently and radically the task of improving prisoners' quality of life, and politicians to take action to reduce the size of, and resource pressures on, the prison system and to bring a significantly greater measure of justice to the running of prisons.

At the same time, the Government was concerned to set the direction of policy and practice in the Prison Service for the remainder of the century. The reforms proposed in the White Paper published on 17 September 1991, moved slowly in the direction recommended by Woolf, but without the changes advocated by reformers and without the additional resources the POA saw as necessary. The reforms advocated were located in the imperative of maintaining control of an expanded prison system through improved security, and lacked a clearly timetabled prior commitment to the resources required to benefit prisoners substantially. The consideration of Woolf's recommendations to deal with overcrowding by holding the authorities accountable for it was postponed until 1995. Additional immediate spending of £23m on improved security was to be diverted from elsewhere in the existing prisons budget. Woolf's insistence on national accredited standards for all aspects of the prison regime was diluted in the White Paper to the goal of providing basic necessities and facilities 'towards which establishments would work as resources allowed'. (*Guardian*, 17 September 1991)

5 Responses to Prison Riots

> Crushing power exercised relentlessly by and without hesitation is really the merciful, as it is the necessary, course to be pursued.
>
> (Molineux, 1884, p. 15)

Examination of responses to rioting presents considerable difficulties. Research into responses to riots tends to be based on hindsight and, to the extent that riots are rarely predictable, serendipity as far as accurate, standardized data are concerned. There is an ambiguity in the term 'responses'. Responses to prison riots include policies and practices at the time of specific incidents and subsequent actions after the riot is over in the prison and at the level of penal policy. Every action also can be considered as a response to other, usually preceding and perhaps anticipated, actions. So the actions of prisoners in rioting, which precipitate responses by the authorities, are themselves responses to other factors which need also to be considered as consequences, in more or less a succession. Taking cognizance of these factors, this chapter considers how responses by the authorities to prison riots have changed over time.

Smith argues that since prison riots arise from unresolved conflicts due to power differentials between staff and prisoners, four possible responses are possible at the point where the conflict becomes manifest: negotiating between the parties, one party withdrawing from the conflict, physical combat between the parties, or a third party being called in to mediate the conflict (Smith, 1973). This simple typology may be used to demonstrate how responses to prison riots have moved from combative confrontation to negotiation and, latterly, towards a more mixed response, which is a hybrid of these.

FORCEFUL SUPPRESSION: A TRADITIONAL RESPONSE

The history of prison rioting has been intimately bound up with measures taken by the authorities to prevent, curb and control rioting in the community. In Western Europe since the end of the eighteenth century, and in the US since the mid-nineteenth century, the traditional response to intercommunal riots has been forceful suppression, buttressed by respectable citizens' acute fear of unruly gangs, mobs, hooligans, outlaws and minority groups such as immigrants and people displaced from traditional ways of life (Pearson, 1983). Part of the societal response to these fears has involved the generation of organized means of quelling riots and maintaining public order (Tilly, 1989, p. 89).

By 1870, the penitentiary systems in Britain and the US were overdue for reform. It was realized that as reforming agents these prisons were a failure. They had long since lapsed into a custodial habit, increasingly punitive and constrained by lack of money to run them efficiently (Hawkins and Alpert, 1989, p. 48). Prison systems in search of a mode of operation which was above reproach increasingly adopted the military style of management (Hawkins and Alpert, 1989, p. 50). The new reformatories which began to be built in the US from 1876 offered jobs to many former Unionist and Confederate veterans, just as new and existing prisons in Britain absorbed many former soldiers from the Crimea.

Accordingly, the military model of forceful suppression came to be viewed as the logical and natural response to prison riots. Ironically, however, the extent and intensity of violence perpetrated by states in Europe and the US increased through the nineteenth and twentieth centuries, as powerful more or less federated nation states were built (Tilly, 1989, p. 93). In direct contrast, what Tilly describes as the 'repertoires of contention' became more various, which sometimes meant less violent, as traditions of mutiny and invasions and escapes associated with penal institutions were supplanted with a range of less immediately confrontational and violent means of protest.

Not only shaming ceremonies, but also invasions of posted fields, seizures of grain, expulsions of unwelcome representatives of authority, machine-breaking, destruction of dishonored houses, and a number of other forms of direct action were well-known violence-producing routines in the eighteenth century that almost disappeared during the nineteenth. In their place, meetings, demonstrations, rallies, strikes, petition drives, electoral campaigns, and other forms of contention having relatively low probabilities of producing violence grew more and more common. The change of repertoires significantly reduced the proportion of all claim-making that involved violence. The change emerged from a century of struggle for the right to strike, the right to assemble, the right to vote, the right to form unions, parties, and other associations, the right to have a say in government policy.

(Tilly, 1989, p. 92)

The policing of riots changed. European and US police forces played a more prominent and a more explicitly political role (Tilly, 1989, p. 91). Prison staff involved in riot control often worked closely with police and with the military. The consequences of increased policing included:

> . . . far greater control by the authorities over the short-run extent and timing of collective violence, especially attacks on persons rather than property, than their challengers had. This was true for several reasons. Authorities usually have the technical and organizational advantage in the effective use of force, which gives them a fairly great choice among tactics of prevention, containment and retaliation. Limits on that discretion are more likely to be political and moral – Could they afford to show weakness? Could they open fire on women and children? – than technical. If the criterion of success is simply the minimization of nonstate violence, repression often works.

(Tilly, 1989, p. 91)

There is some similarity between the patterns of waves of rioting in both Britain and the US. But the scale of prison riots in the US has consistently been greater than that in Britain, if by 'scale' is meant the matrix of the size of establishment, the number of prisoners involved, the degree of violence involved for both prisoners and the authorities and the outcome in terms of deaths, injuries and damage to property.

The military model of management and practice outlasted other more precarious rationales for imprisonment, such as the betterment of prisoners (Street, Vinter and Perrow, 1966). One consequence in Britain and the US was the restriction of the officers' and guards' roles largely to custodial activities. In the US, guards became an armed force, often totally cut off from informal interaction with prisoners. This had crucial implications for the way in which riots were responded to.

In the US, the early years of the twentieth century witnessed the incidents of rioting, rarely reporting as they were, used increasingly by the authorities as the rationale for tightening up areas of slackness and maladministration in prisons. The 1913 Sing Sing riot, for instance, sparked a more public debate than hitherto about the assumed correlation between poor administration and disorder within prisons and set the scene for future riots to be dealt with more forcefully and decisively.

In 1917, the occasion arose, when the Joliet Penitentiary riot was suppressed brutally (see Chapter 3). Again, when prisoners rioted at Folsom Prison, California, in 1927 and held seven guards hostage in a cellblock following a failed escape attempt in which two guards were injured and a prisoner killed, the authorities decided to quell the riot with force when the prisoners refused an ultimatum to go back to their cells. In the attack which followed, eight inmates were killed and one guard died of 'excitement' (Garson, 1972, p. 413).

In 1929, prisoners at Colorado State Prison barricaded themselves in after trying to escape. Again the assumption of the authorities that once hostages had been taken force should be used proved expensive in terms of human casualties:

> More guards arrived and localized the disturbances, but the prisoners held seventeen guards hostage and issued an ultimatum threatening to kill three of them if a car and a clear escape road were not provided. When these conditions were refused, four guards were killed and thrown from the cellhouse window one at a time over a two-hour period. The officials began their attack by dynamiting the inmates' stronghold. This forced inmates back into another part of the cellhouse, which was also dynamited. The inmates were running out of ammunition and, as authorities mobilized machine guns and a 75 mm. cannon for a final assault, the inmate leader shot his four lieutenants and himself, ending the revolt.
>
> (Garson, 1972, pp. 413–14)

This policy of forceful suppression of prison riots by the authorities was pursued by the authorities in the US, in five of the incidents in the 1929–30 wave of prison riots, at a cost of nineteen prisoners' lives. In contrast, in cases where no force was used by the authorities, there were no casualties (Garson, 1972, p. 414). Garson reviews the profile of responses to prison riots in the US over more than a century and concludes that:

> First, there is no evidence that when prisoners' demands are granted there is either more or less rioting than when they are ignored. Second, to the extent that officials have granted prisoners'

demands, prison reform has been advanced. Indeed, prison rioting
has been one of the main vehicles for prison reform, each riot
series re-awakening and promoting further advances in reform.

(Garson, 1972, p. 419)

NEGOTIATION: IN THE HEYDAY OF REHABILITATION

One spin-off from the ascendancy of the rehabilitative ideal was the
presence in and around penal systems in Western 'developed' countries after the Second World War of sociologists and psychologists
with an interest in exploring a range of responses to violence, in
individual and group situations. Research into rioting and its prevention and control followed a similar trajectory to research into prisons
themselves, away from a preoccupation with functionalist management and towards an appreciation of the experience, and therefore
the mental state, of the rioter. There was a growing interest in ma-
nipulating the interaction between the authorities and rioters so that,
with the minimum of risk of injury, the authorities came out on top.

By 1952, some officials in the US were moving towards a more
conciliatory style of response to prison riots. There was an increased
impulse towards penal reforms which had been shelved through
resource and other constraints during the Second World War.

A review of 25 prison riots in the 1950s which involved hostages
being taken indicates that no hostages were killed, regardless of
whether the riot was ended by force or in a more restrained way. 'This
demonstrated that the safety of hostages was not a plausible justification for a strategy of force, particularly when this strategy often led to
inmate deaths' (Garson, 1972, p. 415). In contrast, in twelve riots
which took place in the 1950s, force was used and deaths occurred. In
nine of these cases, guards shot prisoners while executing a policy of
force. These were reportedly the first deaths in prison riots since the
Alcatraz riot of 1946 (Garson, 1972, p. 415).

But the evidence against force is not unequivocal. At least 27 of the
prison riots which occurred in the 1950s did not involve deaths,
despite the fact that the authorities employed a policy of force in
curbing them (Garson, 1972, p. 416). On the other hand, practically
all deaths in riots were in situations where force *was* used.

In 1955, the response to mounting unrest in the New York Reformatory on Rikers Island and the nearby Women's Detention House
was the Estimates Board vote to hire twenty psychiatrists, psycho-

logists, social workers and rehabilitation counsellors. Similarly, in Britain, the softening of responses to riots was much influenced by the 'Spaghetti House Siege', where the police used talk rather than force.

REASSERTION OF CONTROL THROUGH CONFRONTATION

The quotation at the beginning of this chapter, from the nineteenth-century handbook on riot control by General Molineux, might have been prepared for use in the US in the score of years beginning with the Attica prison riot of 1971. Attica marked the turn away from a low-key, negotiating response to rioting by prisoners. The decision to use force to quell the Attica riot was justified at the time by the authorities, but has been criticized since (Garson, 1972, p. 419). Spiro Agnew, in the wake of Attica, concluded that

> In taking the necessary steps to end the confrontation at Attica, Governor Nelson Rockefeller acted courageously. Those who would have had him act otherwise have yet to learn the paramount lesson of our century: that acquiescence to the demands of the criminal element of any society only begets greater violence.
>
> (Garson, 1972, p. 419)

The violent quelling of the Attica Prison riot symbolized the growing conviction of the prison authorities in the early 1970s that a firm demonstration of control was needed to suppress rioting.

A DIVERSITY OF RESPONSES

In the post-rehabilitation prison, uncertainty about which penal philosophy is, or should, be dominant has been reflected in responses to riots. Responses to them have varied from ignoring them to suppressing them, through various attempts to manipulate rioters and potential rioters and making more or less significant attempts to reform the running of prisons. So, since the late 1970s there have been instances both of shifts towards more placatory styles of management and towards more violent interventions in riots.

The responses by the authorities to prison disturbances in the 1980s were more violent in Scotland than in England or Northern Ireland. A controversial SAS raid ended the siege at Peterhead prison in early October 1987 (*The Sunday Times*, 4 October 1987, p. 1g). In contrast, the Home Office intervened during April 1990 actually to prevent the governor of Strangeways prison taking direct action to retake the prison (Woolf and Tumin, 1991, p. 108).

Ignoring Riots

The widespread tendency for the prison authorities in Britain to attempt to ignore, or to try to persuade the mass media to ignore, the increasing incidence of collective rioting since the Second World War has not been paralleled in the US, where the context of problems arising in prison policy and practice has encouraged openness and public debate. But in both Britain and the US, responses at the time to curb prison riots have tended not to be ignored by the authorities. Attempts publicly to deny the existence of prison riots may be motivated partly by defensiveness and partly by the theory that, if ignored, somehow the spread of waves of riots between institutions can be prevented.

Withdrawal of the authorities from a near or actual riot situation does not necessarily amount to ignoring the riot, especially if they are still in evidence as a potential threat to the rioters. In some notable cases, withdrawal by the authorities at the point of the outbreak of a riot actually has been followed by a rapid escalation. This criticism was made of the handling of the Hull prison riot in 1976 (Thomas and Pooley, 1980). In a notable intercommunal riot in St Paul's, Bristol, in South West England, the police withdrew to gather reinforcements and the riot in early April 1980 escalated. Hundley associates withdrawal with the need for the authorities at this point to communicate immediate concessions to the rioters, whereupon legitimate leaders in the rioters' community can be enabled to exert control (Hundley, 1975, p. 129). Similarly, the act by the authorities of posting forces simply to observe the riot 'further promotes the emergence of norms which allow deviant activity' (ibid.). Thus it is believed that passive withdrawal is less likely to curb rioting than withdrawal associated with positive concessions to the rioters by the authorities.

Various blends of deviant subcultural theory combine with control theories to inform the view that prison staff may co-opt dominant inmates in the process of maintaining order. The 'grass' in the British penal system is equivalent to the 'snitch', 'stooly', 'fink' or 'rat' in the US system. Contrary to some popular portrayals, these 'rats' are by no means marginal, outcast or weak. Clavell's fictional *King Rat* is much nearer the mark, running a successful contraband business inside the wartime camp (Clavell, 1975). The memoirs of former prisoners, also, give insights into the dynamics of the informal negotiations between 'rats' and staff (Solzhenitsyn, 1963; Rigby, 1965; Charrière, 1970). Research in a south-western state penitentiary indicates the processes by which staff use a network of 'rats' to maintain social order and try to prevent violence such as riots (Marquart and Roebuck, 1985).

Colvin notes that in the 1980 New Mexico riot, in the face of great violence by inmates, the authorities re-established control without any injuries or hostages among inmates or staff. His analysis of this riot focuses on what he sees as escalating violence by inmates as a consequence of staff disrupting the existing pattern of informal and formal controls shared with inmate gangs over a number of years. He follows Thomas and colleagues (Thomas *et al*, 1981) who argue for positive measures to enable prisoners to organize themselves 'around mutually beneficially and non-violent activities' (Colvin, 1982, p. 460).

The wider issue this raises is how to encourage the development in prisons of a culture less dependent on violence as the currency for maintaining stability and security in the experience and expectations of staff as well as prisoners.

More subtle preventive strategies have been adopted by the authorities over the years in relation to violence in general and riots in particular. Discussion concerning responses to riots tends to be located within the tacit parameters of their preventive social control. Order is maintained in the prison not simply by overt repression but also by 'institutionalized preventive social control . . . in which the subjects do not even feel that they are being restrained or repressed – the thought of challenging the existing order does not even occur to them' (Turner and Killian, 1975, p. 113).

A related feature of prisons is the use of prisoner elites to control other prisoners and thereby reduce violence, perhaps by arbitrating informally among warring groups (Jacobs, 1974). An illuminating study of the building tender (BT) system in the Texas Department of Corrections (TDC) reveals some strengths of weaknesses of such strategies (Marquart and Crouch, 1984). What were known as 'BT' prisoners were organized hierarchically and in some, such as maximum security, prisons managed the older, more violent and escape-prone prisoners (Marquart and Crouch, 1984, p. 495). In some prisons, they were virtually given 24-hours a day freedom, carried weapons and were ready to use force to control other prisoners (Marquart and Crouch, 1984, p. 499).

The demise of the BT system in the wake of the *Ruiz* v. *Estelle* court case in 1980 by implication may be viewed as a cause of the increasingly fragmented violence between prisoner cliques after the mid-1970s. But research suggests that prisoner élites tend to control other prisoners for their own ends rather than those of the institution or the authorities (Marquart and Crouch, 1984, p. 492). The research into the BT system in the TDC confirms this. Whereas some BTs were fair, others were thugs who developed a reputation for toughness or *machismo*, 'men who used their positions to coerce, exploit, and engender fear' (Marquart and Crouch, 1984, pp. 504–5). Further, BTs depended on prison staff and usually acted in a way condoned or even ordered by them. 'Moreover, officers themselves at times meted out the same type of physical discipline attributed to BTs' (Marquart and Crouch, 1984, p. 505).

Some predictable negative consequences of the ending of the BT system include deteriorating control of prisoners and increasing inter-prisoner violence as staff struggle to build up their own authority over prisoners formerly controlled for them by the BTs and other prisoners try to move into the power vacuum (Marquart and Crouch, 1984, p. 507). BTs traditionally brought information to top-level staff, but in their absence the task of control may tend to fall to less experienced mid-level staff (Marquart and Crouch, 1984, p. 508).

In contrast, some good outcomes followed from the ending of the BT system, including decreased tension among prisoners, who 'no longer live with the threat of violence at the hands of guards and their inmate agents' (Marquart and Crouch, 1984, p. 506).

Suppressing Prison Riots

The widespread use of active means of suppressing riots in the US and Britain tends to be reinforced by learning theory, which argues that unless riots are discouraged by force, the behaviour of prisoners will get worse and repeated riots will result. On the other hand, frustration-aggression theory suggests that the use of force actually produces greater frustration and anger in prisoners, who, consequently, are more than ever likely to behave violently.

There is debate about whether offensive action by the authorities acts to damp down or escalate potential or actual riots. 'The vast majority of literature pertaining to riot control operations is based, in varying degrees, on the military concept, military tactics, and military formations' (Brown, 1975, p. 127). The authorities generally set out three linked objectives: to contain the riot, isolate it and disperse the rioters. This last 'is the offensive action aimed at destroying the mob's organization, breaking its will to resist, and restoring law and order. Speed and decisiveness, coupled with an impressive show of force, should pervade this tactical situation' (Brown, 1975, p. 128).

Hundley noted, in the light of ghetto riots in the US in the late 1960s, that overt activity by the authorities is only likely to curb rioters if the presence of guards, police or militia is perceived as legitimate. 'However, even if the original activity is viewed as legitimate, but the policemen are observed as being rude, impolite, unfair, or brutal, then these activities can precipitate a riot' (Hundley, 1975, p. 129). This finding confirms the need for the authorities to hesitate before deciding to use force to quell prison riots. Despite this, there was controversy on the overriding by a Prison Department manager of the governor of Strangeways' wish to use control and restraint teams forcibly to retake the prison during the 1990 riot. Significantly, the official investigation tends to support the governor's argument for the use of such force at that point (Woolf and Tumin, 1991, p. 108).

The effectiveness of a show of force may be compromised by the wish of some rioters actually to provoke the authorities into capturing a number of hostages, as a way of promoting solidarity (Brown, 1975, p. 128).

In the late 1940s, a manual for the Chicago Park District Police proposed five techniques for intervening in potential riots: removal or isolation of individuals, dividing the milling crowd into small units, removing leaders without use of force, diverting the crowd from its focal points, isolating the crowd and preventing the spread of the riot (Lohman, 1947, quoted in Brown, 1975, p. 128).

But the assumption of the authorities that established leaders may be enlisted to help in negotiating with rioters may be undermined by the emergence of new leaders, previously unrecognized by the authorities, during the riot (Brown, 1975, p. 129).

The Lockdown

In the US, the lockdown (see pp. 182–3) epitomizes the controlling response to prison riots. For example, a lockdown of nine to ten months resulted from an uprising by prisoners at Pontiac Correctional Centre, Illinois, which involved the deaths of three guards and extensive damage to property (Olivero and Roberts, 1987, p. 240).

The advantage of the lockdown from the standpoint of the authorities is that it unambiguously demonstrates that control is re-established and that there is no real challenge to the authorities' power to control the fate of prisoners (Olivero Roberts, 1987, p. 241). However, the lockdown necessarily curtails the rights of prisoners, acts as a focus for confrontation and collective aggression on the part of prisoners and staff, and in some instances, notably the Marion Penitentiary lockdown of 1983 (see Chapter 7), may lead to escalating violence by staff.

The Riot Squad

Traditionally, the authorities have called in military or quasi-military forces from outside the prison to quell riots. In October 1943, after the Detroit and Harlem riots, the Committee on Race Discrimination of the American Civil Liberties Union, chaired by Pearl Buck the novelist, produced a pamphlet entitled *How to Prevent a Race Riot in Your Home Town*. This advised communities on 'how to call in federal troops in a hurry' (Shogan and Craig, 1964, p. 138). A similar spirit enveloped responses in the US to many riots up to the 1951–3 wave of prison riots and again after 1970.

An alternative is to train the prison staff themselves to reassert control by force. In 1979, evidence of a hardening attitude to riot control in Britain was provided by the first use of the MUFTI squad in the Wormwood Scrubs disturbance of 31 August (*Abolitionist*, 1979, No. 4, p. 14) and by the use of high-powered water jests by prison officers clad in helmets with shatter-proof visors, metal riot shields, breast and back plates and leg guards, in the response to the Peterhead prison riot of August 1979 (*Abolitionist*, No. 4, pp. 14–15). After the Wormwood Scrubs incident where the MUFTI (Minimum Use of Force Tactical Intervention) squad broke up the peaceful protest, at first the Home Office denied that any prisoners had been injured, but later it emerged that 53 prisoners had been injured, many requiring stitches. 'No prison doctor spoke up after either of these incidents, and both are used as evidence by those who argue that prison doctors identify too much with the authorities' (Smith, 1983a, p. 1522).

Concentration and Segregation of Rioters

In the postwar period, one response to prison disturbances has been to attempt to identify potentially disruptive prisoners and isolate them. Consequent policies have passed through several phases, most involving segregating such prisoners, isolating them from other prisoners and, often, from each other. Additionally, policy responses have moved from concentration through dispersal to re-concentration in the social and physical architecture of new-generation prisons.

Arguments about the dangerousness of a number of inmates since the 1930s in the US and since the 1960s in Britain have been used to justify viewpoints concerning either their concentration or their dispersal. In the US, Alcatraz was used by the Federal Bureau of Prisons, from 1934, to concentrate all the problem prisoners from medium security federal prisons throughout the US. In 1963, following increasing criticism of concentration, Alcatraz was closed, with the onset of the emphasis on rehabilitation (Olivero and Roberts, 1987, p. 236).

In Britain, the US experience was drawn on as a justification of arguments for dispersal, notably by a subcommittee of the Advisory Council on Penal Reform chaired by Radzinowicz (Advisory Council on the Penal System, 1968), in pursuance of the recommendations of the otherwise influential Mountbatten report on prison security (Mountbatten Report, 1966). The Home Office in Britain adopted a policy of dispersal and in subsequent reviews, notably in 1983–4, this policy was reviewed and retained, since:

> All our American witnesses agreed that when Alcatraz was closed and its inmates dispersed to other very secure prisons, the majority settled down into their new communities. A small proportion of these prisoners were still very dangerous disruptives, but the regime of the other prisons was not jeopardized. This American experience reinforced our view that to move the most recalcitrant prisoners to a small maximum security prison, and to leave them there is likely to increase the number of apparently incorrigible prisoners with whom the system as a whole has to cope.
> (Control Review Committee, 1984, pp. 55–6)

It is significant that substantially the British authorities, as the annual reports of the Home Office demonstrate, have attempted to locate debates about riot-proneness of prisoners and prisons under the heading of security. Within this, the active and ongoing debate about how to categorize and effectively isolate – and hopefully therefore render powerless – a relatively small number of prisoners viewed as intractable and disruptive is linked in the 1970s and 1980s with controversial innovations such as control, maximum security and segregation units.

During 1979, the campaign continued to close the punishment 'cages' at Porterfield prison, Inverness, in Scotland. The 'silent cell' there was a concrete cell with a further concrete cell inside, designed with no sanitation, so that a prisoner could hear nothing outside at all (*Abolitionist*, no. 4, p. 20).

Sudden transfers or 'ghosting' formed part of the tactics of control though constant disruption to prisoners' sense of group identity. The prison officer in charge of the punishment block at Armley prison, a local prison in Leeds in the North of England catering for over 1100 prisoners in 1979, described how staff prevented those whom they anticipated would fight the system from becoming trouble-makers:

> The way we stop the subversives is by getting in early and shanghai-ing them before the roof blows off. It's known round here as ghost-training. When the security officers get wind of what's going on, we make a plan to grab the ringleaders when they aren't expecting it, when they're on their own. Get them straight out under guard into a taxi and whip them away to another institution. Keep 'em on the move.
>
> (Kettle, 1979, p. 294)

In the US, the Federal Bureau of Prisons revived the policy of concentration in 1973 by sending problem prisoners from other prisons to a major 'control unit' in the Federal Penitentiary at Marion, Illinois (Olivero and Roberts, 1987, p. 237). Criticism of concentration in the US has focused on the 'lockdown' at Marion Penitentiary since 27 October 1987, which has turned the whole prison into one large top security unit for prisoners who cannot anticipate release in the foreseeable future. Lockdown is a situation where prisoners stay in their cells the whole time, apart from being unlocked for very short periods for specific purposes such as feeding or court appearances. Critics allege that the lockdown at Marion was an overreaction, since isolated violent incidents rather than a collective riot were used to justify it (Olivero and Roberts, 1987, p. 240). Further, they maintain that the lockdown was disastrous on a number of counts, not least of which was increased brutality of staff towards prisoners. Apparently, staff from other federal prisons were asked to volunteer to serve there and prisoners allege that many of these volunteers were militantly aggressive towards them (Olivero and Roberts, 1987, p. 241). Also, a special operations squad of staff was formed known as the 'A Team', whose task was the tactical control of riots and other disturbances. They were trained by a similar squad from Leavenworth prison. 'These officers were outfitted with riot helmets, other riot control devices and special uniforms. They trained Marion staff in techniques such a conducting forced cell movements and controlling resistant prisoners.' (Olivero and Roberts, 1987, p. 241) On 7 November 1983, a 'security shakedown' was reportedly used as the guise for 'a calculated police riot' (ibid., p. 243), in which all the 300–400 prisoners were removed from their cells and had their belongings taken. Olivero and Roberts quote extensively from several investigative reports (Marion Prisoners' Rights Project, 1974; Breed and Ward, 1984; Cunningham and Susler, 1983) and illustrate how confrontational responses to prisoners labelled as ultimately dangerous may escalate. Using Cunningham and Susler's study as a source, they state:

> The officers who came to the cells were wearing jump suits without name tags, flak jackets, helmets, face masks (thus, unidentifiable), heavy boots, and gloves, and each officer carried a double metal-studded, three-foot riot baton. The prisoners were shoved or dragged from their cells naked or clad only in their underwear. They were handcuffed with their hands behind their backs. While restrained in this fashion, many were struck with fists, pushed, kicked, and prodded or beaten with riot batons. Continually during the ordeal, the prisoners were verbally threatened and badgered (Cunningham and Susler, 1983, pp. 4–5). The officers said such things as, 'Who runs this prison? We do!' they demanded that the inmates respond 'Yes sir!' Those who protested the beatings or had presented problems in the past were singled out for extra-severe beatings. (These prisoners were beaten in their cells or taken to the hallways and stairwells to be beaten.)
>
> (Olivero and Roberts, 1987, p. 242)

Prisoners alleged that their rights were violated as the lockdown continued into its second year. Access to chaplains, rabbis and the spiritual leaders of North American Indians were restricted. Fasting Indian prisoners and Jews were threatened with force-feeding (Olivero and Roberts, 1987, p. 244). Prisoners stated that the Federal Bureau of Prisons tried to prevent them taking court action by curtailing their rights of legal representation and not returning their legal papers confiscated during the original security shakedown (Olivero and Roberts, 1987, p. 245).

Democratization of Prisons

Reforms aiming to reduce prison violence have included offering prisoners more power, through structures which enable them to participate more in the management of the prison. The evidence is patchy and by no means conclusive but suggests that such efforts alone do not achieve this.

In Britain the Prison Department did not encourage the spread of experiments, monitored by the Prison Psychological Service, in increasing prisoner participation in prison management, carried out in such prisons as Long Lartin in the 1970s (Shapland et al., 1972). In the US, progress made up to the mid-1970s in several correctional institutions was subsequently reversed (Stastny and Tyrnauer, 1982).

A prisoner council called the Adult Basic Learning Experience (ABLE) was introduced as a means of improving staff–prisoner communication regarding prisoners' grievances. But prisoners involved tended to be from a number of gangs in the prison who consequently monopolized the ABLE (Engel and Rothman, 1983, p. 98).

Efforts at Soledad prison in the mid-1970s to reduce violence by offering prisoners participation in running the prison seemed fruitful at first, but later were marked by further collective fighting between prisoners, leading to two deaths (Engel and Rothman, 1983, p. 99).

Encouraging Resistance

At another extreme is the strategy of actively encouraging collective responses by prisoners. This should be viewed, perhaps, in the same light as the contrast between mass unionization in a single union, in, for example, the car industry in West Germany, and fragmentation among the many unions involved in car production in Britain.

Irwin's discussion of the impact of long-term imprisonment concludes with his recommendation that, far from trying simplistically to suppress gangs:

> Gang involvement has a history, and I certainly would not want prison administration to plan strategies against it. I think providing other alternatives is the approach . . . If I were running a prison, I would do everything to encourage formal collective resistance. Organizing persons into political organizations that would come forth with grievances and the members of which would be angry if the organizations were not accepted is healthy. These organizations

could file petitions or get lawyers to file petitions for them, they could contact outside organizations that would take complaints to the press, and so forth. I would encourage such actions and would consider such resistance completely unthreatening. But I would consider it a very serious rule violation if a person committed violence against another prisoner or a guard, attempted escape, or destroyed property.

(Irwin, 1981, p. 59)

'Reform Increases the Incidence of Riots'

A similar argument to the 'appeasement produces more trouble' thesis has been advanced in respect of reform movements. Engel and Rothman conclude that 'the overall effects of the reform movement have been the dissolution of the inmate social order and heightened violence' (Engel and Rothman, 1983, p. 105), Marquart and Crouch adopt a similar viewpoint (Marquart and Crouch, 1985, p. 584).

Such arguments are inherently conservative. In the past, they have been used to justify maintaining the status quo. In 1913, the observation of a Commission (Penitentiary Investigating Committee, 1913, p. 29) investigating conditions in prisons in Texas that the use of the strap should not be suspended (although in the event it did not recommend its retention) was based partly on statistics taken to indicate that disciplinary problems had increased where the strap was abolished (Ekland-Olson, 1986, p. 414).

A variant on such theories is the cyclical view of trends in prison policy and practice. According to cyclic theory, the often mutually contradictory purposes of imprisonment lead to the pendulum of reform swinging in a 'paradoxical cycle of crisis and equilibrium' (Ekland-Olson, 1986, p. 416), though it would be cynical to use this to justify doing nothing in the face of, by this view, inevitable waves of rioting and intervening 'truces'.

INQUIRIES AND INVESTIGATIONS

On the whole, responses at the inquiry stage tend to be framed in terms of how riots can be curbed or prevented in future, rather than examining discourse about riots themselves, how they are understood and how imprisonment itself may be questioned.

The catalogue of controversies surrounding the various investigations into numerous major prison riots in Britain and the US suggests

that the larger and more newsworthy the riot, the more vested interests are brought into conflict over the production of a so-called
comprehensive, independent inquiry report. One sign of this is a
multiplication of inquiry reports. Thus, in Britain the Hull riot in
1976 generated three inquiry reports, Peterhead in 1987 two. In the
US, the McKay report into the 1971 Attica riot was followed by journalists' (see, for instance, Bell, 1985; Wicker, 1975; Fitch and Tepper,
1971) and prisoners' own versions (Harsh, 1972), while the attorney
general's report into Santa Fe in 1980 was followed by Morris's account based on available documentary and interview information
(Morris, 1983).

The majority of official investigations into prison riots tend to
reinforce existing penal policy and practice rather than to present an
analysis of their origins with recommendations which work through
its implications for changes and reforms. In this, they are consistent
with the general trend of investigations into intercommunal riots in
the US. Lipsky and Olson argue that the main purpose of inquiries
commissioned into major riots, such as the investigation of the urban
riots of the 1960s called for by President Lyndon B. Johnson, 'is
symbolic, minimizing the impact of the crisis without appreciably
changing the conditions which gave rise to it' (Turner and Killian,
1975, p. 130). Against this trend was the Scarman inquiry into the first
of the most significant wave of intercommunal riots in Britain in 1981,
which was critical of policing policy and practice in Brixton, London,
and the two most far-ranging investigatory reports into prison riots, in
Attica 1971 (New York State Special Commission, 1972) and
Strangeways 1990 (Woolf and Tumin, 1991).

The way official investigations into riots are handled and responded
to is further evidence of the contested nature of riots (Chapter 1). On
the whole intercommunal and institutional riots in both Britain and
the US have tended to be accompanied or followed by controversy
about whether they are followed by 'whitewash' reports conducted by
the authorities. In the wake of such controversy, some riots have
attracted what prisoners and many reformers have regarded as more
independent inquiries. These have tended to allocate responsibility
and blame more fairly, often incriminating the authorities or their
employees. For example, after the Hull prison riot of 1976, the Fowler
Report found the prison staff not responsible, but in 1978 after two
further reports, one by a local MP and one by PROP, the prisoners'
rights movement, eight prison officers were found guilty in York
Crown Court of charges arising from the riot. But it should be remem-

bered that the Fowler inquiry excluded dealing with allegations by prisoners of brutality against them at the end of the riot, because they allegedly occurred on 4 September and lay outside the brief to examine events between 31 August and 3 September (Evans, 1980, p. 90). But the question as to why there was a five-month delay before the policy inquiry into those allegations began, the following February, remains unanswered (Evans, 1980, pp. 90–1).

In Britain, the Home Office has a history of secrecy and defensiveness when it comes to responding to criticism of the penal system. As long ago as 1922, when the Prison System Inquiry Committee reported, because it went ahead in 1919 sponsored by the Labour Research Department albeit with distinguished members without Home Office sanction, 'the Home Office declined to provide the Committee with information, and prohibited the members of the staff from assisting the Inquiry: Nevertheless, the report has frequent quotations from the secret Standing orders, and more than 50 prison officials of all grades are stated to have given evidence' (*Westminster Gazette*, 26 February 1922).

Official inquiries are one means of addressing the requirement that riot incidents be investigated with a degree of rigour and independence from those involved at the time. There are pragmatic reasons why official inquiry reports, such as Fowler (Home Office, 1977a), Woolf (Woolf and Tumin, 1991) and Attica (New York State Special Commission, 1972), conducted in the immediate aftermath of riots, contain limited detailed testimony about the riot by participants. Accounts by staff and prisoners may be *sub judice*. This is one reason why more information often emerges during subsequent court cases than the official inquiry process itself.

Apart from the alleged partiality of official reports and inquiries, more general criticisms have been made of the parameters within which inquiries tend to work. 'Invariably official inquiries are restricted by their terms of reference. While occasionally they move beyond their remit and offer a critical perspective it is more usual for fundamental questions to be ignored or for already established policy initiatives to be repeated.' Instancing the Royal Commission on the Police (1962), the May Inquiry (1979) and the Scarman Report on the 1981 communal riots in Brixton, London (1981), the Independent Committee of Inquiry report into the Peterhead disturbances continues: 'In the post-war period there has been a range of state-sponsored inquiries and commissions on most aspects of the criminal justice process yet their recommendations often have been ignored, if they propose fundamental changes, or when there has been a response there has been little effective structural change' (Independent Committee of Inquiry, 1987, p. 13).

Defensiveness and protectiveness have played a part in previous 'official' investigations into rioting by prisoners. A pattern emerges, discernible also in some of the reports of race riots in the US. Often the official inquiry comes first and is later counterpointed by investigations carried out, perhaps, on behalf of others affected by the riot, which tends to be more critical of the authorities.

An official inquiry into a prison riot may have its critical commentary on actions by staff attacked by a member of staff. A month after the Commission investigating the Attica riot reported, Russell G. Oswald, Commissioner of Correctional Services of New York, produced a book, defending the actions of staff (Oswald, 1972).

Bell's book on the Attica riot and investigation is a painstaking study carried out from his informed position, as the lawyer appointed as chief assistant to the special state prosecutor, with the task of investigating the shootings by the police during the riot. From Bell's account, it is clear that the initial weight of the investigation was put into the four homicides by prisoners. Later, Bell's sustained attempt to assemble evidence against police involved in the 39 homicides from police gunfire was blocked and the single indictment of a police official only followed Bell's public declaration of a cover-up. Even then, no correctional or police official was ever found guilty, because at that time Governor Hugh Carey issued a pardon for all those involved in the riot (Bell, 1985, viii).

Bell confirms the accuracy and concision of the McKay report, but draws attention to its omissions – including 'the worst that had happened at Attica, individual criminal acts' (Bell, 1985, p. 49). In contrast to Governor Rockefeller's praise of the State Police in the wake of the retaking of the prison for 'doing "a superb job" and for showing "skill . . . courage . . . and . . . restraint" in saving hostages and holding down casualties', Bell notes that 'too many had died at Attica for the Governor's words to ring true. He hadn't been there. Being responsible for the retaking, he had every reason to say it went well, whether it did or not' (Bell, 1985, p. 49). The McKay Report noted that 'in the cellblocks, on the catwalks, and in D Yard there was much unnecessary shooting' (New York State Special Commission, 1972, p. 402). 'That suggested much criminal shooting, if McKay rather than the Governor was right' (Bell, 1985, p. 49).

The development of an independent inquiry account of a prison riot in its immediate aftermath is both desirable and inherently problematic. In the wake of the 1971 Attica riot, there were at least four special commissions, basing their reports on testimony from observers, police, state correction staff and prison reformers. But, on the whole, prisoners refused to take part in these, fearing that their statements might be used against them in court. The 40 prisoner rioters held in cellular isolation after the riot refused to testify to the McKay Commission, criticizing its lack of 'minority community representation' (Harsh, 1972, p. 127). It was 1972 before the first interview with a member of the prisoners' negotiating committee, by Robert Harsh, was published (Harsh, 1972).

Wicker's articulate autobiographical account of Attica in 1971 highlights the way the prisoners underestimated the extent to which the authorities would respond violently to their bluff when they took eight of the hostages to visible locations and threatened each with a blade (Wicker, 1975, pp. 274–6). It highlights also the blunder which led the authorities to entrust the rescuing of the hostages to a large number of untrained and, by then, exhausted toopers, instead of using a small force of crack shots. 'The result was a massacre, not just of the inmates but of the hostages whose rescue was the aim of the assault' (Carney, 1975, p. 153).

The outcomes of official investigations into riots often leave many traces of unfinished and unresolved business. This applies partly to prisoners' actions, such as the failure to prosecute the violence by prisoners to prisoners during the Attica riot, but especially to the actions of staff. For example, 'various inquiries into official criminality at the New Mexico prison were sent to state or federal agencies where they would languish or be quietly dismissed for the usual lack of evidence' (Morris, 1983, p. 212).

Independent Judicial Procedures and Inspections

One argument for bringing into the process of official responses to riots an independent body is the marked contrast which repeatedly occurs between the evidence of the authorities and the perspective of the rioting prisoners. For example, in a period when there were continual disturbances and riots, reports of HM Inspectorate of Prisons for Scotland repeatedly claimed that the satisfactory conditions at Peterhead prison were well-liked by most prisoners and that disturbances such as attacks on staff were caused by a small minority of prisoners, 'encouraged in their activities by the attention of the media and the support and interests of external agencies' (HM Inspectorate of Prisons for Scotland, 1985, pp. 7–8). Again, two days before the riot at Strangeways prison on 1 April 1990, the report of an inspection was published which concluded by saying that 'standards of cleanliness and kit control were not as high as they should be but on the whole there was much more to praise than to decry in an establishment clearly going in the right direction and with an optimistic momentum' (HM Inspectorate of Prisons, 1990, p. 86).

In Britain, the systems of petitioning by prisoners and punishment of prisoners are not accountable to independent bodies outside both the prison and the prison service so as to ensure that justice is done. Although in theory the courts can intervene in prison matters, in practice, European courts apart, they have shown a reluctance to do so.

In the US, in contrast, court cases are said to have led to improvements in the accountability and justice of prison systems: 'The court actions, many of which have been over medical matters, have come about because various bodies, including the American Medical Association, have produced minimum standards for various prison activities, and prisoners have been quick to sue those prisons that do not meet the standards' (Smith, 1983c, p. 1708).

Systems of inspection, by Boards of Visitors and by the Prison Inspectorate, could be said also to be compromised. Boards of Visitors 'are limited in their ability both to make useful inspections and to make any changes happen as a result . . . The independence of the inspectorate is questionable not only because it remains part of the Home Office but also because most of the inspector's staff come from the prison department, and some of them are going to return there' (Smith, 1983c, p. 1708).

The *Campbell* v. *Fell* case arose from disciplinary proceedings subsequent to the Albany riot of September 1976, when a number of prison officers were injured while trying to end a demonstration by prisoners who were subsequently charged and found guilty before the Board of Visitors. They lost remission and challenged the ruling under Article 6 of the European Convention on Human Rights, which required a decision as to whether the disciplinary charges were in respect of 'criminal' offences (Harding and Koffman, 1988, p. 31). This case and a number of others including *R* v. *Hull Prison Board of Visitors, ex p. St. Germain and others* (1979) 1 All ER 701 (CA), and *Engel*, 8 June 1976, *Publications of the European Court of Human Rights*, Series A, vol. 22, raise the linked issues as to whether a privilege is treated the same as a right and what the dividing line is between offences against discipline dealt with inside the prison and offences considered to be more grave, dealt with by the use of judicial processes and bodies outside the prison (Harding and Koffman, 1988, p. 32).

A Research Response

There is a place for a response to prison riots by researchers, partly as a means of encouraging critical reflection by the authorities, into their response to them. There is also a place for research into other responses to riots. For instance, in the Strangeways riot, did the prisoners act up to the cameras and reporters from the press and television, thereby prolonging the riot? On the other hand, did the use of negotiators shorten this riot? At one level, there is a question about whether, for example, military-style intervention would have shortened the riot. This raises issues of a moral and political order, beyond the technicalities of responses to rioting, to which we return in Chapter 7.

CONCLUSIONS

This review of the trend of official responses to prison riots suggests that over a lengthy period of time, in both the US and Britain, there has been a tendency for punitive measures to suppress riots to predominate over more conciliatory responses to them. It is clear that attempts at more conciliatory responses to rioting were a feature of the period when the rehabilitative ideal was in the ascendant. Subsequently, the post-rehabilitation era has witnessed a variety of responses to rioting by prisoners. Over time, though, the predominant strategies for responding to riots have tended at the time to focus on controlling rather than understanding them. The consequence, more often than not, has been a confrontational response from prisoners, thus confirming the rationale for their original use. This last statement raises an important question in relation to preventing riots from escalating. It implies also that attention should be paid to the origins of riots and we turn to this in the next chapter.

6 Explaining Prison Riots

Riots are the voices of the unheard.

(Martin Luther King Jr)

PROBLEMS OF RESEARCH

One 'obvious' focus for this book would have been to have presented in an early chapter a single theory explaining the origins of prison riots. Unfortunately, no such theory has been produced to date and there is no ready agreement among researchers even about what questions to ask and the perspective from which to address them. This is not surprising, given the contested concept of riots and their changing nature over the years. So, this chapter has a more limited objective. It deals first with a number of general problems which need to be addressed in explaining prison riots before different theories of their origins are assessed. Then it simply puts forward, in the light of the research and theories reviewed, the ingredients considered essential to an adequate explanation of them.

Positivist or Non-Positivist Research

According to a positivist view, the causes of prison riots can be studied objectively by scientific criteria and methodology. Positivist research tends to treat the subject matter of social investigation as of the same order as the subject of natural scientific research. There is an emphasis on causes which can be deduced from an hypothesis, rather than on origins which are shaped in a less 'inevitable' way. Positivism asserts a distinction between facts, which can be specified objectively, and values, which are matters of opinion. Positivist research suffers from the weakness that the distinction cannot be made in practice, since even the words describing it are at once descriptive *and* evaluative, partly because the subject matter of the social sciences is *intrinsically and qualitatively* different from that of the natural sciences, partly because the concept of 'science' itself is under attack (Kuhn, 1970), partly because the complexity of social happenings in the prison precludes the application of scientific method to research therein, and finally partly because disputes about the meaning of the concepts used by researchers into prison riots 'are essential to their value as concepts and are, therefore, indeterminate' (Calvert, 1990, p. 27).

Observing Behaviour or Understanding Experience

In Britain, the work of Cohen and Taylor (1972) used the experience of prisoners themselves in the top security unit at Durham prison as the basis to challenge traditional research, weighted towards observing prisoners' behavioural adjustment to long-term imprisonment, producing, for instance, the finding that this adjustment gives them a positive outlook on 'doing time' (Flanagan, 1981, pp. 201–22), rather than asking them what they felt and experienced.

Lack of General Explanation

In the latter quarter of the twentieth century, social scientists have not been optimistic about the prospect of explaining communal rioting. In 1968, the year of the Chicago and Washington communal riots, Geertz comments that 'domestic disorder is a product of a long sequence of particular events whose interconnections our received categories of self-understanding are not only inadequate to reveal but are designed to conceal' (Geertz, 1968, p. 25).

Some penologists argue that the variety of circumstances in which prison riots arise makes it unproductive to seek a general explanation for them. Prison riots may occur anywhere, at any time, given a sufficient 'background' level of dissatisfaction among prisoners with the conditions of their imprisonment. It is preferable to focus attention, as Ditchfield has done (Ditchfield, 1990), on the implications of such disturbances for the managers of prisons rather than to expend energy on relatively unproductive speculation. Fox goes as far as to suggest that prison riots are spontaneous, set off rather like bombs, by unplanned events (Fox, 1972). This viewpoint makes it easier to dismiss the discontinuities and fragmentariness of the history of prison riots as 'randomness'. But it turns aside from, for example, the tension between the apparent spontaneity of riots and the tendency for waves of riots to happen in some circumstances and not others.

Difficulties of Historical Study

At the macro-level, there is a striking lack of historical comparison of riots in different historical periods and locations. In a rare example of such an approach, Martin examines former prison riots in the US in the light of the incidents of 1951–3 and compares them. He identifies several differences: earlier riots were bloodier, with less negotiation and more murder; prison conditions were a feature of both periods, but earlier riots were often linked with escape attempts, whereas the 1951–3 riots were generally 'purely riots of protest'; hostage-taking, while not new, was more a feature of the 1951–3 riots; only two riots were 'touched off by racial hatred' – in 1912 when in Wyoming white prisoners lynched a 'Negro' prisoner and in 1953 when, in Alcatraz, white prisoners rioted when they were put in cells near 'negroes' (Martin, 1955, p. 202).

A growing literature examines the viability of theories concerning 'traditions', 'cycles' and 'waves' of collective protest and violence in society at large. The question is whether such communal and intercommunal incidents can be linked in an explanatory way with happenings inside prisons.

At first sight, an overview of the major incidents of collective violence in both the US and Britain, before 1968, does not bear this out. In a wide-ranging review of what he calls 'group violence' in the US, Gurr observes that, between 1850 and 1989, the only period of relatively sustained peace occurred between the mid-1920s to the mid-1950s (Gurr, 1989, p. 20). Two of the three major periods of prison rioting, 1929–30 and 1951–3, occurred during this period. We could also attempt to correlate significant riots and waves of rioting with major national and international social and political upheavals. But whilst this works well for some dates it is less helpful for others. If we take significant riot incidents in the US, 1929–30 is the period of stock market collapse, 1951–3 the Korean War, 1971 is in the middle of the Vietnam War. In Britain, 1932 is in the middle of the economic depression of the 1930s. But, there are three fundamental problems with this form of analysis. First, it is not clear what causal connections are proposed between these general events and specific prison riots. Secondly, there are other years in which social events occur but there are no corresponding prison riots. Thirdly, there are significant prison riots in years with no sign of commensurate social disturbances. To be adequate, our theory would need to deal with these issues and explain, for instance, why Santa Fe (1980) and Strangeways (1990) occurred when they did and why there were apparently no comparable riots during the Cuban crisis of the early 1960s, the Falklands War of the early 1980s or the Gulf War of the winter of 1990–1.

Limitations of Single-Factor Explanations

At the other extreme, it is tempting to fasten the outbreak of riots onto a single factor, such as climate or an aspect of the regime. Despite Baron and Ransberger's finding that in the seven days before a civil riot, the temperature increased significantly and then decreased significantly after the riot (Baron and Ransberger, 1978), other researchers have found no significant correlations between such factors as temperature, humidity, tidal forces, the time of the month (Atlas, 1984, p. 283), and disciplinary offences (Megargee, 1977), violence or rioting. A prolonged attempt to apply catastrophe theory to the prediction of prison riots (Zeeman *et al.*, 1977) was built on theories beyond the competence of all but theoretical physicists and expert mathematicians (Thom, 1972). It attempts to plot tension (defined as frustration and distress) against alienation (defined as division, lack of communication and polarization) and adding local 'noise' such as trigger events (Zeeman *et al.*, 1977), but has proved unproductive and inconclusive. The argument that riots are assumed to be 'obviously' caused by such an obvious key feature does not stand up in the face of known evidence about their incidence. The reality is that riots are brought about in a variety of settings and circumstances and that the task of teasing out and prioritizing the factors related to the origins of a particular riot is at the best complex and at worst impossible. Prisons are complex organizations. Consequently, as Shapland notes, 'it becomes easy to call a precipitating factor, like poor food, the *cause* of a disturbance and proceed to overlook more intangible things, like staff-inmate relationships, because they are so difficult to unravel' (Shapland, 1973, p. 20).

Riots Viewed as the Sum of Individuals' Behaviour

Some researchers use psychological or small-group theories to reduce the explanation of collective incidents to the sum of individual or small-group behaviour. An extreme faith in psychological factors was demonstrated by Kinsey, who wrote in 1955 that sexual frustrations in some 'normal' prisoners bring about tensions which cause riots (quoted in Fox, 1956, p. 305). Lee and Humphrey's analysis of the Detroit 'race riot' of 20 June 1943, in which more than forty people died, presents the outbreak of riots atomistically, as 'the end-products of thousands of irritants in an atmosphere of growing tension' (Lee and

Humphrey, 1943, p. 6). They argue that people need to feel a sense of importance and this may be achieved through feeling superior to others, through ethnocentrism or group-egotism. In the absence of a socially acceptable way of feeding their egos, people are prone to seek scapegoats on whom to blame their frustrations, who may be bosses, or members of other ethnic groups (ibid., p. 5). At this point, 'a demogog immediately appears who builds his power on this unmistakable indication of social sickness' (ibid.). Over and above the fact that 'riots are in the making when irritating frictions ignite latent intolerances (ibid., p. 6), a trigger is needed, 'a single spectacular event (which) can unleash a torrent of accumulated emotional hatreds and bitterness that can temporarily be directed – with little restraint – against an easy scapegoat' (ibid., p. 7). Of course, prison riots differ in that they often are initiated *by* rather than *against* an oppressed group. Further, building up an explanation of a riot's origins simply from individuals militates against considering social factors.

Outsiders and Agitators as Scapegoats

Nevertheless, identifying psychological factors which motivate individuals to engage in violent behaviour or rioting is very popular. One theory argues that race rioting, for example, like other forms of social violence, occurs when people are 'misled' by 'extremists' and 'militants'. In widespread police and media reports of the British urban riots in 1981, it was alleged that extremist agitators 'from outside the area' may play a key role in fomenting rebellion and rioting (Kettle and Hodges, 1982, pp. 187–8).

Glazer and Moynihan's research in New York City, first published before the New York race riots, maintained that urban black people would tend to follow the same path as white people, from poverty and slum-dwelling to respectability and a good living standard. It was republished after the disturbances, prefaced by the explanation that they had failed to predict the power of black militants to influence people in the direction of deviance (Glazer and Moynihan, 1970).

Attributing Riots to Pathology of Leaders

To the extent that theories explaining riots simply in terms of the activities of militant leaders tend to emphasize the roles of individuals in the institution and deflect attention from structural features of prisons as social and political systems (Rubenstein, 1989, p. 310), riots may be explained in terms of the pathology of their prisoner leaders. Ohlin rejects the view that psychopathic or otherwise 'sick' prisoner leaders are significantly responsible for the outbreak of prison riots, pointing out that such leaders are always present but would be powerless to bring about a riot which was not accompanied by major widespread discontent (Ohlin, 1956, p. 25). Much research has been done on the ways in which staff and prisoner groups and cultures interact. Through prisoner gangs, for instance, it is known that prisoners in general may become more politicized. 'Black consciousness and the political ramifications of incarceration have become salient issues. In contributing to the transformation of a group of inmates in itself to a group for itself, the gangs can be said to have contributed to the politicization of the prison' (Jacobs, 1977, p. 154). But research has generally neglected the contribution made by staff groups and cultures to riot situations in prisons. So at best, through the concentration on individuals, we see half a situation.

Mass Movements and Economic Reductionism

Olson attempts to reduce to an economic basis the explanation of collective action, distinguishing between the rationality of small groups in seeking their interests and sometimes those of other people as well, and the non-rationality of mass movements (Olson, 1965). In the early 1960s, Olson's typology suited the prevailing view that mass movements were a feature of unstable countries rather than stable, orderly Western democracies like the US and Britain, in that period when Bell wrote of the end of ideology in politics (Bell, 1960). Thus Olson explains mass movements in psychological rather than political terms. He quotes Kornhauser's view (Kornhauser, 1959) that individual supporters of them tend to be alienated and argues that 'this alienation produces a psychological disturbance or disequilibrium', in circumstances typified by 'fanatic devotion to an ideology or leader . . . on the 'lunatic fringe''' (Olson, 1965, p. 162). Unfortunately, however, the upsurge of widespread protest movements in these so-called peaceful Western countries before the end of the 1960s made this psychologically-based location of mass movements at the edge of lunacy difficult to sustain.

Penal policies in general provide another tempting distraction from the specifics of the origins of riots. The complexities of the task are multiplied because of the need to correlate political, geographical and penological differences and then relate them to riots. Whereas in Britain, comparison only is possible between England, Wales, Scotland and Ireland, the states of the US provide a much broader canvas for comparisons. Nagel ranks states of the US according to their crime rates and incarceration rates, plotting these against other variables. He finds that there is no significant correlation between a state's racial composition and its crime rate, but a great positive correlation between its racial composition and its incarceration rate (Nagel, 1977, p. 162). He constructs a conservatism–liberalism ranking of states based on the voting records of all senators over a period of twenty years and observes that conservative states have significantly higher incarceration rates than liberal states. He finds that the crime rate in a state tends not to correlate positively with the incarceration rate, yet the incidence of black populations does. But he concludes that crime rates have little to do with differing policies regarding prison building (Nagel, 1977, p. 164). It seems unlikely, therefore, that, given the problematic status of data concerning the incidences of rioting by prisoners, attempts to make specific correlations between them and these wider factors would be any more productive.

Architectural Determinism

A powerful architectural lobby has fastened onto the 'obvious' fact that riots occur in inadequately designed prisons, using the historical evidence that over the centuries the design of prisons has reflected the kind of regime the authorities intended them to employ (Johnson, 1973). In the mid-1980s, a Home Office Working Party report entitled (New Directions in Prison Design enthused key officials in the British Home Office about introducing some 'new generation' prisons, based on those designed and built in the US so as to isolate prisoners in relatively small, even landscaped and 'villa-style', self-contained units. But the physical layout of a prison is only a contributory factor to a situation where the management style and relationships between staff and prisoners is central. Decentralization, for instance, has been identified as a key factor increasing tension and ever-more punitive reaction by staff to minor incidents in different sectors, during the 1951 to 1953 prison riots in the US (Ohlin, 1956, pp. 23–4).

Critics of such architectural determinism dismiss new generation architecture as simply 'one of the latest penological fads' (Rutherford, 1985, p. 408). Rutherford compares two new generation prisons in the US: Oak Heights, Minnesota, and Mecklenberg, Southern

Virginia. The decentralized regime and closer prisoner–staff relationships of Oak Park Heights are associated with reduced violence and problems of control. In contrast, the location of the warden's office at Mecklenberg outside the perimeter fence symbolizes a management style associated with greater unrest by prisoners (Rutherford, 1985, p. 410). Rutherford instances the civilizing influence of Frank Wood, warden of the maximum security state prison at Stillwater. Wood says that with a change in management style, regardless of architecture, Oak Park Heights could become 'the most regressive dungeon-like volatile environment that you'd find anyplace in the world because its architecture gives it the capacity to be very restrictive. It has the capacity to be abused dramatically. If they gave me the choice between having Oak Park Heights and an incompetent, dishonest staff or a tent and competent, honest staff I'll take the tent and the competent honest staff' (Rutherford, 1985, p. 410).

Crowding, Overcrowding and Riots

Research into the association between crowding and overcrowding and violence and rioting in prisons (Nacci, Teitelbaum and Prather, 1977, p. 26; D'Atri, 1981, p. 36; D'Atri *et al.*, 1981, p. 103; Ellis, 1984, pp. 277–308; Megargee, 1977; Cox *et al.*, 1984; Gaes and McGuire, 1985, pp. 41–65; Ekland-Olson, 1986, p. 393; Gove and Hughes, 1980, p. 864; Farrington and Nuttall, 1980, p. 230) has been no more conclusive than attempts to correlate it with the social climate of correctional institutions through such measures as the Social Climate Scale (Moos, 1968, pp. 174–88) and, later, the Correctional Institutions Environment Scale, with its 86 items and nine scales of measurement (Wenk and Moos, 1972). Ultimately, like catastrophe theory, and despite Moos' hint that such research may enable correlations to be developed between the nature of the setting and predictions about 'behaviour', such investigations consume large amounts of research resources but shed little or no light on the origins of collective disturbances in prisons (James and Jones, 1974, pp. 1110).

Lack of Adequate Theories

With the exception of some of the case studies (Scraton *et al.*, 1991; Useem and Kimball, 1989), there is a notable tendency for accounts of specific riots, such as reports of official investigations, to be long on

detailed description and short on discussion about theoretical perspectives on riots and their social origins. The lack of theoretical
consideration of the origins of riots in prisons relates to the lack of
attempts by social scientists to explain collective violence in prisons
(Wilsnack, 1976, in Cohen *et al.*, p. 61). There is much presumption
in commentary, especially in media commentary. In contrast, there is
little research evidence, and what there is, is confined largely to the
US. While the report on the Attica riot of 1971 (New York State
Special Commission, 1972) is an outstanding exception to the general
shortcomings of official inquiries, the report into the 1990 Strangeways
and associated riots (Woolf and Tumin, 1991) contains nearly 600
pages of impeccably detailed narrative. But it leaps from descriptive-
ness to assertions about 'what is wrong with prisons', without making
clear the conceptual connection, save in the obvious equation of
'prisoners' grievances cause rioting'.

Wilsnack views the lack of adequate conceptualization as a weakness of research into the origins of prison riots:

> The basic problem with theories of collective violence in prisons is
> that there are no theories. There are many conclusions and gener-
> alizations about prison violence, and some of these may help us
> understand particular incidents or may serve as starting points for
> theories. However, no one has yet offered a general explanation of
> collective violence in prisons that applies unambiguously to observ-
> able events, and that has been tested systematically against history
> or the experience of a large number of prisons.
>
>   (Wilsnack, 1976, p. 61)

THEORETICAL DEBATES AND EXPLANATIONS OF RIOTS

This section reviews briefly the main currents of research and theorizing about prisoners and prisons which bear directly on the problems
of explaining the origins of prison riots.

Contagion and Convergence Theories

As indicated in Chapter 1, the problem is partly one of the domination of such research as has been carried out by structural-
functionalism. In the wake of the French Revolution, theorists from
Le Bon in the mid-nineteenth century have attempted to manage

public fears about the destructive power of rioting crowds by producing explanations of their origins. Contagion and convergence theories dominated research into the origins of intercommunal rioting until the 1970s. These theories, whether directly or indirectly, have contributed to what we may call a 'social disorganization' perspective on prison riots, rather than the less popular 'resource mobilization' perspective.

Le Bon (Le Bon, 1952) develops a *contagion* theory from a pessimistic view of human nature, that violence and rioting are infectious to the extent that the atmosphere of the riot is capable of stripping away the thin veneer of civilization and reducing the intelligence of the crowd to no more than the intelligence of its least intelligent member.

Contagion theories make possible a non-political appraisal of the outbreak of riots. On the whole, they have been used by the authorities to justify their existing situation. Thus, in the US, they are popular with white people as explanations which 'derogate the rioters and rob the event of political significance' (Sears and McConahay, 1973, p. 18). A typical contagion theory argues that the rioters were manipulated by political agitators, possibly travelling in from outside the area.

The significance of the rapid spread of prison riots has been the subject of much speculation. Ohlin suggests that the contagious development of the 1951–3 prison riots in the US points to the strength of prisoners' identification throughout the US as 'a consciously identified prisoner community', many of them moving from prison to prison and maintaining this (Ohlin, 1956, p. 23). He cautions against attempting to explain the occurrence of prison riots until much more is known about the nature of the social structure of the prison and the impact of policies on it (Ohlin, 1956, p. 25).

Convergence theories can be used to justify a conservative or a liberal position. They may lead either to a non-political or a political view. From a conservative standpoint, the rioters may be seen as 'riff-raff'. They may be described as 'deviant and disreputable, as hardened criminals, as ungodly drifters, as lazy and chronic trouble-makers, as rebellious youths working off their "animal spirits"' (Sears and McConahay, 1973, p. 18). The view that there is an 'underclass' of victims of social problems, who sometimes riot, is a variant on this theory (Sears and McConahay, 1973, p. 20).

In one popular, liberal, version, convergence draws attention to factors such as personal and social problems produced and aggravated by poverty, unemployment, inadequate education, discrimination and oppression which contribute to the riot. But, convergence theories enable the authorities still to parcel up the riot as the outcome of the activities of particular groups, whether these be civil rights agitators, police or the rioters themselves. In the case of race rioters:

> The whites proposing the theories were not to blame. Secondly, since the theorists were not responsible, others would have to make the sacrifices necessary to bring about change. Blacks would have to resist their criminal impulses or invite control by the police forces. Southern whites would have to change their ways so that southern blacks would not want to migrate to Los Angeles. Civil rights leaders would have to tone down their rhetoric. A minimum of inconvenience for the theorist was involved.
>
> (Sears and McConahay, 1973, p. 19)

Social explanations of rioting which neither attribute their outbreak to the pathology of the rioters, nor deny any political aspirations they may have towards change, lie at the further end of the continuum. These theories tend to state or imply that all or part of the riot has come about through some defect of society and the political order.

Smelser attempts to produce a theory of the origins of riots which encapsulates different levels and kinds of factors. He argues that there is no particular type of communication or interaction which is a central defining characteristic of collective behaviour such as riots (Smelser, 1962, p. 11). According to Smelser, the determinants of such incidents are of six kinds, the components of each of which operate together and cumulatively. There are *structural* factors of two kinds: conduciveness such as panics, structural strains such as real or anticipated deprivations and the growth and spread of generalized beliefs among the participants. *Precipitating* factors, are significant, since 'it is nearly always a dramatic event which precipitates the outburst of violence' (Smelser, 1962, p. 16). But, Smelser adds that a precipitating factor cannot operate thus, except in the context of the other determinants. The participants need to be mobilized for action and in this process the actions of leaders are important. Finally, social controls are crucial, since the responses of the authorities, for example, may either suppress or escalate the riot (ibid., p. 17).

Smelser's functionalism, the 'dualist' distinction between structural and precipitating factors, the emphasis on the 'behaviour' of the rioters and the prominence of the precipitating incident, downplay the social context of the last factor he lists as contributing to the incident, namely social control. His comment that 'in certain respects this final determinant arches over all the others' is not born out in the structure of his essay. A detailed case study into the conduct of the miners' strike in Britain in 1984 rectifies this imbalance, according prominence to the importance of the trajectory of policies, strategies, anticipations and preparations made by the authorities in bringing about confrontations with protesters (Waddington, Jones and Critcher, 1989).

Social Disorganization and Resource Mobilization Theories

Theories about the origins of prison riots cluster round two theoretical traditions which relate closely to contagion and convergence theories but, because of their institutional dimension, are not totally compatible. They are termed here social disorganization and resource mobilization. The labels used by different commentators vary. Tilly and colleagues, whose comparative study of collective violence in Italy, Germany and France includes a critical survey of theories of their origins, use the terms breakdown and solidarity theories respectively. (Tilly, Tilly and Tilly, 1975)

Social disorganization
Social disorganization theories can be traced back to Le Bon's contagion theory, and thence through functionalism. They argue that riots arise because of a dislocation or breakdown in the established functioning of the prison.

From Durkheim, the key elements of social disorganization theories as they apply to collective prison violence, can be distilled:

That collective violence is a by-product of structural rearrangements in society, associated with the breakdown of existing controls over anti-social activity.

That collective violence often arises in conditions where rising living standards raise expectations faster than possible achievements.

That collective violence is one aspect of the unstable period, between the status quo before the violence and the new period of equilibrium in its aftermath.

(Tilly, Tilly and Tilly, 1975, p. 4)

Researchers in the late 1950s and early 1960s proposed that collective incidents arose in many different settings in society:

- intercommunal disturbances and strikes in industry, for instance;
- when the traditional structures of solidarity, such as the church, family and voluntary associations, which encouraged people to conform socially, broke down (Kornhauser, 1959; Smelser, 1962).

Social disorganization theories offer two alternative views of the significance of leaders in bringing about riots. According to one version, common in the wake of the Hull prison riot in Britain, the concentration of a number of prisoners seen as trouble-makers – in this case IRA prisoners convicted of terrorist offences – in appropriate conditions can allow them to play a leading role in fomenting disorder. According to the other view, it is the *removal* of such leaders which disturbs the pattern of informal control over other prisoners which staff tacitly or overtly allow them to build up over time, and may precipitate a riot. Thus, Hartung and Floch argue that the prison riots in the US in the early 1950s occurred when these controlling prisoners were no longer present. In this version of events, it was ironic that 'when such inmate control was removed, during periods of reform, and not replaced with other avenues for inmate self-expression, problems resulted. The aggressive inmates then became a destructive force' (Reid, 1981, p. 206).

Such theories make the assumption that in 'normal' conditions people will not become involved in collective action such as rioting. Two conditions predispose people to rioting. First, if they are uprooted from their usual surroundings, they may experience isolation and, in Durkheimian fashion, anomie. Second, the anomic, isolated individual is more likely to experience discontent, to develop potentially unfulfillable desires, to develop 'irrational' beliefs about how to achieve them, through collective action (Useem, 1985, p. 677).

An example is Colvin's study of the origins of the New Mexico Prison riot of 1980 which identifies the disruption of established patterns of control, whereby staff relied heavily on controls exerted informally and formally by dominant gangs and groupings of prisoners (Colvin, 1982, p. 449). The strength of this approach is that it identifies correctly the need to set prisoner's actions in the context of their interaction with staff. One limitation is that it tends to set aside structural features of the system and dismisses specific dynamics such as features of the prison regime. This is surprising, since Colvin refers explicitly to Foucault's work and the need to consider the class structure (Colvin, 1982, p. 460). But there is a lack of consideration in his work of the specific dynamics associated both with oppressive features of imprisonment and, for example, how oppressed groups such as black prisoners are affected by these and respond through rioting. More generally, he exemplifies what Liazos has identified as the tendency for sociologists of deviance to focus on the deviant and, thereby, intensify the signification of deviance itself (Liazos, 1977), to the continued neglect of the structures of knowledge and power in whose context that signification occurs.

More significant still, by focusing attention on seemingly 'marginal' categories of prisoner, this approach lacks the potential either to explain the mass riots involving *all* the prisoners in an institution, or from the 1970s the spread of riots in Britain to categories of prisoner such as those on remand, or those considered low security or with short-term sentences and hitherto outside the category of long-term prisoners who were the 'obvious' potential rebels.

Another variant is Gurr's theory of relative deprivation, defined as 'a perceived discrepancy between men's value expectations and their value capabilities' (Gurr, 1970, p. 13). Gurr uses the concept of perceived relative deprivation as the basis for theorizing about the causes of collective political violence. Discontent is the fundamental cause of collective violence. It becomes politicized and then actualized in actions. He argues that the greater the frustration, the greater the intensity of deprivation and the greater the quantity of aggression against the source of frustration, that is more people will riot more violently (Gurr, 1970, p. 9). From the standpoint of 'relative deprivation', the argument is that as people's living standards improve, the 'revolution of rising expectations' leads to their aspirations rising faster than is realistic (Caplan and Paige, 1968, p. 15).

Tilly and colleagues summarize the critique of Gurr's work. They dissent from Gurr's identification of relative deprivation as the fundamental cause of collective violence (Gurr, 1970), partly on the grounds that the political factors are undervalued in his analysis (Tilly, Tilly and Tilly, 1975, pp. 296–8). Social disorganization theories have become 'part of our common-sense explanation of most varieties of disorder' (ibid., p. 6). They are inherently conservative. 'There is the nostalgia for an ordered social life, the approval of moderation, the resentment and fear of pushy, strident, angry people' (ibid., p. 5).

Associated with this question is the issue as to whether riots are a gesture of despair in a declining situation or are a claim to more in a period of improvement. The Attica riot of 1971 occurred in a matrix of factors which brought into the foreground questions about the nature and purposes of imprisonment. Campaigns for equal rights and the full range of citizens' rights for minorities, poor people, criminals and prisoners amounted to what Bell calls a revolution of rising entitlements (Bell, 1976, p. 232), 'fear of public disorder, and a decline in confidence in public institutions' (Useem and Kimball, 1989, p. 11). The question is whether riots occur because of improving conditions or because of raised consciousness and a degree of empowerment. The latter provides a more convincing basis for explaining prison riots, given the problem of finding evidence to support the view that prisoners actually *experienced* better conditions across the board, even if in some areas the authorities *claimed* conditions had improved.

But this research does not bear out the hypothesis that tighter security will curb prison violence. In four high security prisons in California in 1973, research found that a decline in some forms of violence tended to be accompanied by an increase in other forms, and particularly in more serious incidents (Bidna, 1975, p. 44). Individual prisoners may even be more at risk from violence in the more crowded situations brought about by increased security. It seems that prisoners cannot be coerced into becoming less prone to violence and rioting.

Resource mobilization
An equally powerful theoretical tradition starts from two propositions:

(a) that 'the conditions that lead to violent protest are essentially the same as those that lead to other kinds of collective action in pursuit of common interests' (Tilly, Tilly and Tilly, 1975, p. 7);
(b) that the people involved in such collective incidents are no different physiologically or psychologically to those engaged in other aspects of social life.

Resource mobilization theorists vary widely. The great range of theoretical positions is represented here in terms of three viewpoints: non-Marxist, and less and more sophisticated Marxist versions.

An example of non-Marxist theorizing is Kerr's hypothesis about the lifecycle of working class protest, which 'rises and then falls off again as the process of commitment advances' and 'finally, in the over-committed worker . . . tends to disappear' (Kerr, 1960, p. 353, quoted in Tilly, Tilly and Tilly, 1975, p. 8).

In the idealist-Marxist version of the theory, changes in a society's organization of production 'realign the fundamental class divisions within the society, define new interests for each class, and (through an awakening awareness of those interests promoted by interaction with both class allies and class enemies) eventually produce new, expanding forms of class conflict' (Tilly, Tilly and Tilly, 1975, p. 7). The major criticisms of the crude Marxist version have been around the difficulty of correlating the groups involved in collective action with the major societal divisions defined by the mode of production, and also in the failure of industrial societies to move towards the class conflict predicted by the economic crisis of capitalism. The collapse of several communist East European regimes in the winter of 1989–90 has undermined this determinist view of history still further.

Thompson's classic study of the making of the English working class avoids this lack of subtlety and simplistic Marxist theorizing (Thompson, 1963). By painstakingly constructing 'histories from below', 'in his discussions of Luddism, Chartism, and the other major working-class protests of the early nineteenth century, Thompson is at great pains to demonstrate that precisely those groups of working men with the most highly-developed sense of class divisions led the assault on their enemies' (Tilly, Tilly and Tilly, 1975, pp. 7–8).

Resource mobilization theories are prone to problems. They can lead to viewing protest as both the outcome and the evidence of collective consciousness and action by the rioters. They do not readily explain those incidents which might be termed reactionary, or are led by, say, government officials such as police, troops or militias (Tilly, Tilly and Tilly, 1975, p. 8). Ralph Banay, consultant to the US Bureau of Prisons, argues that the proneness to riots of those prisons with regimes lagging behind others is increased by prisoners' increased awareness of the means by which those in the community make their protests. (Banay, 1959, p. 8)

In the light of detailed research, Useem shares with Colvin the belief that social disorganization theories explain the outbreak of the 1980 New Mexico Prison riot more convincingly than resource mobilization theories (Colvin, 1985; Useem, 1985). Useem concludes: 'There is no evidence that the prison riot occurred in 1980 because of an increase in inmate resources or solidarity, which resource-mobilization theorists say must precede collective action' (Useem, 1985, p. 686).

First, resource-mobilization theorists hold the critical edge over social disorganization theorists in four respects:

(a) They assert that people's grievances are sufficiently widespread throughout society at all times to make it difficult to correlate grievances with variations in the incidence of specific forms of collective action, such as rioting.
(b) They maintain that disorganized groups are the least likely to take collective action, since they are, of all people, the most likely to lack access to the necessary resources and skills.
(c) They argue that collective action arises from well-defined, well-organized groups.
(d) They point to evidence that the incidence of collective action does not correlate positively with measures of disorganization, such as personal sickness, crime and suicide rates, non-membership in primary and secondary groups and changes in deprivation levels (Useem, 1985, p. 678).

Secondly, before proceeding, we need to take up a debate central to research into social life in prisons. This revolves around the extent to which riots in them are generated primarily in the institution or with reference back to the culture in which prisoners are rooted, outside the prison.

Assimilation and Prisonization

Typically, prisons are coercive institutions. That is, staff rely on the ultimate sanction of controlling prisoners by physical force (Goffman, 1961) in carrying out the primary function of guaranteeing their custody (Etzioni, 1975, p. 117). In both the US and Britain, prisons, in the wider context of the criminal justice system, are not accountable to the public (Thomas and Petersen, 1977, p. 14). The tendency for prisons to 'strip' new prisoners of many aspects of their social role and position (Goffman, 1961) contributes towards the process by which they adjust to, and encourages them collectively towards, a subcultural response as prisoners to their incarceration (Thomas and Petersen, 1977, p. 49). A wealth of research confirms that the nature of the inmate subculture varies according to the character and regime of the prison (Grusky, 1959; Glaser 1964; Street *et al.*, 1966; Berk, 1966), and that frequently the consequent alienation of prisoners generates a culture in opposition to that of the authorities and staff

(Schrag, 1961; Tittle, 1972). The conditions for prison riots arise from the positive correlation between increasing deprivations of prisoners and their increasing integration into the oppositional inmate culture (Clemmer, 1958; Wheeler, 1961).

Since the 1950s, a long tradition of studies of prisoner cultures has shifted from a conceptualization of them as a reaction specific to imprisonment (Clemmer, 1958; Sykes, 1958), to an acknowledgement that they are rooted in the community (Giallombardo, 1966). Prison subcultural theories divide between prisonization and importation perspectives. Prisonization is 'the taking on, in greater or lesser degree, of the folkways, mores, customs and general culture of the penitentiary' (Clemmer, 1940, p. 279). This process is assumed to replace prisoners' societal values with the more criminal ones of the prison. Conventionally, the *informal* prisoners' social system is viewed as opposed to the official system (Clemmer, 1940; McCorkle and Korn, 1958; Sykes, 1958). Tittle distinguishes primary organization among prisoners, found in treatment-oriented institutions, from collective organization, found in more custodial institutions (Tittle, 1972). Fry found that opposition by prisoners to the official values did not necessarily prevent the achievement of institutional treatment goals (Fry, 1976).

The concepts of 'assimilation' and 'prisonization' are both used to describe ways in which prisoners adapt to the existing culture of the prison. Clemmer identifies assimilation, which he describes as a process by which a person learns enough of a culture to make him or her characteristic of it, as perhaps much slower than the process of prisonization (Clemmer, 1977, p. 175). Tittle examines how men and women relate to prison life and concludes that, while women tend to affiliate in primary groups, men 'display greater tendencies towards integration into an overall sym-biotic organization', that is into the prisoner subculture in their interaction with the staff culture. 'In general, the data seem to justify the conclusion that inmate organization is largely a response to institutional conditions' (Tittle, 1969, p. 503). Research into prison 'rats', who turn against the inmate code and give information to the staff, has been used to illustrate how the confinement of a prisoner produces isolation from outside society and leads to adjustment to unfamiliar values and relationships in prison (Johnson, 1961, p. 528). Some 'rats' are assimilated and then violate the inmate code; others are unassimilated, but are still attacked by other prisoners for breaking it (Johnson, 1961, p. 530). The inmate code which inhibits prisoners from 'snitching', when combined with an administration which encourages 'rats' to 'snitch', reinforces the gulf between staff and prisoners, polarizes them and makes for greater rigidities and tensions (Wilmer, 1965, p. 49).

Whichever term they adopt, however, commentators tend to agree about the character of the prison as an institution which deprives its inmates. But deprivation theory itself is constrained by the functionalist assumptions which underpin it. Fundamentally, from this perspective inmates in total institutions adjust to conditions as they are. It does not take on board the argument that prison is inherently a 'wrongful system', a corollary of Zimbardo's finding that even volunteer novices within a short period of time began to behave brutally towards mock captives, when placed in an artificially created prison (Zimbardo, 1973).

Joan Moore's study of the Chicano gangs from distinct territorial bases who serve sentences for drugs and related offences in Californian prisons presents dramatic evidence of the importation of their minority group culture into the world of the prison (Moore, 1978, pp. 124–8). The prison is not a total institution in the sense of being totally cut off from society. If nothing else, the constant flow of staff, prisoners and visitors in and out of prisons maintains their close relationships with other systems. The 'deprivation' view fails to account adequately for the nature and intensity of some prisoners' opposition to staff (Thomas and Petersen, 1977, p. 51) and restricts consideration of wider influences associated with the way prisons run, and the processes involved in the passage in and out of prisons of staff, prisoners and other people.

Research into women's experiences in prison illustrates the dangers of attributing responses to prison to one set of factors. Ward's study of a British women's prison examines reasons for the lack of solidarity among women prisoners and the extent to which the lack of sanctioning of women who 'snitch' or 'grass' is symptomatic of this. She criticizes the studies of Giallombardo (1966) and Ward and Kassebaum (1965), who:

> . . . attribute a lack of solidarity to the essentially individualistic interpretation of events by women, whose place in American society forces them into a stance of rivalry in their efforts to ensnare a man who will provide them with a home and a life in a society where women derive their status largely from the man they marry and not from their own efforts . . . the explanation is couched in terms of

the femininity of the inmates, whose different socialisation had not fitted them for more co-operative behaviour.

(Ward, 1982, pp. 234–5)

Ward argues that the explanation lies partly in these women's pre-prison experiences and partly in what happens to them in prison. Thus:

An apparent lack of solidarity is not a direct result of the prisoners being women but that, given a diversity of pre-prison careers and a structure and organisation which exacerbate the differences, then the diversity of 'cross-cutting ties' will enable people to escape from the consequences of their actions, since they can always withdraw into another group. As was hinted at in the reference to research into 'rats' above, if one of the chief 'pains' of imprisonment is then a perceived uncertainty, and that uncertainty can be mitigated by grassing, then grassing will result.

(Ward, 1982, p. 256)

Beyond Historical Relativism

Now we are in a position to address the historical relativism inherent in the possible ways of addressing the respective strengths and weaknesses of these theories referred to above, by arguing that each may have relevance in given historical and social circumstances (Useem, 1985, p. 687).

Thus we could assert that in the context of the late 1960s and early 1970s, when there were strong movements among not only inmates but also oppressed groups such as black people and women towards the collective redressing of social and political injustices and discrimination, resource-mobilization theories would seem most appropriately to provide an explanatory model for the occurrence of protests in the form of the communal riots of the late 1960s and the Attica prison riot in 1971. Thus, we would latch readily on the analysis of the Kerner Commission on the 1967 riots in the US, which identified the ingredients of increasing racial divisions in the US, widespread discrimination and segregation, black ghettos, frustrated aspirations and negative police–civilian relations in ghettos as part of the recipe for rioting (National Advisory Commission, 1968, p. 206). 'Nevertheless, the essential *explanation* of ghetto violence they offered was that grievances accumulated, organized protest movements sharpened those grievances, then small incidents were enough to touch off an "explosion"' (Tilly, Tilly and Tilly, 1975, p. 292).

From the mid-1970s, when prevailing social conditions were moving away from the mass expression of coordinated grievances by organized groups in society, the argument runs that social disorganization theories came into their own as a means of explaining such incidents as the Miami riot by black people in 1980 and the 1980 New Mexico prison riot. At the bleakest surface of the social disorganization perspective, Caplan and Paige develop riff-raff theory, which maintains that rioters are irresponsible, criminal, unassimilated migrants, disturbed members of an underclass, essentially marginal to society (Caplan and Paige, 1968, p. 15).

The McCone Commission on the Watts riot of Los Angeles in 1964 locates major responsibility for the riot in the consequences of a tenfold increase of the black population between 1940 and 1965.

> To those who have come with high hopes and great expectations and see the success of others so close at hand, failure brings a special measure of frustration and disillusionment . . . When the rioting came to Los Angeles, it was not a race riot in the usual sense. What happened was an explosion – a formless, quite senseless, all but hopeless violent protest – engaged in by a few but bringing great distress to all.
> (Governor's Commission, 1965, pp. 4–5, quoted in Tilly, Tilly and Tilly, 1975, p. 292)

Superficially, it may appear that social disorganization and resource mobilization theories refer simply to different phases of the same protest, or that different varieties of violent protest arise from disorganization and from resource mobilization, or that they are the same phenomenon viewed from a conservative and radical perspective respectively (Tilly, Tilly and Tilly, 1975, pp. 8–9). But Tilly and colleagues refute this on the grounds that there is a fundamental divergence between the perspectives of these theories regarding the recruitment of rioters, the distinctiveness of social protest, and the most likely conditions for protest:

> It cannot be true *both* that revolutionary crowds recruit their members mainly from the marginal, floating population of the city *and* that revolutionary crowds draw most heavily on groups strongly integrated into the collective life of the city, although it is possible

that the activists are well-integrated, while the floating population supplies most of the bystanders. It cannot be true *both* that crime, mental illness, and rebellion spring from the same basic strains *and* that there is no connection among them, unless those strains are so pervasive as to have no predictive value. It cannot be true *both* that raw, swelling centers of new industry are ripest for protest *and* that settled industrial cities are most likely to produce movements of protest, although the truth could well be more complicated than either alternative.

(Tilly, Tilly and Tilly, 1975, p. 9).

Towards Reforms of Wrongful Aspects of Prisons and Imprisonment

Lawyers in the US (Anon, 1981), the Council of Europe (*Guardian* 13 December 1991, p. 20) and HM Chief Inspector of Prisons in Britain (*Guardian*, 13 December 1991, p. 2), have all condemned aspects of prisons and prison systems in Britain and the US as wrongful. But it is difficult to see how such fundamental criticisms can readily be translated into penal reforms which the authorities will take on board. Interpretations of prison riots need to recognize how the nature of rioting by prisoners has changed, even if the incidence of prison riots over the latter half of the twentieth century has not demonstrably altered. In examining intercommunal violence, Rubenstein argues the ways in which violence in society has changed, rather than the incidence of violence itself. The lack of major riots, civil disorders and assassinations should not divert attention from the existence of 'anomic individual violence (particularly crime), state violence (particularly against the underclass), and what Johan Galtung calls "structural violence"' (Rubenstein, 1989, p. 309). In this connection, the work of Galtung provides a bridge between psychological and social theories of violence (Galtung, 1964).

Rubenstein observes that 'paradoxically, the very forces militating against a revival of low-intensity mass violence may be opening the door to rebellion of a less inhibited type' (Rubenstein, 1989, p. 311). He concludes that in the likely absence of 'top-down' *perestroika*-style reforms on one hand or mass mobilization of people from beneath, 'it seems likely that the suppressed or inner-directed anger of identity groups outside the current American consensus will again express itself (when hope and desperation rise) in more and less constructive forms' (ibid., p. 325).

Rubenstein's prediction is relevant to the profile and trajectory of prison riots in the US and in Britain when he suggests that a diversity of fragmented, small-scale, locally-based rebellions are a likely response, either of 'any substantial rise in an oppressed group's expectations or [a] dramatic threat to its identity' (ibid., p. 324).

Focusing on Oppression

The commentary of Feagin and Hahn significantly reworks the interpretations of the riots of the 1970s, describing the ghetto riot as one act in a continuing struggle between different urban groups. Far from incidents arising from the failure of people to adjust satisfactorily, or from consequent strains they experienced, riots are viewed as:

> . . . occasioned by the failure of the existing urban political system to respond adequately to their desires and aspirations, to allow them a proportionate role in the urban structure of power. Ghetto rioting, therefore, reflected an attempted reclamation of political authority over ghetto areas and a type of political recall, not necessarily of specific public officeholders, but of the entire political apparatus that had failed to grant a reasonable share of the political pie to ghetto residents.
>
> (Feagin and Hahn, 1973, p. 53, quoted in Tilly, Tilly and Tilly, 1975, p. 293).

Although they find no typical rioter and suggest that the kinds of people involved change to some extent as the violence proceeds. Feagin and Hahn dispel the idea that participants in collective ghetto violence came disproportionately from the ghetto's marginal, depressed, disorganized populations. They bring out the selectivity of attacks on stores and other property. They conclude that the police and the National Guard did almost all the killing. Finally, they emphasize the extent to which injustice and discrimination (rather than, any, absolute or relative material hardship) dominated the complaints of people in the areas which experienced major conflicts.

> (Tilly, Tilly and Tilly, 1975, p. 293)

A similar conclusion is drawn in Porter and Dunn's case study of the Miami riot of May 1980, in which 18 people died and $80m damage was done to property in disturbances marked by the contrast with earlier riots – black people apparently setting out deliberately to attack white people (Porter and Dunn, 1984, p. xiii). The authors note that 'one of the more striking findings of this study was the degree to which the riot in Miami appeared to have drawn in the "good" people of the community . . . Many held jobs, were normally law-abiding and did not otherwise fit the stereotypical image of a "rioter"' (Porter and Dunn, 1984, p. 183). They quote Lieberson and Silberman's analysis of riots in the US between 1913 and 1963, which notes that cities sampled which have not experienced any riots actually have higher unemployment rates than those which have experienced them. They conclude that riots are not caused by deprivation but by conditions which lead to people feeling left out of the system, when grievances are not resolved by normal, routine means (Lieberson and Silverman, 1965).

So, discrimination against rioters – for example, white discrimination against black people – excludes them from systems and opportunities. Thus rioting is not a problem of the rioters, as the first two theoretical positions imply, but a problem of white institutions, which need to be changed if rioting is to be prevented (Caplan and Paige, 1968, p. 15).

Caplan and Paige distinguish rebellions, where people set out to destroy the system, from riots, where they attempt to get access to the system they feel excludes them. 'One is led to conclude that the continued exclusion of Negroes from American economic and social life is the fundamental cause of riots' (Caplan and Paige, 1968, p. 21).

This is an interpretation familiar to, though not necessarily popular among, commentators on terrorism. Rubenstein, for example, insists that terrorists do not possess the characters of extremists and psychopaths, but resemble the person next door. He associates state violence with the violence of terrorism and argues that the solution to terrorism is to connect the terrorists with political means to achieve their aims (Rubenstein, 1987).

Beyond Dualism

Martin reflects Smelser's distinction between structural and immediate factors in his distinction between two conditions – 'underlying unrest, and a spark to touch off the explosion' – leading to prison rioting. 'As we have seen, the experts who investigated at Jackson concluded that Jackson's bigness, its heterogeneous population, and its overcrowded condition combined to produce a powder keg that was ignited by the combination of the untrained guard and the unstable inmate in cell-block 15. The causes of riots elsewhere were not very different' (Martin, 1955, p. 203). Wilsnack produces a more sophisticated, multi-level theory. His study of 51 of the largest prisons in 50 states of the US, plus the district of Columbia, concludes that three levels of factors contribute to the outbreak of three-quarters of prison riots: 'inmate deprivation and social disintegration, administrative conflict and instability, and pressure and publicity from outside the walls' (Wilsnack, 1976, p. 72). Wilsnack distinguishes 'non-riot resistance' involving prisoners making demands from 'riot resistance' where the demands are associated with them taking over territory in the prison. This distinction enables Wilsnack to hypothesize that non-riot resistance will occur where prisoners can engage in some form of negotiating with staff, whereas riots will tend to occur where negotiation with the authorities is not perceived by prisoners as likely to be productive, either because of prisoners' own lack of cohesion, staff unresponsiveness or a combination of these (ibid., p. 73). Ironically, therefore, 'rioting may be a response to failures of less violent or smaller scale protest. In the course of nonriot resistance, administrators may prove unwilling or unable to negotiate meaningfully, and inmate organization may prove inadequate. The powerlessness felt from these failures can set the stage for more desperate action' (ibid., p. 74).

The purpose of this chapter has not been to develop a general theory of riots. But so far, the above discussion points to the need for the social origins of prison riots to be understood in terms of a meta-perspective: that is, from outside the dominant discourse of the day, which has influenced both social disorganization and resource mobilization perspectives. The pursuit of explanations of rioting by prisoners needs to take on board two considerations: the social factors leading to higher rates of imprisonment both in absolute terms and for particular oppressed groups, especially those liable to racial discrimination; and the implications of the assumption that the prison system is wrongful. So the explanation of the origins of rioting by prisoners needs to be sought in the matrix of penal values, policies and practices in society, and in institutional, organizational, group and personal levels or oppression, experienced by prisoners. It is clear that prison riots arise from the dynamic interaction of factors at different levels: social, political, penal policy and practice, prisoner cultural, prison, group, interpersonal and personal. As we have noted elsewhere (Adams, 1987; Adams, 1991), an adequate analysis of the origins of riots depends crucially on the dialectic between the observed and experienced realities of those who are parties to institutional life.

CONCLUSIONS

This discussion demonstrates the complexity of the task of researching the origins of prison riots. There is a tendency, inevitably perhaps, for research into the origins of riots to reflect the particular concerns of the era in which they are undertaken. Thus, Martin Luther King's statement at the start of this chapter is redolent of the concerns of black civil rights agitators of the 1960s.

But some general comments can be made. Research does tend to make dualist distinctions between disciplines and intra- and extra-institutional factors, for instance. The task is to frame the study of the origins of prison riots so as to enable the different levels and dimensions of interacting factors to be appreciated, incorporating the dialectic between structural and experienced conditions, so as to move beyond a normalist focus on the rioters and categorizations of the divisions between different 'types' of riots and rioters to an interpretation of prison riots as a critical commentary on the wrongful aspects of imprisonment.

7 Prospects of Prison Riots

> Tyranny sets up its own echo-chamber; a void where confused
> signals buzz about at random; where a murmur or innuendo causes
> panic: so, in the end, the machinery of repression is more likely to
> vanish, not with war or revolution, but with a puff, or the voice of
> falling leaves . . .
>
> (Chatwin, 1989, p. 120)

Inevitably, some of the content of previous chapters has spilled over
into the issues which concern this final chapter, namely the evaluation of prison riots. By 'evaluation' is meant examining the impact on
prison riots of trends in penal policy and practice. This leads to a
discussion of the future prospects of lessening the scale of prison
riots, or even preventing them altogether.

POSSIBLE SCENARIOS

This discussion begins with the depressing but realistic observation
that, if history is anything to go by, prison riots are as likely to be a part
of the future of imprisonment as they have been of its past. Collective
resistance to imprisonment is inevitable. But despite the history of
widespread protests by prisoners, and riots as an aspect of their collective resistance, the authorities have tended not to take on board the
social dimension of prisoners' collective actions. Thus, in the information booklet for male prisoners produced by the Prison Service
in Britain in the early 1990s, though there are references in the 'Race
Relations Policy Statement' to 'all prisoners' its substance, including
the section on how to complain, is addressed to prisoners as individuals and not as a group (HM Prison Service, undated, p. 15).

One consequence of the fragmentation of prisoners into cliques
and subgroups in the last quarter of the twentieth century has been to
make it less likely that their collective actions will be perceived as
directed, however obliquely, at the powers which oppress them. Although in one sense prison riots represent the more directly confrontational aspects of collective resistance by prisoners, in another sense,
as the history of protests by pupils shows, such resistance is expressed
also through diversionary and subversive acts (Adams, 1991). The

need has emerged above to examine the changing nature of prison riots and responses to them over time, with a view to establishing how their negative and destructive aspects may be minimized and the likelihood of positive outcomes from them maximized.

Experience demonstrates the close interconnections between the actions of rioting prisoners and those of the authorities, before and after the onset of a riot, though the 'chicken-and-egg' character of their interrelatedness makes this complex relationship difficult, if not impossible, to probe. So, the nature of future prison riots depends on the future nature of prison policies and practices and vice versa.

For many years, well into the twentieth century, the struggles of prisoners to resist the conditions of their imprisonment were denied or ignored by the authorities, the media and by other commentators. In the latter half of the twentieth century, the increasing scale and scope of prison riots in particular has made protests by prisoners impossible to ignore. Two hypothetical alternative scenarios of the future can be envisaged, the more likely prospect of the more rigorous control of potentially riotous prisoners and, on the basis of precedent, the less likely option of their being given more humane treatment by the authorities. The trouble with words such as 'control', 'humane' and 'treatment' is that they have been pretty well worked to death in the penal literature. But any alternatives we might choose – 'authoritarian', 'liberal', and so on – are just as laden with overtones. So, we shall retain these as evocative labels which indicate contrasting directions in penal policies and practices.

Control Scenario

From the standpoint of this 'control' scenario, prison riots are viewed in terms of the overriding preoccupations of the authorities with the more effective control of prisoners *within* the penal system *as it stands,* or rather, in an enlarged system with enhanced facilities for the control, disciplining and, where necessary, segregation of prisoners judged by professionals to be difficult. The fact that the state has moved increasingly towards a *mixed economy* for the provision of facilities for imprisoning people does not override these parameters. If anything, it reinforces them. It find evidence to corroborate the view of prison riots as spontaneous, involuntary or preconscious, unconscious, instinctive reactions by subrational, or even subhuman, prisoners.

In the 1980s and early 1990s, in both Britain and the US there has been an increased tendency by the prison authorities to target rioters, and those viewed as potential rioters, for more effective measures of control. In Britain, post-Strangeways, the Home Secretary has referred to the need for the introduction to the penal code of the offence of prison mutiny, Bifurcation is the term used by Bottoms (1977 p. 90) to refer to the renaissance of the concept of dangerousness, which involves sorting out dangerous, that is riot-prone, prisoners and segregating, confining and even applying tough behavioural methods to them.

In the nineteenth century, the impulse of prison officials to silence, separate and isolate prisoners associated reformative zeal with the purpose of abolishing corruption and disruption by prisoners. In the late twentieth century segregation has become a sophisticated system of warehousing, Messinger (1969) uses the term 'strategies of control' to describe the systems of management of prisoners by segregation in separate isolation blocks, segregation units or adjustment centres, developed in Californian prisons since the early 1960s. Cohen refers to Messinger's work:

> One adjustment centre in which disruptive inmates were segregated ended up by spawning its own segregation unit to deal with those beyond its reach. The 'complicated Chinese box effect' which results 'with inmates in the innermost box ideally required to traverse each enclosing one on the way to relative freedom' is very much the way most prison systems are developing. As Messinger notes, the 'logic' of the segregation strategy is simple enough: 'identify potential troublemakers as early as possible, try to bring them to heel, if you fail, segregate them.' Whether this works or not in minimising disruption, what is clear is that 'the strategy of segregation leads to more segregation'. Given the organizational imperative of control, officials point out quite plausibly that other strategies are ineffective: force can only sometimes be used (in riots or disturbances) and anyway cannot make inmates want to do things: motivation through punishments and rewards are limited and one cannot freely select into or reject from the institution. With restrictions on the legitimate use of force, the control issue – which dominates the daily routine of prison officials at all levels – resolves itself into motivating prisoners to do things the management wants or else neutralizing the recalcitrants.
>
> (Cohen, 1977, p. 222)

The consequences of such segregation and confinement may be increasing power attracted to the lower grades of prison staff. In one scenario, which Cohen elaborates a few years later as 'applied behaviour analysis' and 'behavioural criminal justice', staff control the detailed daily living patterns and actions of prisoners (Cohen, 1985, p. 147). 'Out of a combination of internal system demands and external pressures, then, the Chinese box effect will slowly develop. The prisoner in the innermost box – the segregation wing, the isolation block – can look forward not to release, but, if he satisfies the staff that he is "prepared to co-operate", transfer to the next box' (Cohen, 1977, p. 222).

The incidence of riots following in the wake of such policies and practices is unlikely to be reduced in the institution where control and security rule over humaneness and a positive relationship between staff and prisoners. It is unlikely that devising new measures to segregate rioters, as individuals and in small groups, will deter them from rioting, although at the physical level it is undeniable that, as in the nineteenth-century silent and separate systems, keeping some prisoners locked up and isolated permanently does at least stop them from engaging in collective activities of most sorts. But it is unlikely that threatening prison rioters with enhanced punishments, such as charging them with prison mutiny and lengthening their sentences, will deter those experienced and determined rioters who are already serving very long sentences of imprisonment.

Conditions in prisons in Britain and the US have for the most part been experienced by prisoners as dehumanized and dehumanizing. Inquiries into such prison riots as Attica, Santa Fe and Strangeways refer specifically to the need to humanize them. A common refrain among rioting prisoners in Attica in 1971, recorded in a *Newsweek* commentary, reverberates down the decades: 'If we can't live like human beings, at least we can die like men.' (Edwards, 1972, p. 157)

Humane Treatment Scenario

Many inquiries into prison riots have drawn attention to prisoners' demands for better conditions, better opportunities for meaningful employment in prison and better facilities for association with other prisoners. These issues, most clearly articulated in Attica in the US (New York State Special Commission, 1972) and in Strangeways in Britain (Woolf and Tumin, 1991), generally revolve around the themes of more humane and just prisons for prisoners, linked most obviously by the notion of prisoners having more say in the way they are dealt with and greater areas of freedom and choice, within the necessary parameters of their being kept in prison. There is plenty of support for this, from reformers and from prisoners themselves. As one prison manager put it, 'most rioting prisoners want a bigger slice of bread rather than to take over the bakery.' (Personal communication to author.) Although that may be true, we still need to consider the arguments for and against giving prisoners more say in how resources within the prison are deployed. The question is whether a democratized prison, with prisoners exercising a meaningful level of control over improved facilities rather than the facilities being used simply to control them, would be less riot-prone. In one sense, the official response to riots for many decades in the US has reinforced the desirability of seeking a more humane prison, paying particular attention to the linked themes of justice for prisoners and the democratization of prisons.

In connection with this ideal, repeated statements have been made emphasizing the necessity to listen to what prisoners themselves have to say about their experiences of imprisonment. In the 1950s a consensus view predominated that most prisoners still accepted the legitimacy of the system (Sykes, 1958). Within a decade, that legitimacy was being questioned by prisoners. The assumption that power belongs with the people spread into prisons, and with it a conflict view, of the institution riven by the gulf between guards and prisoners. As long ago as 1965, a Government Commission in the US recommended that 'all institutions should be run to the greatest possible extent with rehabilitation a joint responsibility of staff and inmates. Training of correctional managers and staff should reflect this mode of operation' (US President's Commission, 1967, p. 174).

According to this view, the key to preventing further rioting lies not so much with the authorities taking action in the light of what they guess prisoners are expressing, but rather in empowering prisoners to take action themselves by more legitimate and socially approved means.

Prisoners, in theory, form a unique and irreplaceable part of the network of groups and organizations which contribute to the formation and implementation of penal policy and practice. It is true that a great range of bodies take part in this process. These include not just representatives of government and the penal authorities themselves, but also, over the years, a number of advisory groups. For instance, in Britain, the Advisory Council on the Penal System existed between 1966 and 1979, created by the government as an *ad hoc* body to give advice on penal affairs (Morgan, 1979). But neither the authorities nor advisory bodies, essentially set up at the behest of government and controlled by them, could provide the independent, critical commentary on penal policy and practice of the reform groups and, of course, prisoners themselves. Further, until the 1970s, penal reform groups in Britain, such as NACRO and the Howard League for Penal Reform, occupied a liberal reformist rather than a radical position, as the publications of the latter illustrate (Klare, 1962; Rose, 1961). It may be symptomatic of the marginal situation of British prisoners as a group that they are not mentioned in Morgan's significant paper reviewing the influence of different groups and organizations considered relevant in relation to penal policy and practice in Britain (Morgan, Part 3, pp. 24–33). It needs to be appreciated how rioting by prisoners, individually, in groups and as larger collectivities, may act as a challenge to the compound impact of the depriving and oppressive features of imprisonment.

This prospect of prisoners as potential contributors to prison reforms takes for granted that:

Both the overt contradictions and covert functions of incarceration in that society must be grasped if change is to become controlled and goal-oriented or even if, at some distant future, prison abolition is adopted as a societal aim. We must also develop more understanding of the positive role of conflict – now seemingly coextensive with senseless and pervasive violence – in effecting structural changes in institutions.

(Stastny and Tyrnauer, 1982, p. 206)

But it may be asking too much of professionals in the penal systems of Britain and the US, and the public at large, to take on board prisoners' collective critiques of imprisonment.

In practice, the voices of rioters cannot always be read or heard with the same readiness that laws, manuals and reports illustrating official perspectives of prison policies and practices can be located. In part, however, prison riots draw their legitimation from beliefs in wider society about penalty and prisons and from the repeated criticisms of prison conditions, reformers and prison staff alike. In the US, alliances between the low status guards, who were as likely to be searched for contraband as the prisoners, in Jackson prison, Michigan, at the time of the riot in 1952, may have been implicit rather than overt but they were no less real for that. In Britain, the 1986 riots were not the only cases where there was talk of prison officers actively encouraging rioting by prisoners to further the staff's own industrial claims (Prison Reform Trust, undated, p. 19). One former governor of a large prison commented that just as prison officers have been known to wish for a riot partly because it justifies their intervention and reassertion of control over prisoners, so governors themselves have been known to view the riot as a chance of bidding for increased resources (personal communication by governor to the author).

The complaints of the rioting prisoners in many ways are constructed using edited versions of the criticisms of prison staff and reformist organizations about poor food, outdated accommodation, lack of resources, overcrowding and so on. But in the democratized prison, the prisoners' own actions reconstruct these items in their own distinctive agenda. Specifically, for example, the rioters regard direct action as legitimate. Then, prison riots may be viewed as a pattern of social protest which reflects a widespread consensus among prisoners and other similarly oppressed groups with whom they identify – and sometimes staff as well – as to the shortcomings of the prison system.

Stastny and Tyrnauer use the history of Walla Walla to argue that once prisoners have become politicized, the clock can never be put back.

> Prisoners' groups and organizations became politicized interest groups; and the conflict between these newly formed interest groups led to fundamental changes in the social structure. Thus, even as the memory of the reforms at Walla Walla wanes, many of these changes in structure and consciousness persist . . . As the silence of the penitentiary was ruptured, so also, it seemed, was the consensus. The relationship between rulers and ruled changed from that of more or less benevolent despotism to a polarization and suppressed warfare.
>
> (Stastny and Tyrnauer, 1982, pp. 206–7)

Then, when the legitimacy of the prison was challenged by prisoners in the 1960s, imprisonment became seen by many prisoners as an instrument of social and political control. 'The result was a polarization between keepers and kept, a feeling that each represented a life-threat to the existence of the other' (Stastny and Tyrnauer, 1982, p. 207).

Not only is the history of prison riots in Britain and the US particularly unenviable, and in the US bloody as well, but incarceration rates in Britain in 1990 were the highest in Europe and those in the US were the highest among Western countries, if not the entire world. In contrast, Scandinavia and the Netherlands, where incarceration rates have been among the lowest in the Western world for most of the second half of the twentieth century, have also experienced very few large-scale prison riots. In the case of the Netherlands, with its emphasis on small prisons and short sentences with rapid transitions of even life sentence prisoners to community facilities and supervision, prison riots are extremely rare. In these countries, the climate of penal policy is so much less punitive than in Britain and the US that it may be argued that comparison is pointless. Yet it is worth noting that in both the Netherlands and Scandinavia articulate and well-organized prisoners' organizations have existed for many years. Whilst needing to bear in mind that all in these prisons is not perfect – an American visitor to Sweden, for instance, notes the repetitive, boring work of Tillberga factory prison and the 'sterile, bombproof' character of Kumla prison with its 'bland and oppressive atmosphere' (Ward, 1979, p. 95) – there are positive features of the history of collective activity by prisoners from which much can be learned.

In the Netherlands, for example, the BWO, or Union of Law Breakers, was founded in 1973, by a group of prisoners who had produced a number of accounts of their experiences in the Dutch prison system and a series of pamphlets called K69. Over the years, the BWO struggled to retain its critical voice in relation to penal policy. The struggle had its ups and downs. Latterly, the BWO adopted at first sight a self-contradictory stance, simultaneously pragmatic and idealist. Its pragmatic aim was to stress the legal rights of prisoners, as a positive aim of prison reform within the system. Its idealist aim, depenalizing rather than decriminalizing, was the abolition of prisons themselves (van Swaaningen, 1990, p. 15).

In Sweden on the other hand, the history of collective organization by prisoners to bring about changes in their conditions of imprisonment is generally acknowledged to have begun in the 1960s when groups of prisoners began to meet to talk about these matters. The formation of the first advisory council of prisoners in Hall prison in 1969, the succeeding unrest which led to strikes and other demonstrations, the often painful process of negotiations with staff in other prisons, the hunger strike in Österåker Central Prison, the formation of KRUM, the Swedish prisoners' reform organization, and the failure of efforts to introduce democracy to prisons, have provided a case study from which much can be drawn:

> An additional feature of the prison democracy experiment merits attention. This experiment provides an example of prison conflict in which inmate resistance involved work stoppages, hunger and thirst strikes, and appeals for political support through the mass media. It did not produce the physical violence that has characterized inmate-staff confrontations in American prisons.
>
> (Ward, 1979, p. 126)

Further:

> In Sweden the manner in which all parties have sought to deal with the problem has differed, and the substantive issues of concern to Swedish prison reformers and prisoners are far more sophisticated than those of most of their colleagues in the United States. Movements towards those more advanced issues require that American prisoners first win some basic rights; most important is the right to organize in behalf of their own interests. The failure of prison democracy – an experiment that would not have been given serious consideration in any American prison system – does, however, provide evidence of the difficulty inmates have in bringing about fundamental changes in even the most enlightened system.
>
> (Ward, 1979, p. 126)

Whilst democratizing prisons would seem in theory to offer a more optimistic future prospect for prisoners than simply controlling them, in practice the history of attempts to democratize prisons in Britain and the US has been one of failure. Can the roots of this failure be related to the persistence of prison riots in these countries?

Put at its most stark, there is a patent gulf between the discipline of the prison to which the inmate is expected to conform and the (claimed) freedom of the democratic situation in the society to which she or he returns. The twentieth century has seen attempts to reduce this incongruity. In the US, the most notable experiments began with Thomas Mott Osborne in Auburn in 1913 and continued with Superintendent Howard B. Gill in the community prison of Norfolk, Massachusetts, beginning in the late 1920s, and, in separate innovations, in Washington State Penitentiary at Walla Walla in the 1970s (Stastny and Tyrnauer, 1982, Chs 4 and 7). The four-year experiment in Walla

Walla focused on 'detotalizing' the power in the institution. All of these endeavours eventually failed and were terminated (Stastny and Tyrnauer, 1982). In Britain, in the 1920s, the rather dubious efforts of Homer Lane with young offenders had a mixed reception at the time and were followed by more limited explorations of prisoner participation. The most notable were in Grendon Underwood, influenced by the therapeutic community movement, and Long Lartin prison at the turn of the 1970s (Shapland et al, 1972).

The purpose of democratizing prisons may be claimed to be therapy in the treatment-oriented regime of an institution such as Grendon Underwood, or, in other initiatives, to make the prison more like the community 'out there'. But if a few exceptions tempt sentencers to use imprisonment more, or encourage the pretence that prisons are not fearsome, this is misguided. The fact remains that most prisons are awful for most of the time.

Ohlin attempts to bridge the gulf between control and democratization strategies, in putting forward several principles towards which penal policy regarding the confinement of offenders in prison should be directed. In summary, these amount to avoiding typing some prisoners as highly dangerous and some institutions as catering specifically for them and concentrating on fostering conditions in prison which encourage inmate subcultures which in turn support the official cultures concerned with control (Ohlin, 1981, pp. 177–81). However, they remain speculations rather than realized in practice.

If such reforms are difficult to engineer from outside prisons, they are no less difficult for those inside them. In general, prisons have remained relatively impervious to reforms initiated by those most involved in working in them. To the extent that riots have been perceived by the authorities as crises of control, subsequent inquiries have at least provided some brief snapshots of what goes on in prisons. Regular visitors to prisons who are not part of the custodial hierarchy in theory are relatively well placed to act as critical monitors of prison conditions. But in practice their sensitivity may become dulled through close regular contact with an institution. In Britain, the vulnerability of probation officers, generally seconded for short periods to work as 'outsiders' in prisons, to incorporation into the culture of the institution, requires sensitive, and sometimes assertive, counter-measures on the part of practitioners themselves (Williams, 1991). Even members of Boards of Visitors, who act as adjudicators of prisoners' disciplinary offences not considered serious enough for police investigation, and inspect aspects of the regime directly on behalf of the Home Secretary, may find it difficult to sustain a role as involved critics (Martin, 1980, pp. 85–101; Adams, 1981, pp. 6–8).

In short, the inescapable reality of imprisonment seems to be that the pattern of locking offenders up for relatively long periods in rather large institutions inevitably produces anger and hostility in them, which manifests itself from time to time in conflict with the authorities and on occasions collective rioting. Moreover, the prison mirrors the culture of the society in which it is located. The features of the riot and responses to it – its militaristic, confrontational nature – mirror to a large extent the culture of the prison system itself. In turn, features of the prison as an institution reflect aspects of society, displayed in responses to crime and collective protests and rioting. These comments are in the nature of reflections rather than a proven syllogism. But they raise the question which exercises the final part of this chapter, as to whether anything can be done to change the nature of prison riots, so as either to reduce their scale and impact or to prevent them altogether.

REDUCING OR PREVENTING PRISON RIOTS

There is little doubt that the issue of reducing or preventing prison riots, to the extent that it involves making decisions which will change the current trajectory of prison policies away from expansionism and large institutions, is primarily political. An associated political issue concerns the development of an adequate philosophy of imprisonment, in the post-rehabilitation era, not centred on containment but, for example, on anti-oppressive, non-discriminatory values. A corollary of these changes, in Britain and the US, would be more open, self-critical and self-aware, non-defensive approaches to managing prisons by the authorities, at all levels from government administrations to day-to-day work in prisons.

The above statements imply that only a cultural revolution in the running of penal systems and in the societies which endorse them will lead to the abolition of prison riots as we know them. However, it is also apparent that in the last quarter of the twentieth century, the post-rehabilitation prison has generated two contrasting streams of prisoner struggles, one reflecting the dominant macho values of imprisonment and the other challenging them.

Rutherford uses the illustration of the ambiguous sexual, racial and political identity of T.E. Lawrence – 'Lawrence of Arabia' – to reproduce the image of the desert, at the margins of society, as the setting for Lawrence's personal revaluation of his identity and values and his realization that his Arabian experience had liberated him from his traditional Englishness but not made him an Arab (Rutherford, 1990, p. 10). The prison riot is a setting similarly at the margins of society, yet capable of highlighting the centrality to society of what is happening. The displacement of the reformative and reha-bilitative ideals still allows the prison, partly through the challenging actions of prisoners, to provide the site for values taken for granted to be revaluated and reformed.

The fragmented riots of the 1970s onwards displayed the tendency for prisoners' actions in relation to imprisonment to be displaced from confrontation with the authorities into internecine conflicts among different groups. Complex issues arise when one considers not just prisoners in this connection, but the entire network of people associated with prison, as inhabitants and visitors. Some groups of staff may be almost as disempowered as prisoners. Other staff may wield disproportionately great power.

In some senses, then, riots in the post-rehabilitation prison hark back to the turn of the eighteenth century, when jailors and the more powerful prisoners were in alliance together. But nowadays often the consequence is anarchic violence. In another sense, there is the prospect of the courts ruling increasingly over increasing protest-prone and litigious prison populations. Alternatively, some commen-tators argue that the legislatures that control the prison budgets will tend to call the tune (Stastny and Tyrnauer, 1982, p. 208).

The context of prison riots coexists with them reflexively. The changes brought about by the political development of the market economy of many Western 'developed' countries since the 1970s have contradictory consequences in the penal field. The diversification of providers of penal and correctional facilities is demonstrated by the evidence of the presence of a rapidly growing private sector in the prison systems of the US (Bronick, 1989; General Accounting Office, 1991; Thomas, 1989) and Britain (Matthews, 1989), producing a novel and significant crop of political, economic and ethical issues.

Ironically, this plurality of providers strengthens the likelihood that the future of the prison will be viewed more and more in terms of a greater diversity than formerly of relationships between the custodians as providers, and the prisoners as consumers, of penal services. Consumerism individualizes the prisoner and does not take on board the social dimension of the state of imprisonment and, if being a consumer of prison services is not accompanied by real choices and spending power, it impoverishes as well. The market philosophy potentially impacts on the power relations between prisoners and their custodians. It has consequences for the identities of prisoners in terms of increased ambiguities and therefore enhanced possibilities for cultural innovation. For instance, they may be able to explore the extensive continuum between the identities of 'captive criminal' and 'empowered user' of the facilities of the prison. Even recognizing that the administration and management of correctional systems is more decentralized in the US than in Britain, the introduction of the market economy into prisons still contradicts the pressing logic of discipline and hierarchy which sustain these institutions at every level and in every sector of their operation.

Arendt's analysis of totalitarianism in the twentieth century invites a speculation about the danger of 'unorganized' rioting in the post-rehabilitation, fragmented prison, in that it may be the fruit of, and the germ of, prison regimes of terror and uncertainty (Arendt, 1973, p. 478). The fragmentation of the collectivities binding social order in the community and in the prison offers both hope and the horrifying psychotic nightmare, realized, for instance, at Santa Fe in 1980 in the carnage inflicted by prisoners on each other.

The trauma of riots persists for many years. The associations of 'Attica' and 'Strangeways' linger, memories of these riots of 1971 and 1990 far outweighing the actual knowledge people have of the prison itself. The confidence of staff and prisoners between themselves and in each other is shaken. Divisions among them are intensified.

Three ways forward can be envisaged: first, by making prisons eccentric rather than concentric to penal policy and ensuring that the penal institution is less central to bearing the burden of responsibility for public order.

Far too much effort by the authorities has been placed in the past on making prisons more secure and riotproof, with all the negative consequences of that for human relationships within the institutions. It would be more constructive to examine ways of making prisons less central, symbolically and materially, in penal systems. The mere fact that community-based ways of dealing with offenders tend to be labelled not in their own right but as 'alternatives to prison' illustrates the centrality of the image of the prison to most debates about penal policy and practice. Of course, shifting prisons from this central position is only the first stage, as Stastny and Tyrnauer recognize:

The first step in a constructive course of public policy will be to place much less reliance on imprisonment, except for the 'dangerous.' Next, the courts must stand firm in their insistence on constitutional standards. Finally, on the 'inside,' more open environments must be created, attuning the prison regime to democratic values.

(Stastny and Tyrnauer, 1982, p. 214)

Research indicating that two-thirds of those sentenced to probation are re-arrested within a 40-month follow-up period implies the need for the creation of meaningful alternative disposals between probation and prison, used in conjunction with a sentencing policy that takes into account predictors of the risk of re-offending, in the context of a 'just deserts' model. Using this, courts would base disposal decisions mainly on the conviction offence and then refer to factors correlated positively with recidivism to determine the nature of the community disposal or the length of sentence, the possibility of parole and so on (Petersilia *et al*, 1985, pp. 379–91).

Secondly, if prisons are to survive as prisons, there is a need for a positive philosophy for imprisonment to be created. It is easy to make this point, but, it has to be said, difficult in this present connection to envisage it being achieved in the immediate future.

The prison and its context are in a constant state of flux, as is the relationship between the prisoner and the institution. In such circumstances, the process by which the rioting prisoner, or indeed any inhabitant of the prison, staff included, attains an identity, is 'an interchange between self and structure, a transforming process. If the object remains static, ossified by tradition or isolated by a radically changing world, if its theoretical foundations cannot address that change, then its culture and politics lose their ability to innovate. Its symbolic language can only conjure up the past, freezing us in another moment' (Rutherford, 1990, p. 14). From a post-modern vantage point, the search for a new overarching philosophy for imprisonment is itself mistaken. It is akin to what Schon criticized as the illusory search for the stable state (Schon, 1970).

Thirdly, there is a need to transcend the fragmentation exemplified in riots of the post-rehabilitation prison. Irwin comments that the move towards significant prison union organizations and somewhat receptive prisoner administrations in California in the early 1970s collapsed in the wake of the disturbances of 1975 and January 1976:

In fact, across the country the concept of prisoners' having the right to organize and participate in decisionmaking now seems ludicrous to most prison administrators and the public. In the meantime, I have become more convinced that formal prisoner organizations with input in decisionmaking and access to independent grievance processes will be necessary to reestablish a safe prison and to establish for the first time a prison free from excessive punishment and arbitrary and malicious practices. Without this formal structure, many prisoners will remain divided into hostile factions and the majority will withdraw in fear. Administrations will continue in or lapse into self-serving and arbitrary practices.

(Irwin, 1980, p. 246)

The final official report into the causes and prevention of violence in the US emphasizes the need to avoid 'a decaying cycle in which resistance grows and becomes ever more violent'. This depends on a shift from purely punitive and controlling responses to a more balanced approach involving remedial action (National Commission on the Causes and Prevention of Violence, 1969, p. 2).

A more radical set of proposals for preventing prison riots arises from the user-perspective on their significance, which emphasizes the participation of prison users. It should be emphasized that users of prisons include all grades of full- and part-time staff and visitors, as well as the prisoners who live in them. According to this view, the key to preventing further rioting lies not so much with the authorities taking action in the light of what they guess prisoners are expressing, but rather in empowering prisoners to take action by more legitimate and socially approved means themselves. Participation by prisoners in the running of aspects of their prisons was tried in a few institutions in Britain in the early 1970s. The experiment in consultative management at Long Lartin prison was one of the few to be monitored with any degree of rigour (Shapland *et al.*, 1972). Such initiatives were precarious, prone to halting, by either the Home Office, as at Long Lartin, or a change of governor, as at Hull in the build-up to the riot of 1976. Yet a decade later, the rhetoric of democratic participation of prisoners in such 'safe' aspects of the regime as educational and creative activities, still persisted, at any rate, in Europe. (Council of Europe, 1986, p. 16) To date, the only area where this has been seriously considered in Britain is in the field of prison architecture. The value of the Prison Architecture Research Unit in London lies partly in its emphasis on prisoner participation. Audrey Lennox, its director, comments:

> A major problem is that people who plan and design prisons have never lived and worked within them. There is a two-way communication block; the providers do not really understand users and the way they go about their jobs, nor do users really understand designers' problems and what they are trying to do. The involvement of users and understanding of the social impact of design and the interaction of design and use are inescapable correlates of effective prison design and planning.
>
> (Personal communication to the author)

This approach needs to be extended to the running of Prisons as well.

After a tour by the American Foundation of prisons in the US in 1972, its director commented on the tokenism which underlay changes made to the architecture of prisons, arguing that *social* resistance to change is a feature of prison systems, at *all levels*:

> The prison experience too often corrodes those who guard and those who are guarded. This reality is not essentially the product of good or bad architecture. It is the inevitable product of a process that holds troubled people together in a closed and limited space, depriving them of their freedom, their families, and their humanity.
>
> (Nagel, 1977, pp. 154–5)

From a radical perspective, the rioters of Attica emerge as challenging not just the *use and abuse* of power by the authorities but its *legitimacy*. Their struggles are linked with the struggles of liberation movements in the US and the Third World, using arguments based on the common basis of domestic and foreign oppression to fuel revolutionary theory and practice. 'The prisoners at Attica were unlike their counterparts in the 1950s because they had no trust in the prison officials with whom they were dealing. Indeed, they challenged the ideology and structure of both the penal system and the large society' (Johnson and Dorin, 1978, p. 35).

From a radical perspective also, prisoners are not resigned to compliance or conformity, yet they do not revolt collectively. Their resistance is individual and fragmented. They adopt a pragmatic, survival-oriented individualized approach to 'making-out' in prison.

Johnson and Dorin's research illustrates this perspective. Their survey of inmates in all maximum security penal institutions in New York State and two major jails in New York City between 1871 and 1973 suggests that only three out of 146 prisoners in the total sample adopted a revolutionary stance, even though radical or militant in their views. The results suggest that the oppressed, typically black, prisoner on the receiving end of injustice develops strategies of coping, as a victim. Whilst some prisoners strike back angrily and violently, the majority curb and divert their rage:

> The sequence in which injustice spawns rage, which in turn must be suppressed or ventilated in indirect (safe) ways, is a theme that is related to the 'cool role' of black ghettos. The man who must live in a world comprised of arbitrary and often powerful others must cultivate a pose of detachment – whenever possible he must avoid trouble and refrain from actions that are likely to invite unmanageable confrontations . . . [So] experiences of victimization and resentment in prison thus typically spawn a pragmatic and cynical 'militancy,' not the uncompromising stance of the ideologue.
>
> (Johnson and Dorin, 1978, pp. 47, 49)

Prison riots themselves have changed. Since the 1960s, prison riots in the US and to a lesser extent in Britain have passed through a period of libertarian concern with social issues which seemed novel from the vantage point of the institution – race, poverty in the Third World, employment. For a decade or more, the challenges to imprisonment by prisoners were sustained by the simple polemics of anti-oppressive activity. From the mid-1970s, however, the practice of this simplistic assertion of collective unity was fragmenting and over the following decade, as the idealist Marxist positions and their derivatives fell apart in the politics of the Reagan and Thatcher years, it became clear that it was no longer sufficient for every issue to be collapsed into the uni-dimensional analysis of class politics or the activities of trade unionists. In Britain, Nemesis came in the 1984–5 miners' strike. The rhetoric of the now anachronistic Socialist Workers' Party and Militant continued. But it seemed increasingly authoritarian and inflexible in the face of the emerging realities of the strike, which were, for instance, that groups of women, regarded as marginal to cooperation, production and solidarity by men, and trade unionist miners especially, now assumed central importance as they organized national, regional and local networks for the collection and distribution of money, fuel and food, largely outside established bureaucratic Labour Party or trade union channels. Meanwhile, researchers were caught up in narrating the much more appealing and dramatic confrontations between miners and the authorities, which simply confirmed the traditional patterns of interaction between the machismo of both parties to the conflict.

One lesson for the study of prison riots is to examine the silences in the text. The account in preceding chapters inevitably follows the dominant preoccupations of discourse about prisons and rioting. Of course, this partly reflects the various processes, summarized in an adjacent context by Jupp (Jupp, 1989), by which research into riots has been channelled by the authorities. But the collapse of the treatment philosophy opened up the possibility of the surfacing of new and more complex formulations of the enduring antagonism between prisoners and the authorities, organized around heterogenous penal issues affecting women prisoners, black prisoners, Irish prisoners and remand prisoners. Through this process there was the possibility of the simplistic anachronism of class politics to be transcended as these categories, formerly marginalized or ignored, were now experienced as the primary bond between prisoners. What was learned from the experience of prison riots since the 1970s was that the identity of prisoners in all their diversity is not reducible to the deterministic logic of social class. For a dramatic illustration, the moving memoirs of Lady Lytton, imprisoned and force-fed during the suffragette protests, are echoed across divisions of race, religion and class in the various campaigns of women prisoners since the beginning of the twentieth century for the Irish republican cause (Lytton, 1976). What is significant is not simply the way women and men have protested without violence in Northern Irish prisons, but also the way this has generally been ignored by commentators.

Post-rehabilitation riots provide the stimulus to deconstruct the universalist assumptions of the Marxist analysis which in various forms sustained their predecessors during the consciousness-raising period. One outcome of this deconstruction may be what Rutherford calls a cultural politics of difference (Rutherford, 1990). Thus, whilst research has accurately identified issues such as long-term imprisonment (Scraton *et al.*, 1991) as central to the explanation of protests by prisoners in the latter quarter of the twentieth century, it is crucial that this factor does not dominate and exclude from consideration *any* experience of imprisonment which offers the setting for political antagonism between the authorities and prisoners.

The fragmented character of incidents points to the need to transcend the former globalized unities sought by rioters without replicating them. Post-rehabilitation riots put onto the agenda of discourse about penalty the diversity of prisoners and the issues of imprisonment. They offer the opportunity of responding to riots in ways which transcend and transform the dominant values of hierarchy, militarism, machismo, oppression and violence in the prison systems of Britain and the US, 'not attempting to construct oppositions based on hierarchies of value and power, not through the politics of polarity, but in the recognition of the otherness of ourselves, through the transformation of the relations of subordination and discrimination' (Rutherford, 1990, p. 26). The task is to move beyond the multifaceted oppressions replicated in repeated riots to an explanation of their politics which enables their differences to be reconciled, without containing them in false unity. This has repercussions for all people involved in prisons, as participants in, witnesses of, and respondents to riots. Prison riots are not so much a product of prison conditions as of the condition of imprisonment. It is the condition of imprisonment to which critical attention should now be addressed.

CONCLUSIONS

The origins of prison riots are inextricably associated with the way prisons are run. More broadly, the roots of prison riots lie in pervasive features of social control in society and in accompanying strategies of penal policy.

Overwhelmingly, prison riots in both the US and Britain have taken the form of confrontations between prisoners and their guards, which have often involved considerable violence on both sides. The traditional pattern of rioting took the form of *ad hoc* responses by prisoners, not involving an articulation by them of any specific demands, and often simply expressed by mutinying and trying to escape. The twentieth century, however, has witnessed a number of waves of prison riots, usually distinguished by prisoners making a number of complaints about prison conditions. In the second half of the century, there has been a trend towards prisoners engaging in more explicitly socialist, consciousness-raising rioting. Whereas earlier riots had focused attention on conditions *within* prisons, these later riots often challenged the dominant rehabilitative ideal of imprisonment.

In the last quarter of the twentieth century, as the philosophy of rehabilitation through imprisonment was discredited and declined, the nature of riots has changed. In this period, prison riots in the US and Britain have shifted the site of their challenges to the authorities from an exclusive focus on the macho confrontations between the 'heavy end' of long-sentence prisoners and the authorities to a more diversified continuum of rioting. In the process, the centrality has been confirmed of categories of prisoners hitherto shoved to the margin or rendered invisible, such as women prisoners, black prisoners, Irish republican prisoners, mentally ill and remand or trial prisoners.

The proliferation of institutional settings for challenges by prisoners has involved them often demonstrating abilities not simply to oppose, but to transcend the equations of violent confrontation which have for more than a century provided the rationale for a closed circle of repression by the authorities and counter-challenges by the prisoners. In this way, the riots of the post-rehabilitation period have kept open the opportunity for the reformulation of the sociology of the prison riot, around the proliferation of different social and political antagonisms and identities of imprisoned people.

It remains to be seen whether the trend towards a more public and pluralistic debate about the conditions of prisons that was furthered by Santa Fe, Hull and Strangeways will lead to improved conditions of imprisonment in Britain and the US. The challenge is to project a future for prisoners which transcends the patterns of violent confrontation which have been a feature of the intense divisions made more evident by these riots between prisoners and between prisoners and staff. Even if prison riots do not arise solely because of the inhuman and degrading impact of imprisonment on prisoners, they draw attention to the need for urgent penal reform.

Bibliography

Abbott, J.H., *In the Belly of the Beast: Letters from Prison* (New York: Random House, 1981).

Abeyie, D.G. (ed.), *The Criminal Justice System and Blacks* (New York: Clark Boardman, 1984).

Abolitionist, The No. 4, 1979, pp. 14–19.

Ackroyd, P., 'Crisis in the prisons', *The Spectator*, 27 January 1979 pp. 11–12.

Adams, G., *Cage Eleven* (Brandon, 1990).

Adams, R.W., 'Outsiders inside penal establishments: servants or reformers?' *AMBOV Quarterly*, No. 2, July, 1981, pp. 6–8.

Adams, R., 'Protests by Pupils', *Youth and Policy*, Vol. 21, 1987, pp. 28–35.

Adams, R., *Protests by Pupils: Empowerment, Schooling and the State* (London: Falmer Press, 1991).

Advisory Council on the Penal System *The Regime for Long-Term Prisoners in Conditions of Maximum Security*, Report of the Advisory Council on the Penal System, (Radzinovicz Report), (London: HMSO, 1968).

American Correctional Association, *Prison Riots and Disturbances* (New York: American Correctional Association, 1953).

American Correctional Association, *Causes, Preventive Measures and Methods of Controlling Riots and Disturbances in Correctional Institutions*, 3rd edn (New York: American Correctional Association, 1990).

Anon., 'Why convicts riot', *US News and World Report*, Vol. 33, 19 December 1952, pp. 18–21.

Anon., 'Aftermath of riot', *The Prison Journal*, Vol. 34, 1954, entire issue.

Anon., *Disturbances in British Prisons in 1976*, unpublished paper, Prison Service Staff College Library (Wakefield, 1976).

Anon., *United Troops Out Movement*, pamphlet, 1979.

Anon., 'Complex enforcement: unconstitutional prison conditions', *Harvard Law Review*, Vol. 94, 1981, pp. 626–46.

Arendt, H., *The Origins of Totalitarianism*, new edn (San Diego: Harcourt Brace Jovanovich, 1973).

Atlas, R., 'Violence in prison: environmental influences', *Environment and Behaviour*, Vol. 16, No. 3, 1984, pp. 275–306.

Baker, J.E., *The Right to Participate: Inmate Involvement in Prison Administration* (Metuchen, NJ: Scarecrow Press, 1974).

Banay, R.S., 'Why the prison alarm sounds', *New York Times Magazine*, 26 July 1959, pp. 8, 24–5.

Banfield, E.C., 'Rioting mainly for fun and profit', in Wilson, J.Q. (ed.), *The Metropolitan Enigma* (Cambridge, Mass.: Harvard University Press, 1968).

Barnes, H.E., *The Evolution of Penology in Pennsylvania: A Study in American Social History* (Montclair, NJ: Patterson Smith, 1968).

Baron, R.A., 'Aggression as a function of ambient temperature and prior anger arousal', *Journal of Personality and Social Psychology*, Vol. 21, 1972, pp. 183–9.

Baron, R.A. and Bell, P.A., Aggression and heat: mediating effects of prior provocation and exposure to an aggressive model', *Journal of Personality and Social Psychology*, Vol. 31, 1975, pp. 825–32.

Baron, R.A. and Bell, P.A., Aggression and heat: the influence of ambient temperature, negative affect, and a cooling drink on physical aggression', *Journal of Personality and Social Psychology*, Vol. 33, 1976 pp. 245–55.

Baron, R.A. and Lawton, S.F., 'Environmental influences on aggression: the facilitation of modelling effects by high ambient temperatures', *Psychonomic Science*, Vol. 26, 1973, pp. 80–2.

Bartollas, C., Miller, S. and Dinitz, S., *Juvenile Victimisation: The Institutional Paradox* (New York: Halstead Press, 1976).

Bateson, C., *The Convict Ships* (Glasgow: Brown, Son and Ferguson, 1985).

Beaumont, G. de and Tocqueville, A. de, *On the Penitentiary System in the United States and its Application in France* (Carbondale, Ill.: Southern Illinois University Press, 1979).

Bell, C. and Newby, H. (eds), *Doing Sociological Research* (London: Allen & Unwin, 1977).

Bell, D., *The End of Ideology* (Illinois: Free Press of Glencoe, 1960).

Bell, D., *The Coming of Post-Industrial Society: a venture in social forecasting* (New York: Basic Books, 1976).

Bell, M., *The Turkey Shoot: Tracking the Attica Cover-up* (New York: Grove Press 1985).

Berk, B.B., 'Organizational goals and inmate organization', *American Journal of Sociology*, Vol. 71, 1966, pp. 522–34.

Berkman, R., *Opening the Gates: The Rise of the Prisoners' Movement*, (Lexington, Mass.: D.C. Heath, 1979).

Bernat, B. 'NPP Lawyer Ed Koren: Attica started it all', *National Prison Project Journal*, No. 16, Summer 1988, pp. 12–14.

Bianchi, H., Simondi, M. and Taylor, I. (eds), *Deviance and Control in Europe: Papers from the European Group for the Study of Deviance and Social Control* (London: John Wiley, 1975).

Bidna, H., 'Effects of increased security on prison violence', *Journal of Criminal Justice*, Vol. 3, 1975, pp. 33–46.

Bok, C. *Star Wormwood* (New York: Knopf, 1959).

Bottomley, A.K., 'Implications for future policy and research', in Bottomley, A.K. and Hay, W. (eds), *Special Units for Difficult Prisoners* (Hull: University of Hull, 1991), pp. 105–14.

Bottoms, A., 'Reflections on the renaissance of dangerousness', *Howard Journal of Penology and Crime Prevention*, Vol. 16, No. 2, 1977, pp. 124–40.

Bottoms, A.E. and Light, R. (eds), *Problems of Long-term Imprisonment* (Aldershot: Gower, 1967).

Boyle, J., *A Sense of Freedom* (London: Pan, 1977).

Boyle, J., *The Pain of Confinement: Prison Diaries* (London: Pan, 1985).

Bramham, P., *How Staff Rule: Structures of authority in two community schools* (Farnborough, Teakfield, 1980).

Braswell, M., Dillingham, S. and Montgomery, R. Jr. (eds), *Prison Violence in America* (Cincinnati, Oh.: Anderson, 1985).

Breed, A. and Bright, B., 'An examination of the forces that influence criminal justice policy and its administration in England and Poland', in Wilson, T. (ed.), *Penal Services for Offenders: Comparative Studies of England and Poland 1984/85* (Aldershot: Avebury, 1987), pp. 23–37.

Breed, A. and Ward, D., *The United States Penitentiary, Marion, Illinois: A Report to the Judiciary Committee, United States House of Representatives* (Washington DC: House Judiciary Committee).

Brody, S.R., *The Effectiveness of Sentencing*, Home office Research Study No. 35 (London: HMSO, 1976).

Bronick, M.J., *The Federal Bureau of Prisons' Use of Private Correctional Facilities to Relieve Subpopulation Pressures* (Washington: Federal Bureau of Prisons, 1989).

Bronstein, A.J., 'Neglect of prisons reaps high costs for society, *National Prison Project Journal*, No. 7, Spring 1986, pp. 12–15.

Brown, R.M., 'The American vigilante tradition', in Turner, R.H. and Killian, L.M. (eds), *Collective Behaviour*, 3rd edn (Englewood Cliffs, NJ: Prentice-Hall, 1975).

Buckley, M., *The Jangle of the Keys* (Dublin: James Duffy, 1938).

Bunker, E., 'War behind walls', *Harper's Magazine*, February 1972, pp. 39–47.

Burns, H., 'Remembering Attica', *National Prison Project Journal*, No. 13, Fall 1987, pp. 5–7.

Butler, K., 'The Muslims are no longer an unknown quantity', *Corrections Magazine*, Vol. 4, Part 2, 1978, pp. 55–7, 60–3.

Cahalan, M., 'Trends in incarceration in the United States since 1880: a summary of reported rates and the distribution of offences', *Crime and Delinquency*, Vol. 25, 1979, pp. 9–41.

Caird, R., *A Good and Useful Life: Imprisonment in Britain Today* (London: Hart-Davis, MacGibbon, 1974).

Calvert, P., *Revolution and Counter Revolution* (Milton Keynes: Open University Press, 1990).

Campbell, D., 'Switching of disruptive prisoners "inhumane"', *Guardian*, 6 May 1991, p. 4.

Caplan, N.S. and Paige, J.M., 'A study of ghetto rioters', *Scientific American*, Vol. 219, No. 2, August 1968, pp. 15–21.

Carney, J.T., 'Wicker at Attica', *Yale Law Journal*, Vol. 85, 1975, pp. 150–8 (review of Wicker, 1975).

Cavadino, P., 'The research case for shorter prison sentences', *New Society*, Vol. 56, No. 961, 1981, pp. 91–3.

Chambliss, W.J., 'The state, the law and the definition of behaviour as criminal or delinquent', in Glaser, D. (ed.), *Handbook of Criminology* (Chicago: Rand-McNally, 1974), pp. 7–43.

Charrière, H., *Papillon* (New York: Basic Books, 1970).

Chatwin, B., *Utz* (London: Pan, 1989).

Christianson, S., 'Corrections law developments: prison labor and unionization – legal developments', *Criminal Law Bulletin*, Vol. 14, 1978, pp. 243–7.

Clavell, J., *King Rat* (London: Hodder & Stoughton, 1975).

Cleaver, E., *Soul on Ice* (New York: Dell, 1968).

Clemmer, D., *The Prison Community* (New York: Rinehart, 1940).

Clemmer, D., *The Prison Community*, 2nd edn (New York: Holt, Rinehart & Winston, 1958),

Clemmer, D., 'The process of prisonization', in Leger, R.G. and Stratton, J.R.

(eds), *The Sociology of Corrections: A Book of Readings* (New York: John Wiley, 1977), pp. 175–80).

Cloward, R.A., 'Social control in prison', in Cloward, R.A. *et al.* (eds), *Theoretical Studies in Social Organization of the Prison* (New York: Social Science Research Council, 1960).

Cloward, R.A., 'Social control in the prison', in Leger, R.G. and Stratton, J.R. (eds), *The Sociology of Corrections: A Book of Readings* (New York: John Wiley, 1977), pp. 110–32.

Cloward, R.A. *et al.* (eds), *Theoretical Studies in Social Organization of the Prison* (New York: Social Science Research Council, 1960).

Cohen, A.K., Cole, G.F. and Bailey, R.G. (eds), *Prison Violence* (Lexington, Mass.: D.C. Heath, 1976).

Colvin, M., 'The 1980 New Mexico Prison riot', *Social Problems*, Vol. 29, No. 5, June 1982, pp. 449–63.

Cohen, S., 'It's all right for you to talk: political and sociological manifestos for social work action', in Bailey, R. and Brake, M. (eds), *Radical Social Work* (London: Edward Arnold, 1975), pp. 75–95.

Cohen, S., 'Prisons and the future of control systems: from concentration to dispersal', in Fitzgerald, M. *et al.* (eds), *Prisoners in Revolt* (Harmondsworth: Penguin, 1977), pp. 217–28.

Cohen, S., *Visions of Social Control: Crime, Punishment and Classification* (Cambridge: Polity Press, 1985).

Cohen, S. and Taylor, L., *Psychological Survival: The Experience of Long-term Imprisonment* (Harmondsworth: Penguin, 1972).

Cohen, S. and Taylor, L., 'Talking about prison blues', in Bell, C. and Newby, H. (eds), *Doing Sociological Research* (London: Allen & Unwin, 1977), pp.

Cohen, S. and Taylor, L., *Prison Secrets* (London: Radical Alternatives to Prison/National Council for Civil Liberties, 1978).

Coleman, J., *Against the State: Studies in Sedition and Rebellion* (London: BBC Books, 1990).

Colvin, M. 'The 1980 New Mexico prison riot', *Social Problems*, Vol. 29, No. 5, June 1982, pp. 449–63.

Conrad, J.P., 'The researcher's work is never done', in Goodstein, L. and Mackenzie, D.L. (eds), *The American Prison: Issues in Research and Policy* (New York: Plenum Press, 1989), pp. 273–86.

Council of Europe, *Prison Regimes*, European Committee on Crime Problems, Strasbourg: Council of Europe, 1986.

Cox, V.C. *et al.*, 'Prison crowding research: the relevance for prison housing standards and a general approach regarding crowding phenomena', *American Sociologist*, Vol. 39, 1984, pp. 1148–60.

Cressey, D.R. (ed.), *The Prison: Studies in Institutional Organization and Change* (New York: Holt, Rinehart & Winston, 1961).

Cressey, D.R., 'A confrontation of violent dynamics', *International Journal of Psychiatry*, Vol. 10, No. 3, September 1972, pp. 93–108.

Cullen, F.T. and Gendreau, P., 'The effectiveness of correctional rehabilitation: reconsidering the "nothing works" debate', in Goodstein, L. and MacKenzie, D.L. (eds), *The American Prison: Issues in Research and Policy* (New York: Plenum Press, 1989), pp. 23–44.

Dickens, C., *American Notes* (London: Collins, 1906).

Cunningham, D. and Susler, J., *A Public Report About a Violent Mass Assault Against Prisoners and Continuing Illegal Punishment and Torture of the Prison Population at the US Penitentiary at Marion*, Illinois (a public release by attorneys of the Marion Prisoners' Rights Project, 1984).

D'Atri, D.A., 'Measuring stress in prison', in Ward, D.A. and Schoen, K.F. (eds), *Confinement in Maximum Custody* (Lexington, Mass.: D.C. Heath, 1981), pp. 27–38.

D'Atri, D.A. *et al.*, 'Crowding in prison: the relationship between changes in housing mode and blood pressure', *Psychosomatic Medicine*, Vol. 43, No. 2, April 1981, pp. 95–105.

Davidson, R.T., *Chicano Prisoners: The Key to San Quentin* (New York: Holt, Rinehard & Winston, 1974).

Davies, J.C., 'Toward a theory of revolution', *American Sociological Review*, Vol. 27, No. 1, February 1962, pp. 5–19.

Dillingham, S.D. and Montgomery, R.H., 'Prison riots: a corrections' nightmare since 1774', in Braswell, M., Dillingham, S. and Montgomery, R. Jr. (eds), *Prison Violence in America* (Cincinnati, Oh.: Anderson, 1985), pp. 19–35.

Ditchfield, J., *Control in Prisons: a review of the literature*, Home Office Research Study No. 118 (London: HMSO, 1990).

Doleschal, E., 'Rate and length of imprisonment: how does the United States compare with the Netherlands, Denmark, and Sweden', *Crime and Delinquency*, January 1977, pp. 51–6.

Downes, D., *Contrasts in Tolerance: Post-war Penal Policy in the Netherlands and England and Wales* (Oxford: Clarendon Press, 1988).

Du Parcq, H., *On the Circumstances Connected with the Recent Disorder at Dartmoor Convict Prison*, Cmd 4010 (London: HMSO, 1932).

Eckstein, H. (ed.), *Internal War: Problems and Approaches* (New York: Free Press of Glencoe, 1964).

Edwards, G., 'Symposium – Prisoners' Rights: foreword – penitentiaries produce no penitents', *Journal of Criminal Law, Criminology and Policy Science*, Vol. 63, No. 2, 1972, pp. 154–61.

Ekland-Olson, S., 'Crowding, social control, and prison violence: evidence from the post-*Ruiz* years in Texas', *Law and Society Review*, Vol. 20, No. 3, 1986, pp. 389–421.

Ellis, D., 'Crowding and prison violence: integration of research and theory', *Criminal Justice and Behaviour*, Vol. 11, No. 3, 1984, pp. 277–308.

Engel, K. and Rothman, S., 'Prison violence and the paradox of reform', *The Public Interest*, Vol. 73, 1983, pp. 91–105.

Erikson, K.T., *Wayward Puritans: A Study in the Sociology of Deviance* (New York: John Wiley and Sons, 1966).

Etzioni, A., *A Comparative Analysis of Complex Organizations* 2nd edn (New York: Free Press, 1975).

Evans, P., *Prison Crisis* (London: Allen & Unwin, 1980).

Evans, R., *The Fabrication of Virtue: English Prison Architecture 1750–1840* (Cambridge University Press, 1982).

Farrington, D.P. and Nuttall, C.P., 'Prison size, overcrowding prison violence, and recidivism', *Journal of Criminal Justice*, Vol. 8, 1980, pp. 221–31.

Featherstone, M., *Consumer Culture and Postmodernism* (London: Sage, 1991).

Feldman, A., 'Violence and volatility: the likelihood of revolution', in Eckstein, H. (ed.), *Internal War: Problems and Approaches* (New York: Free Press of Glencoe, 1964).

Fillmore, J., 'Strike', in R.J. Minton (1971), pp. 69–80.

Fine, B. *et al.* (eds), *Capitalism and the Rule of Law: From Deviancy Theory to Marxism* (London: Hutchinson, 1979).

Fitch, T. and Tepper, J., 'No time to talk, hour by hour at Attica', *Christianity and Crisis*, 18 October 1971, pp. 211–16.

Fitzgerald, M., *Prisoners in Revolt* (Harmondsworth: Penguin, 1977).

Fitzgerald, M. and Sim, J., *British Prisons*, 2nd edn (Oxford: Blackwell, 1982).

Fitzgerald, M. *et al.* (eds), *Welfare in Action* (London: Routledge & Kegan Paul, 1977).

Fitzmaurice, C. and Pease, K., 'Prison sentences and population: a comparison of some European countries', *Justice of the Peace*, Vol. 146, 1982, pp. 575–9.

Flanagan, T.J., 'Dealing with long-term confinement: adaptive strategies and perspectives among long-term prisoners', *Criminal Justice and Behaviour*, Vol. 8, No. 2, June 1981, pp. 201–22.

Flynn, F.T., 'Behind the prison riots', *Social Service Review*, Vol. xxvii, No. 1, March 1953, pp. 73–86.

Foucault, M., *Madness and Civilization*, trans. Richard Howard (London: Tavistock, 1967).

Foucault, M., *Surveiller et Punir: Naissance de la Prison* (Paris: Gallimard, 1975); trans. by Sherridan, A. as *Discipline and Punish: The Birth of the Prison* (London: Allen Lane, 1982).

Foucault, M., *The History of Sexuality, Vol. 1: An Introduction* (London: Allen Lane, 1979).

Fox, V., *Violence Behind Bars* (New York: Vantage Press, 1956).

Fox, V., 'Why prisoners riot', *Federal Probation*, Vol. 3, Part 1, March 1971, pp. 9–15.

Fox, V., 'Prison riots in a democratic society', *Police*, Vol. 16, No. 33, 1972, pp. 40–4.

Frankenberg, R. (ed.), *Custom and Conflict in British Society* (Manchester University Press, 1982).

Franklin, H.B., *Prison Literature in America* (Westport, Conn.: Lawrence Hill, 1982).

Fraser, G., 'Black prisoners embrace new view of themselves as political victims', *New York Times*, 16 September 1971, p. 49.

Friedman, L.M., *A History of American Law* (New York: Simon & Schuster, 1973).

Fry, L.J., 'The impact of formal inmate structure on opposition to staff and treatment goals', *British Journal of Criminology*, Vol. 16, No. 2, April 1976, pp. 126–40.

Fuller, D. and Orsagh, T., 'Violence and victimization within a state prison', *Criminal Justice Review*, No. 2, 1977, pp. 35–55.

Geary, D., *European Labour Protest 1848–1939* (London: Methuen, 1981).

Gaes, G. and McGuire, W.J., 'Prison violence: the contribution of crowding versus other determinants of prison assault rates', *Journal of Research in Crime and Delinquency*, Vol. 22, No. 1, February 1985, pp. 41–65.

Gallego, G., *Hombres en la cárcel* (Madrid: Libertarias-Prodhufi, 1990).

Galtung, J., 'A structural theory of aggression', *Journal of Peace Research*, Vol. 1, No. 2, (1964), pp. 95–119.

Garson, G.D., 'Force versus restraint in prison riots', *Crime and Delinquency*, Vol. 18, October 1972, pp. 411–21.

Geertz, C., 'Is America by nature a violent society?', *New York Times Magazine*, 21 April 1968.

Giallombardo, R., *Society of Women: A Study of a Women's Prison* (New York: John Wiley and Sons, 1966).

Gladstone, H., *Report of the Departmental Committee on Prisons* (C. 7702) London, 1895.

Glaser, D., *The Effectiveness of a Prison and Parole System* (Indianapolis, Ind.: Bobbs-Merrill, 1964).

Glaser, D., *Handbook of Criminology* (Chicago: Rand McNally, 1974).

Glaser, D., 'Politicization of prisoners: a new challenge to American penology', in Peterson, D. and Thomas, C. (eds), *Corrections: Problems and Prospects* (Englewood Cliffs, NJ: Prentice-Hall, 1971), pp. 189–210.

Glazer, N. and Moynihan, D.P., *Beyond the Melting Pot*, 2nd edn (Cambridge, Mass.: Massachusetts Institute of Technology Press, 1970).

Goffman, E., *Asylums* (Harmondsworth: Penguin, 1961).

Goodstein, L. and Mackenzie, D.L., 'Racial differences in adjustment patterns of prison inmates – prisonization, conflict stress and control', in Abeyie, D.G. (ed.), *The Criminal Justice System and Blacks* (New York: Clark Boardman, 1984).

Goodstein, L. and Mackenzie, D.L. (eds), *The American Prison: Issues in Research and Policy* (New York: Plenum Press, 1989).

Goodstein, L. and Wright, K.N., 'Inmate adjustment to prison', in Goodstein, L. and Mackenzie, D.L. (eds), *The American Prison: Issues in Research and Policy* (New York: Plenum Press, 1989), pp. 229–51.

Gosling, D., 'Rawls in the nonideal world: an evaluation of the Rawlsian account of civil disobedience', in Warner, M. and Crisp, R. (eds), *Terrorism, Protest and Power* (Aldershot: Edward Elgar, 1990), pp. 81–95.

Gove, W.R. and Hughes, M., 'The effects of crowding found in the Toronto study: some methodological and empirical questions', *American Sociological Review*, Vol. 45, 1980, pp. 864–70.

Grusky, O., 'Role conflict in organization: a study of prison camp officials', *Administrative Science Quarterly*, Vol. 3, 1959, pp. 452–72.

Gunn, J., Robertson, G., Dell, S. and Way, C., *Psychiatric Aspects of Imprisonment* (London: Academic Press, 1978).

Gurr, T.R., *Why Men Rebel* (Princeton, NJ: Princeton University Press, 1970).

Gurr, T.R., *Rogues, Rebels and Reformers: A Political History of Urban Crime and Conflict* (Beverly Hills, Calif.: Sage, 1976).

Gurr, T.R., 'The history of protest, rebellion, and reform in America: an Overview', in Gurr, E.R. (ed.), *Violence in America, Vol. 2, Protest, Rebellion, Reform* (Newbury Park, Calif.: Sage, 1989).

Gurr, T.R. (ed.), *Violence in America, Vol. 2, Protest, Rebellion, Reform* (Newbury Park, Calif.: Sage, 1989).

Hannum, R.R., 'An experience with inmate attitudes and grievances in a prison riot', *The Prison Journal*, Vol. 33, No. 1, April 1953, pp. 23–4.

Harding, C. and Koffman, L., *Sentencing and the Penal System: Text and Materials* (London: Sweet and Maxwell, 1988).

Harrison, P.J. and Stevens, C.F., 'A Bayesian approach to short-term forecasting', *Operational Research Quarterly*, Vol. 22, 1971, pp. 341–62.

Harsh, R., 'Inside Attica', *Christianity and Crisis*, 29 May 1972, pp. 127–38.

Hartung, F.E. and Floch, M., 'A socio-psychological analysis of prison riots', *Journal of Criminal Law, Criminology and Police Science*, No. 1, May–June 1956, Vol. 47, pp. 51–7.

Harvey, L., *Critical Social Research* (London: Unwin Hyman, 1990).

Hawkins, G., *The Prison: Policy and Practice* (University of Chicago Press, 1976).

Hawkins, R. and Alpert, G.P., *American Prison Systems: Punishment and Justice* (Englewood Cliffs, NJ: Prentice-Hall, 1989).

Hazelrigg, L.E. (ed.), *Prison Within Society: A Reader in Penology* (New York: Doubleday, 1968).

Heaps, W., *Riots U.S.A. 1765–1965* (New York: Seabury Press, 1966).

Hibbert, C., *The Roots of Evil: A Social History of Crime and Punishment* (Harmondsworth: Penguin, 1966).

Hill, P., *Stolen Years: Before and After Guildford* (London: Corgi, 1911).

Hillman, R.G., 'The psychopathology of being held hostage', *American Journal of Psychiatry*, Vol. 138, No. 9, September 1981, pp. 1193–7.

Holland, 'Dying men who stir the boiling pot', *New Statesman*, 5 December 1980, pp. 8–9.

Howard, D.L., *The English Prisons* (London: Methuen, 1960).

Howard, J., *The State of the Prisons* (Abingdon: Professional Books, 1977) (facsimile of 1777 edition).

Hugill, B. and Rose, D., 'No hope in no-go land', *Observer*, 15 September 1991, p. 23.

Hundley, J.R. Jr., 'Interaction between the crowd and social control agencies', in Turner, R.H. and Killian, L.M. (eds), *Collective Behaviour*, 3rd edn (Englewood Cliffs, NJ: Prentice-Hall, 1975).

Hutcheon, L., *The Politics of Postmodernism* (London: Routledge, 1989).

Hyman, R., *Strikes*, 3rd edn (London: Fontana, 1984).

Ignatieff, M., *A Just Measure of Pain: The Penitentiary in the Industrial Revolution* (London: Macmillan, 1978).

Ignatieff, M., 'State, civil society, and total institutions: a critique of recent social histories of punishment', in Tonry, M. and Morris, N. (eds), *Crime and Justice, Vol. 3*, (University of Chicago Press, 1981), pp. 153–92.

Independent Committee of Inquiry, *The Roof Comes Off: The Report of the Independent Committee of Inquiry into the Protests at Peterhead Prison* (Edinburgh: Gateway Exchange, 1987).

Inkeles, A., Coleman, J. and Smelser, N. (eds), *Annual Review of Sociology, Vol. 1* (Palo Alto, Calif.: Annual Reviews, 1975).

Irwin, J., *The Felon* (Englewood Cliffs, NJ: Prenctice-Hall, 1970).

Irwin, J., *Prisons in Turmoil* (Boston, Mass.: Little, Brown, 1980).

Irwin, J., *The Jail: Managing the Underclass in American Society* (Berkeley, Calif.: University of California Press, 1985).

Irwin, J.K., 'Sociological studies of the impact of long-term confinement', in Ward, D.A. and Schoen, K.F. (eds), *Confinement in Maximum Custody* (Lexington, Mass.: D.C. Heath, 1981), pp. 49–60.

Irwin, J. and Cressey, D., 'Thieves, convicts, and the inmate culture', *Social Problems*, Fall 1963, pp. 145–8.

Jackson, G., *Soledad Brother* (New York: Bantam Books, 1970).

Jacobs, J.B., 'Street gangs behind bars', *Social Problems*, Vol. 21, No. 3, 1974, pp. 395–409.

Jacobs, J.B., 'Stateville: the penitentiary in mass society', (University of Chicago Press, 1977).

Jacobs, J.B., *New Perspectives on Prisons and Imprisonment* (Ithaca, NY: Cornell University Press, 1983).

Jacobs, J.B. and Retsky, H.G., 'Prison guard', in Leger, R.G. and Stratton, J.R. (eds), *The Sociology of Corrections: A Book of Readings* (New York: John Wiley, 1977), pp. 49–65.

James, L.R. and Jones, A.P., 'Organizational climate: a review of theory and research', *Psychological Bulletin*, Vol. 81, No. 12, 1974, pp. 1096–112.

Jankovic, I., 'Labor market and imprisonment', *Crime and Social Justice*, Fall–Winter 1977, pp. 17–31.

Jenkins, J.C., What is to be done: movement or organization?', *Contemporary Sociology*, Vol. 8, No. 2, 1979, pp. 222–8 (review of Piven and Cloward, 1977).

Jepson, N., 'Administration: staff structure and training today', in McConville, S. (ed.), *The Use of Imprisonment: Essays in the Changing State of English Penal Policy* (London: Routledge & Kegan Paul, 1975), pp. 17–31.

Jepson, N.A., *Stone Walls Do Not a Prison Make: Institutional Challenge to Education and Social Work*, Thirteenth Mansbridge Memorial Lecture, University of Leeds, 1986.

Johnson, E.H., 'Sociology of confinement: assimilation and the prison "rat"', *Journal of Criminal Law, Criminology and Police Science*, Vol. 51, 1961, pp. 528–33.

Johnson, R. and Dorin, D.D., 'Dysfunctional ideology: the black revolutionary in prison', in Szabo, D. and Katzenelson, S. (eds), *Offenders and Corrections* (New York: Praeger, 1978), pp. 31–52.

Johnston, J.A., *Alcatraz: Island Prison* (New York: Charles Scribner, 1949).

Johnston, N., *The Human Cage: A Brief History of Prison Architecture* (New York: Walker, 1973).

Jones, H., Cornes, P. and Stockford, R., *Open Prisons* (London: Routledge & Kegan Paul, 1977).

Jones, K. and Fowles, A.J., *Ideas on Institutions: Analysing the literature on long-term care and custody* (London: Routledge & Kegan Paul, 1984).

Jupp, V., *Methods of Criminological Research* (London, Unwin Hyman, 1989).

Katz, I., 'Vendetta triggered Cardiff "bread riots", *Guardian*, 3 September 1991, p. 3.

Keller, O.J., 'Cuban detainees face further frustration, unfair treatment', *National Prison Project Journal*, No. 17, Fall 1988, pp. 24–6.

Kettle, M., 'Prison officers, the inside story', *New Society*, Vol. 49, No. 879, 1979, pp. 292–5.

Kettle, M. and Hodges, L., Uprising: The Police, the People and the Riots in Britain's Cities (London: Pan, 1982).

King, R.D. and Elliott, K.W., *Albany: birth of a prison, and of an era* (London: Routledge and Kegan Paul, 1977).

King, R.D., Morgan, R., Martin, J.P. and Thomas, J.E., *The Future of the Prison System* (Farnborough: Gower, 1980).

King, R.D. and McDermott, K., 'British prisons 1970–1987: the ever-deepening crisis' *British Journal of Criminology*, Vol. 29, No. 2, Spring 1989, pp. 107–28.

Klare, H., *Anatomy of Prison* (Harmondsworth: Penguin, 1962).

Korn, R.R. and McKorkle, L.W., *Criminology and Penology* (New York: Henry Holt, 1959).

Kornhauser, W., *The Politics of Mass Society* (New York: Free Press, 1959).

Kovach, W., 'Protesting prisoners in Massachusetts were attuned to Attica', *New York Times*, 3 October 1971.

Krysmanski, H.J., *Soziologie des Konfliktes* (Hamburg: Rohwolt, 1971).

Kuhn, S., *The Structure of Scientific Revolution* (Chicago: University of Chicago Press, 1970).

Le Bon, G., *The Crowd* (London: Ernest Benn, 1952).

Lee, A.M. and Humphrey, N.D., *Race Riot* (New York: Dryden Press, 1943).

Leger, R.G. and Stratton, J.R. (eds), *The Sociology of Corrections: A Book of Readings* (New York: John Wiley, 1977).

Lennox, A., 'De-coding the imagery of prisons: what role for environmental psychology?', *Journal of Environmental Psychology*, Vol. 10, 1990, pp. 273–84 (review article).

Levi, P., *If This Is a Man* (London: Sphere, 1987); trans. by Stuart Woolf from *Se questo è uomo* (Giulio Einaudi, 1958).

Liazos, A., 'Nuts, sluts and preverts [sic]', in Fitzgerald, M. *et al.* (eds), *Welfare in Action* (London: Routledge & Kegan Paul, 1977), pp. 37–47.

Lieberson, S. and Silverman, A.R., 'The precipitants and underlying conditions of race riots', *American Sociological Review*, December 1965, pp. 887–98.

Lindner, R., *Prescription for Rebellion* (London: Gollancz, 1953).

Logan, C.H., 'Proprietary prisons', in Goodstein, L. and MacKenzie, D.L. (eds), *The American Prison: Issues in Research and Policy* (New York: Plenum Press, 1989), pp. 45–62.

Lohman, J.D., *The Police and Minority Groups* (Chicago: Chicago Park District, 1947).

London Armagh Group, 'Strip searches in Armagh jail', *Women Behind the Wire*, No. 2, 1984.

Lopez, M. and Fathi, D., 'The lost meaning of *Whitley* v. *Albers*', *National Prison Project Journal*, Vol. 5, No. 3, Summer 1990, pp. 3–5.

Lukes, S., *Power: A Radical View* (London: Macmillan, 1978).

Lytton, Lady C., *Prisons and Prisoners: experiences of a suffragette* (Wakefield: E.P. Publishing, 1976).

McCleery, R.H., 'The governmental process and informal social control', in Cressey, D.R. (ed.), *The Prison: Studies in Institutional Organization and Change* (New York: Holt, Rinehart & Winston, 1961), pp. 149–88.

McConville, S. (ed.), *The Use of Imprisonment: Essays in the Changing State of English Penal Policy* (London: Routledge & Kegan Paul, 1975).

McConville, S., *A History of English Prison Administration, Volume 1 1750–1877* (London: Routledge & Kegan Paul, 1981).

McCorkle, L. and Korn, R., Resocialization within the Walls, *Annals of the*

American Academy of Political and Social Sciences, No. 293, May 1954, pp. 88–98.

MacCormick, A.H., 'Behind the prison riots', *Annals of the American Academy of Political and Social Science*, No. 293, 1954, pp. 17–27.

McCoy, J., *Concrete Mama: Prison Profiles from Walla Walla* (Columbia, M. University of Missouri Press, 1981).

MacDonald, D. and Sim, J., *Scottish Prisons and the Special Unit* (Edinburgh: Scottish Council for Civil Liberties, 1978).

McGraw, P. and McGraw, W., *Assignment: Prison Riots* (New York: Henry Holt, 1954).

McGuffin, J., *Internment* (Tralee, County Kerry: Anvil Books, 1973).

McGurk, B.J., Thornton, D.M. and Williams, M. (eds), *Applying Psychology to Imprisonment – Theory and Practice* (London: HMSO, 1987).

McKelvey, B., *American Prisons: A Study in American Social History Prior to 1915* (Montclair, NJ: Patterson Smith, 1968).

Mahan, S., 'An "orgy of brutality" at Attica and the "killing ground" at Santa Fe: a comparison of prison riots', in Parisi, N. (ed.), *Coping with Imprisonment* (Beverly Hills, Calif.: Sage, 1982), pp. 65–78.

Marion Prisoners' Rights Project, *Marion Prisoners' Rights Project to the Judiciary Committee* (MPRP attorneys' report to the House Judiciary Committee, November 1984.

Marquart, J.W. and Crouch, B.M., 'Coopting the kept: using inmates for social control in a southern prison', *Justice Quarterly*, Vol. 1, 1984, pp. 491–509.

Marquart, J.W. and Crouch, B.M., 'Judicial reform and prisoner control: the impact of *Ruiz* v. *Estelle* on a Texas penitentiary', *Law and Society Review*, 1985, Vol. 27, No. 3, pp. 554–72.

Marquart, J.W. and Roebuck, J.B., 'Prison guards and 'snitches': deviance within a total institution', *British Journal of Criminology*, Vol. 25, No. 3, July 1985, pp. 217–33.

Martin, J.B., 'The riot at Jackson prison', *Saturday Evening Post*, 6 June 1953, Vol. 225, pp. 17–19, 46, 48, 51.

Martin, J.B., *Break Down the Walls* (New York: Ballantine Books, 1955).

Martin, J.P., *Jellicoe and after – Boards of Visitors into the eighties, Howard Journal*, Vol. XIX, 1980, pp. 85–101.

Martin, S.J. and Eckland-Olson, S., 'Texas prisons: The walls came tumbling down', (Austin: *Texas Monthly Press*, 1987).

Marx, G.T. and Wood, J.L., 'Strands of theory and research in collective behaviour', in Inkeles, A., Coleman, J. and Smelser, N. (eds), *Annual Review of Sociology*, Vol. 1 (Palo Alto, Calif.: Annual Reviews, 1975), pp. 363–428.

Mathiesen, T., *The Defences of the Weak: A Sociological Study of a Norwegian Correctional Institution* (London: Tavistock, 1966).

Mathiesen, T., *The Politics of Abolition: Essays in Political Action Theory* (Oxford: Martin Robertson, 1974).

Mathiesen, T. and Roine, W., 'The prison movement in Scandinavia', in Bianchi, H., Simondi, M. and Taylor, I. (eds), *Deviance and Control in Europe: Papers from the European Group for the Study of Deviance and Social Control* (London: John Wiley, 1975), pp. 85–95.

Matthews, R., 'Decarceration and the fiscal crisis', in Fine, B. *et al.* (eds), *Capitalism and the Rule of Law: From Deviancy Theory to Marxism* (London:

Hutchinson, 1979), pp. 100–17.

Matthews, R. (ed.), *Privatizing Criminal Justice* (London: Sage, 1989).

Megargee, E.I., 'The association of population density, reduced space, and uncomfortable temperatures with misconduct in a prison community', *American Journal of Community Psychology*, Vol. 5, No. 3, 1977, pp. 289–98.

Melossi, D. and Pavarini, M., *Carcere e fabbrica* (Bologna: Il Mulino, 1977); trans. as *The Prison and the Factory: Origins of the Penitentiary System* (London: Macmillan, 1981).

Messinger, S., *Strategies of Control*, unpublished MS, Center for the Study of Law and Society, University of California, Berkeley, 1969.

Minton, R.J., *Inside: Prison American Style* (New York: Random House, 1971).

Molineux, E.L., *Riots in Cities and Their Suppression* (Boston, Mass.: Headquarters First Brigade, 1984.

Moore, J.W. with others, *Homeboys: Gangs, Drugs and Prison in the Barrios of Los Angeles* (Philadelphia: Temple University Press, 1978).

Moos, R.H., 'The assessment of the social climates of correctional institutions', *Journal of Research in Crime and Delinquency*, Vol. 5, 1968, pp. 174–88.

Morgan, R., *Formulating Penal Policy: The Future of the Advisory Council on the Penal System* (London: NACRO, 1979).

Morris, N., *The Future of Imprisonment* (University of Chicago Press, 1974).

Morris, R., *The Devil's Butcher Shop: The New Mexico Prison Uprising* (New York: Franklin Watts, 1983).

Murray, C., *Losing Ground: American Social Policy 1950–80* (New York: Basic Books, 1984).

Murton, T.O., 'Prison management: the past, the present and the possible future', in Wolfgang, M.E. (ed.), *Prisons: Present and Possible* (Lexington, Mass.: D.C. Heath, 1979), pp. 5–53.

Mountbatten Report, *Report of the Inquiry into Prison Escapes and Security*, Cmnd 3175 (London: HMSO, 1966).

Nacci, P.L., Teitelbaum, H.E. and Prather, J., 'Population density and inmate misconduct rates in the federal prison system', *Federal Probation*, No. 41, 1977, pp. 26–31.

Nagel, W.G., *On Behalf of a Moratorium on Prison Construction Crime and Delinquency*, April 1977, pp. 154–72.

Nokes, P., *The Professional Task in Welfare Practice* (London: Routledge & Kegan Paul, 1967).

Ohlin, L.E., *Sociology and the Field of Corrections* (New York: Russell Sage Foundation, 1956).

Ohlin, L.E. *et al.*, 'An overview of issues related to long-term confinement', in Ward, D.A. and Schoen, K.F. (eds), *Confinement in Maximum Custody* (Lexington, Mass.: D.C. Heath, 1981), pp. 177–94.

Olivero, J.M. and Roberts, J.B. 'Marion Federal Penitentiary and the 22-month lockdown: the crisis continues', *Crime and Social Justice*, Vol. 28, Nos 27–8, 1987, pp. 234–55.

Olson, M. Jr., *The Logic of Collective Action: Public Goods and the Theory of Groups* (Cambridge, Mass.: Harvard University Press, 1965).

Orland, L., *Prisons: Houses of Darkness* (New York: Free Press, 1975).

Ostfeld, A.M., Kasl, S.V., D'Atri, D.A. and Fitzgerald, E.F., *Stress, Crowding and Blood Pressure in Prison* (New Jersey: Lawrence Erlbaum, 1987).

Oswald, R.G., *Attica – My Story* (New York: Doubleday, 1972).

Pallas, J. and Barber, R., From Riot to Revolution, *Issues in Criminology*, Vol. 7, No. 2, Fall 1072, pp. 1–19.

Pallas, J. and Barber, R., 'From riot to revolution', in Quinney, R. (ed.), *Criminal Justice in America* (Boston, Mass.: Little, Brown, 1973), pp. 340–55.

Parisi, N. (ed.), *Coping with Imprisonment* (Beverly Hills, Calif.: Sage, 1982).

Pashukanis, E., *Law and Marxism* (London: Pluto Press, 1980).

Paterson, A., *Principles of the Borstal System* (Prison Commission: privately printed and circulated, 1932).

Paulus, P.B. *et al.*, *Prison Crowding; A Psychological Perspective* (New York: Springer-Verlag, 1988).

Pearson, G., *Hooligan: A history of respectable fears* (London: Macmillan, 1983).

Petersilia, J., *et al.*, 'Executive summary of Rand's study, "Granting felons probation: public risks and alternatives"', *Crime and Delinquency*, Vol. 31, No. 3, July 1985, pp. 379–92.

Peterson, D. and Thomas, C. (eds), *Corrections: Problems and Prospects* (Englewood Cliffs, NJ: Prentice-Hall, 1971).

Phillips, R., 'Terrorism: historical roots and moral justifications', in Warner, M. and Crisp, R. (eds), *Terrorism Protest and Power* (Aldershot: Edward Elgar, 1990), pp. 68–77.

Pinard, M., *The Rise of a Third Party: A Study in Crisis Politics* (Englewood Cliffs, NJ: Prentice-Hall, 1971).

Piven, F.F. and Cloward, R.A., *Poor People's Movements: Why They Succeed, How They Fail* (New York: Pantheon Books, 1977).

Poole, E.D. and Regoli, R.M., 'Race, institutional rule breaking and disciplinary response: a study of discretionary decision making in prison, *Law and Society Review*, Vol. 14, 1980, pp. 931–46.

Poole, E.D., Regoli, R.M. and Thomas, C.W., 'The measurement of inmate social role types: an assessment', *Journal of Criminal Law and Criminology*, No. 71, 1980, pp. 317–24.

Poole, R., 'Modernity, rationality and "the masculine"', in Threadgold, J. and Cranny-Francis, A. (eds), *Feminine, Masculine and Representation* (Sydney: Allen & Unwin, 1990), pp. 48–61.

Pope, P., 'Prisoners in maximum security prisons: perspectives upon management and management problems', *Prison Service Journal*, No. 22, May 1976, pp. 2–5.

Porter, B. and Dunn, M., *The Miami Riot of 1980: Crossing the Bounds* (Lexington, Mass.: D.C. Heath, 1984).

Prescott, J., *Hull Prison Riot: Submissions, Observations and Recommendations of Mr John Prescott, MP Hull East*, Presented to Mr G.W. Fowler, Chief Inspector of Prison Services, undated.

Press Council, *Press at the Prison Gates*, Report of the Inquiry by the Press Council into Press Coverage of the Strangeways Prison Riot and Related Matters, Press Council Booklet No. 8 (London: Press Council, 1991).

Presser, S., 'In Pennsylvania, 200 years of practice doesn't make perfect', *National Prison Project Journal*, Vol. 5, No. 3, Summer 1990, pp. 1–3.

Priestley, P. (ed.), *Jail Journeys: The English Prison Experience Since 1918* (London: Routledge, 1989).

Priestley, P., *Community of Scapegoats: The Segregation of Sex offenders and Informers in prisons* (Oxford: Pergamon, 1980).

Prison Reform Trust, *The Riots of '86: Evidence presented to H.M. Chief Inspector of Prisons* (London: Prison Reform Trust, undated).

Prison Reform Trust, *Beyond Restraint* (London: Prison Reform Trust, 1984).

Prison Reform Trust, *Submission to Phase 2 of the Woolf Inquiry into Prison Disturbances* (London: Prison Reform Trust, 1990).

PROP, *Don't Mark His Face: The Account of the Hull Prison Riot (1976) and Its Brutal Aftermath by the Prisoners Themselves* (London: National Prisoners' Movement (PROP), 1976).

PROP, *The Public Inquiry into the Hull Prison Riot* (London: PROP, 1978).

PROP, *Paper of the National Prisoners' Movement*, Vol. 2, No. 6, Winter 1978/9.

PROP, *Wormwood Scrubs: Special report* (London: PROP, 1979).

Pugh, R.D., *Imprisonment in Medieval England* (Cambridge University Press, 1968).

Quinlan, J.M., *Statement of J. Michael Quinlan, Director, Federal Bureau of Prisons, before the Subcommittee on Intellectual Property and Judicial Administration of the House Committee on the Judiciary*, April 24 1991, Washington, Federal Bureau of Prisons, US Department of Justice.

Quinney, R. (ed.), *Criminal Justice in America* (Boston, Mass.: Little, Brown, 1973).

Radical Alternatives to Prison, *Out of Sight: RAP on Prisons* (London: *Christian Action Journal*, Autumn 1981).

Ramirez, J., 'Prisonization, staff and inmates: is it really about us versus them?', *Criminal Justice and Behaviour*, Vol. 11, 1984, pp. 423–60.

Reid, P.R., *The Colditz Story* (London: Coronet, 1950).

Reid, S.T., *The Correctional System* (New York: Holt, Rinehart & Winston, 1981).

Reimer, H., *Socialization in the Prison Community, Proceedings of the American Prison Association* (New York: American Prison Association, 1937), pp. 151–5.

Rigby, R., *The Hill* (London: Mayflower, 1965).

Rock, P.J. and Sevcik, J.G., *The Joliet Correctional Center Riot of April 22, 1975* (Chicago: State of Illinois, Legislative Investigating Commission, 1975).

Rose, G., *The Struggle for Penal Reform: The Howard League and its Predecessors* (London: Stevens, 1961).

Rothman, D.J., *The Discovery of the Asylum: social order and disorder in the New Republic* (Boston, Mass.: Little, Brown, 1971).

Rothman, D.J., *Conscience and Convenience: The Asylum and Its Alternatives in Progressive America* (Boston, Mass.: Little, Brown, 1980).

Rubenstein, R.E., *Alchemists of Revolution – Terrorism in the Modern World* (New York: Basic Books, 1987).

Rubenstein, R.E., 'Rebellion in America: the fire next time?', in Gurr, E.R. (ed.), *Violence in America, Vol. 2, Protest, Rebellion, Reform* (Newbury Park, Calif.: Sage, 1989), pp. 307–28.

Rudé, G., *Protest and Punishment: the story of the social and political protesters transported to Australia, 1788–1868* (Oxford: Clarendon, 1978).

Rusche, G. and Kirchheimer, O., *Punishment and Social Structure* (New York: Russell & Russell, 1968).

Rushdie, S., *Midnight's Children* (London: Pan, 1982).

Rutherford, A., 'The new generation of prisons', *New Society*, Vol. 73, No. 1186, 20 September 1985, pp. 408–10.

Rutherford, A., *Prisons and the Process of Justice* (Oxford University Press, 1986).

Rutherford, J. 'A Place called Home: identity and the cultural politics of difference', in Rutherford, J. (ed.) (1990) pp. 9–27.

Rutherford, J. (ed.) Identity: community, culture, difference, (London: Lawrence & Wishart, 1990).

Salierno, G., *Il Sottoproletariato in Italia: Per un approcio politico e metodologico al problema dell'alleanza tra classe operaia e <<Lumpenproletariat>>* (Roma: E.L. Casalotti, 1972).

Salt, A., *Jottings of a JP* (London: Christopher Johnson, 1955).

Sands, B., *The Diary of Bobby Sands* (Dublin: Sinn Fein Publicity Dept, 1981).

Savas, E.S., *Privatizing the Public Sector; How to Shrink Government* (Chatham, NJ: Chatham House, 1982).

Schon, D.A., *Beyond the Stable State: public and private learning in a changing society* (London: Temple Smith, 1971).

Schrag, C., *The Sociology of Prison Riots, Proceedings of the American Correctional Association,* 1960, pp. 136–46.

Schrag, C., 'Some foundations for a theory of corrections', in Cressey, D.R. (ed.), *The Prison: Studies in Institutional Organization and Change* (New York: Holt, Rinehart & Winston, 1961), pp. 309–57.

Schram, S. and Turbett, J.P., 'Civil disorder and the welfare explosion', *American Sociological Review,* Vol. 48, Part 3, June 1983, pp. 408–14.

Scraton, P., Sim, J. and Skidmore, P., *Prisons Under Protest* (Milton Keynes: Open University Press, 1990).

Scull, A., *Decarceration: Community Treatment and the Deviant* (Englewood Cliffs, NJ: Prentice-Hall, 1977).

Sears, D.O. and McConahay, J.B., *The Politics of Violence: The New Urban Blacks and the Watts Riot* (Boston, Mass.: Houghton Mifflin, 1973).

Serrill, M.S. and Katel, P., 'New Mexico', *Corrections Magazine,* April 1980, pp. 12–16, 20–4.

Shapland, P., *et al.*, *Research into Consultative Management at Long Lartin Prison* (Birmingham, Prison Psychological Service, Midlands Region, 1972).

Shapland, P., 'Thoughts on disturbances in prison', *Prison Service Journal,* No. 11 New Series, July 1973, pp. 18–20.

Shogan, R. and Craig, T., *The Detroit Race Riot: A Study in Violence* (Philadelphia: Chilton Books, 1964).

Silberman, C., *Race, Crime and Corrections, Proceedings of the American Correctional Association, 1979* (College Park, Md.: American Correctional Association, 1980), pp. 5–14.

Silverman, D., *The Theory of Organisations: a sociological framework* (London: Heinemann, 1970).

Smelser, N.J., *Theory of Collective Behaviour* (London: Routledge & Kegan Paul, 1962).

Smelser, N.J., *The Theory of Collective Behaviour, in South Carolina Department of Corrections* (1973) (quoted in Dillingham and Montgomery, op. cit., 1985).

Smith, A., *The Conflict Theory of Riots, in South Carolina Department of Corrections* (1973) (quoted in Dillingham and Montgomery, op. cit., 1985).

Smith, R., 'The state of the prisons: disorder, disillusion and disrepute', *British Medical Journal,* Vol. 287, 19 November 1983a, pp. 1521–3.

Smith, R., 'The state of the prisons: what are prisons for?', *British Medical Journal,* Vol. 287, 26 November 1983b, pp. 1614–18.

Smith, R., 'The state of the prisons: crisis upon crisis', *British Medical Journal*, Vol. 287, 3 December 1983c, pp. 1705–8.

Smith, R., 'The state of the prisons: organisation of prison medical services', *British Medical Journal*, Vol. 287, 17 December 1983d, pp. 1867–70.

Solzhenitsyn, A.I., *One Day in the Life of Ivan Denisovich* (Harmondsworth: Penguin, 1963).

Solzhenitsyn, A.I., *The Gulag Archipelago 1918–1956* (London: Collins, 1974).

Stastny, C. and Tyrnauer, G., *Who Rules the Joint: The Changing Political Culture of Maximum Security Prisons in America* (Lexington, Mass.: D.C. Heath, 1982).

Stephan, E., *Spies in Ireland* (London: MacDonald, 1963).

Stern, V., *Imprisoned by Our Prisons: A Programme of Reform* (London: Unwin, 1989).

Stratton, B., *Who Guards the Guards?* (London: PROP, 1970).

Street, D., 'The inmate group in custodial and treatment settings', in Hazelrigg, L.E. (ed.), *Prison Within Society: A Reader in Penology* (New York: Doubleday, 1968), pp. 199–228.

Street, D., Vinter, R.D. and Perrow, C., *Organization for Treatment: A Comparative Study of Institutions for Delinquents* (New York: Free Press, 1966).

Sumner, C., 'Reflections on a sociological theory of criminal justice systems', in Sumner, C. (ed.), *Censure, Politics and Criminal Justice* (Milton Keynes: Open University Press, 1990), pp. 41–56.

Sumner, C. (ed.), *Censure, Politics and Criminal Justice* (Milton Keynes: Open University Press, 1990).

Swaaningen, R. van, *Pressure Groups for Penal Reform in the Netherlands – A National Report* (unpublished paper).

Sykes, G.M., *Society of Captives: The Study of a Maximum Security Prison* (Princeton, NJ: Princeton University Press, 1958).

Szabo, D. and Katsenelson, S. (eds), *Offenders and Corrections* (New York: Praeger, 1978).

Taylor, I., Walton, P. and Young J., *The New Criminology* (London: Routledge & Kegan Paul, 1973).

Taylor, L. 'Onslaught on Prison Secrecy', *New Statesman*, Vol. 96, No. 2473, 11 August 1978, pp. 172–3.

Teeters, N.K., 'The dilemma of prison riots', *The Prison Journal*, Vol. XXXIII, October 1953, pp. 14–20.

Teeters, N.K. and Shearer, J.D., *The Prison at Philadelphia, Cherry Hill: The Separate System of Penal Discipline: 1829–1913* (New York: Columbia University Press, 1957).

Thom, R., *Stabilité Structurelle et Morphogénèse: Essai d'une Théorie Générale des Modèles* (Reading, Mass.: W.A. Benjamen, 1972).

Thomas, C.W., *The Background, Present Status, and Future Potential of Privatization in American Corrections*, unpublished paper, based on presentation made on 31 March at the 'Privatization: Promise and Pitfalls' conference, Wayne State University, 30–31 March 1989.

Thomas, C.W. and Peterson, D.M., *Prison Organization and Inmate Subcultures* (Indianapolis, Ind.: Bobbs-Merrill, 1977).

Thomas, J.E., *The English Prison Officer: A Study in Conflict* (London: Routledge & Kegan Paul, 1972).

Thomas, J.E. and Pooley, R., *The Exploding Prison: prison riots and the case of Hull* (London: Junction Books, 1980).

Thomas, J., Keeler, D. and Harris, K., 'Issues and misconceptions in prisoner litigation: a critical view', *Criminology*, Vol. 24, No. 4, 1986, pp. 775–97.

Thompson, E.P., *The Making of the English Working Class* (London: Gollancz, 1963).

Thompson, E.P., 'The moral economy of the English crowd in the eighteenth century', *Past and Present*, No. 50, February 1971, pp. 76–136.

Threadgold, T. and Cranny-Francis, A. (eds), *Feminine, Masculine and Representation* (Sydney: Allen & Unwin, 1990).

Tilly, C., 'Collective violence in European perspective', in Gurr, T.R. (ed.), *Violence in America, Vol. 2, Protest, Rebellion, Reform* (Newbury Park, Calif.: Sage, 1989), pp. 62–100.

Tilly, C., Tilly, L. and Tilly, R., *The Rebellious Century 1830–1930* (London: Dent, 1975).

Tittle, C.R., 'Inmate organization: sex differentiation and the influence of criminal subcultures', *American Sociological Review*, Vol. 34, 1969, pp. 492–505.

Tittle, C.R., *Society of Subordinates: Inmate Organization in a Narcotic Hospital* (Bloomington, Ind.: Indiana University Press, 1972).

Tobias, J.J., *Crime and Industrial Society in the Nineteenth Century* (London: Batsford, 1967).

Toch, H., *Men in Crisis* (Chicago: Aldine, 1975).

Tonry, M. and Morris, N. (eds), *Crime and Justice, Vol. 3* (University of Chicago Press, 1981).

Turner, R.H. and Killian, L.M. (eds), *Collective Behaviour*, 3rd edn (Englewood Cliffs, NJ: Prenctice-Hall, 1975).

Tyrnauer, G., 'What Went Wrong at Walla Walla?', *Corrections Magazine*, June 1981, pp. 37–41.

Useem, B., 'Solidarity model, breakdown model, and the Boston anti-busing movement', *American Sociological Review*, No. 45, June 1980, pp. 357–69.

Useem, B., 'Disorganization and the New Mexico prison riot of 1980', *American Sociological Review*, Vol. 50, October 1985, pp. 677–88.

Useem, B. and Kimball, P., *States of Siege: U.S. Prison Riots, 1971–1986* (Oxford University Press, 1989).

Van Voris, J., *Countess de Markievicz* (Cambridge, Mass.: Massachusetts University Press, 1967).

Waddington, D., Jones, K. and Critcher, C., *Flashpoints: Studies in Public Disorder* (London: Routledge, 1989).

Wallace, C., *From Crisis to Collapse?*, Out of sight: RAP on Prisons, Autumn 1981, (St Albans: Christian Action, 1981), pp. 22–3.

Ward, D.A., 'Sweden: the middle way to prison reform?', in Wolfgang, M.E. (ed.), *Prisons: Present and Possible* (Lexington, Mass.: D.C. Heath, 1979), pp. 89–167.

Ward, D.A. and Kassebaum, G., *Women in Prison* (Chicago: Aldine, 1965).

Ward, D.A. and Schoen, K.F., *Confinement in Maximum Custody: New Last-Resort Prisons in the United States and Western Europe* (Lexington, Mass.: D.C. Heath, 1981).

Ward, J., 'Telling tales in prison', in Frankenberg, R. (ed.), *Custom and Conflict in British Society* (Manchester University Press, 1982), pp. 234–57.

Warner, M. and Crisp, R., 'Introduction', in Warner, M. and Crisp, R. (eds), *Terrorism, Protest and Power* (Aldershot: Edward Elgar, 1990), pp. 1–14.

Warner, M. and Crisp, R. (eds), *Terrorism, Protest and Power* (Aldershot: Edward Elgar, 1990).

Waskow, A.I., *From Race Riot to Sit-in, 1919 and the 1960s: a study in the connections between conflict and violence* (New York: Anchor Books, 1967).

Wenk, E.A. and Moos, R.H., 'Social climates in prisons: an attempt to conceptualize and measure environmental factors in total institutions', *Journal of Research in Crime and Delinquency*, Vol. 9, No. 2, 1972, pp. 134–48.

Wheeler, S., 'Socialization in correctional communities', *American Sociological Review*, Vol. 26, 1961, pp. 697–712.

Whitelaw, W., 'Prisons: no easy way out', *The Times*, 5 May 1983.

Wicker, T., *A Time to Die* (New York: Quadrangle, 1975).

Wilkinson, G., *The Newgate Calendar* (London: Sphere, 1991; originally published 1828).

Wilkinson, P., 'Some observations on the relationships between terrorism and freedom', in Warner, M. and Crisp, R. (eds), *Terrorism, Protest and Power* (Aldershot: Edward Elgar, 1990), pp. 44–53.

Williams, B., *Probation Work in Prisons* (Birmingham: Venture Press, 1991).

Wilmer, H.A., 'The role of the "rat" in prison', *Federal Probation*, Vol. 29, 1965, pp. 44–9.

Wilsnack, R.W., 'Explaining collective violence in prisons: problems and possibilities', in Cohen, A.K., Cole, G.F. and Bailey, R.G. (eds), *Prison Violence* (Lexington, Mass.: D.C. Heath, 1976), pp. 61–78.

Wilson, D.P. and Barnes, H.E., 'A riot is an unnecessary evil', *Life*, Vol. 33, 24 November 1952, pp. 138–40, 142, 144, 147–50.

Wilson, J.Q. (ed.), *The Metropolitan Enigma* (Cambridge, Mass.: Harvard University Press, 1968).

Wilson, T. (ed.), *Penal Services for Offenders: Comparative Studies of England and Poland 1984/85* (Aldershot: Avebury, 1987).

Wilson, W.J., *The Truly Disadvantaged: The Inner City, the Underclass, and Public Policy* (University of Chicago Press, 1987).

Wolfgang, M.E. (ed.), *Prisons: Present and Possible* (Lexington, Mass.: D.C. Heath, 1979).

Wright, E.O., *The Politics of Punishment: A Critical Analysis of Prisons in America* (New York: Harper & Row, 1978).

Wright, K.N., *Improving Correctional Classification Through a Study of the Placement of Inmates in Environmental Settings* (Binghampton, NY: Center for Social Analysis, 1987).

Young, A., 'Strategies of censure and the suffragette movement', in Sumner, C. (ed.), *Censure, Politics and Criminal Justice* (Milton Keynes: Open University Press, 1990), pp. 142–62.

Zamble, E. and Porporino, F.J., *Coping, Behaviour and Adaptation in Prison Inmates* (New York: Springer-Verlag, 1988).

Zeeman, E.C., *Levels of Structure in Catastrophe Theory, Proceedings of the International Congress of Mathematicians* (University of Vancouver, 1975), pp. 533–646.

Zeeman, E.C., Hall, C.S., Harrison, P.J., Marriage, P.J. and Shapland, P.H., 'A model for prison disturbances', *British Journal of Criminology*, Vol. 17, No. 3, 1977, pp. 251–63.

Zimbardo, P., 'A Pirandellian Prison', *New York Times Magazine*, Sect. 6, 8 April 1973, pp. 38–53, 56–60.

256 *Bibliography*

OFFICIAL PUBLICATIONS: US

Federal Bureau of Investigation, *Uniform Crime Reports* (Washington, DC: Government Printing Office, 1971).

Federal Bureau of Prisons, *Facilities 1990* (US Department of Justice, (Washington, DC: US Government Printing Office, 1990).

Flanagan, T. and McGarrell, E.F. (eds), *Sourcebook of Criminal Justice Statistics – 1985* (US Department of Justice, Bureau of Justice Statistics, Washington, DC: US Government Printing Office, 1986).

Kerner Report – see National Advisory Commission on Civil Disorders.

National Advisory Commission on Civil Disorders, *Report of the National Advisory Commission on Civil Disorders* (Kerner Report) (Washington, DC: US Government Printing Office, 1968; New York: Bantam, 1968).

National Commission on the Causes and Prevention of Violence, *To Establish Justice, To Insure Domestic Tranquility: Final report of the National Commission on the Causes and Prevention of Violence* (Washington, DC: US Government Printing Office, 1969).

National Institute of Justice, *American Prisons and Jails, Vol. 1, Summary and Policy Implications of a National Survey* (Washington, DC: US Government Printing Office, 1981).

National Institute of Law Enforcement and Criminal Justice, *Prison Population and Policy Choices, Vol. 1: Preliminary Report to Congress* (Washington, DC: US Government Printing Office, 1977).

National Institute of Law Enforcement and Criminal Justice, *Prison Population and Policy Choices, Vol. 2: Technical Appendix* (Washington, DC: US Government Printing Office, 1977).

New York State Special Commission, *Attica: The Official Report of the New York State Special Commission on Attica* (New York: Bantam, 1972).

Penitentiary Investigation Committee, House of Representatives, Texas Legislature, *Report of Committee* (1913).

President's Commission, *The Challenge of Crime in a Free Society: A Report by the President's Commission on Law Enforcement and Administration of Justice* (Washington, DC: US Government Printing Office, 1967).

South Carolina Department of Corrections, *Collective Violence in Correctional Institutions: A Search for Causes* (Collective Violence Research Project, Columbia, SC: State Printing Co., 1973) (quoted in Dillingham and Montgomery, op. cit., 1985).

United States General Accounting Office, *Response to the Chairman, Subcommittee on Regulation, Business Opportunities and Energy Committee on Small Business, House of Representatives* (Washington DC, 1991).

US Bureau of Prisons, *Handbook of Correctional Institution Design and Construction* (Leavenworth, Kansas: Bureau of Prisons, 1949).

OFFICIAL PUBLICATIONS: GB

Committee of Inquiry into the United Kingdom Prison Services, *Report*, Cmnd 7673 (London: HMSO, 1979).

Fowler, G., *Report of an Inquiry by the Chief Inspector of the Prison Service into the Cause and Circumstances of the Events at HM Prison Hull during the Period 31st August to 3rd September 1976* (London: HMSO, 1977).

Hennessey, J., *Report of An Inquiry by HM Chief Inspector of Prisons for England and Wales, into the Disturbances in Prison Service Establishments in England between 29 April – 2 May 1986* (London: HMSO, 1987).

Hobhouse, S. and Brockway, A.F., *English Prisons Today: Being the Report of the Prison System Enquiry Committee* (London: Longmans: Special Edition for subscribers, 1922).

HM Chief Inspector of Prisons, *Report on HM Prison Manchester by Chief Inspector of Prisons* (London: HMSO, 1990).

HM Inspectorate of Prisons for Scotland, *Peterhead, General Assessment, 1985* (Edinburgh: Scottish Office, 1986).

Home Office, *Annual Reports of the Work of the Prison Department* (London: HMSO, various).

Home Office, *Report by Mr Herbert du Parcq, K.C. On the Circumstances Connected with the Recent Disorder at Dartmoor Convict Prison*, Cmnd 4010 (London: HMSO, undated).

Home Office, *Penal Practice in a Changing Society*, Cmnd 645 (London: HMSO, 1959).

Home Office, Managing the Long-Term Prison System: the report of the control review committee (London: HMSO, 1984).

Home Office, *Inquiry Held by the Visiting Committee into Allegations of Ill-treatment of Prisoners in Her Majesty's Prison, Durham*, Cmnd 2068 (London: HMSO, June 1963).

Home Office, *Report of the Inquiry into Prison Escapes and Security* (Mountbatten Report), Cmnd 3175 (London: HMSO, 1966).

Home Office, *Report of An Inquiry by the Chief Inspector of the Prison Service into the Cause and Circumstances of the events at HM Prison Hull during the period 31st August to 3rd September, 1976* (London: HMSO, 1977a).

Home Office, *Prisons and the Prisoner: The Work of the Prison Service in England and Wales* (London: HMSO, 1977b).

Home Office, *Report on the Work of the Prison Department for 1977*, Cmnd 7290 (London: HMSO, 1978).

Home Office, *The Reduction of Pressure on the Prison System: Observations on the Fifteenth Report from the Expenditure Committee* (London: HMSO, June 1980).

Home Office, *Report of Her Majesty's Chief Inspector of Prisons for England and Wales 1981*, Cmnd 8523 (London: HMSO, 1982).

Home Office, *Statement on the Background, Circumstances and Action Subsequently Taken Relative to the Disturbance in 'D' Wing at HM Prison Wormwood Scrubs on 31 August 1979, together with the Report of an Inquiry by the Regional Director of the South East Region of the Prison Department* (London: HMSO, 23 February 1982).

Home Office, *Report of Her Majesty's Chief Inspector of Prisons 1982–89* (London: HMSO, 1983–90).

Home Office, *Report of Her Majesty's Chief Inspector of Prisons for England and Wales 1984* (London: HMSO, 1985).

Home Office, *Report of Her Majesty's Chief Inspector of Prisons for England and Wales 1987* (London: HMSO, 1988).

258   *Bibliography*

Home Office, *Report of Her Majesty's Chief Inspector of Prisons for England and Wales 1989* (London: HMSO, 1990).

Home Office, *Custody, Care and Justice: The Way Ahead for the Prison Service in England and Wales* (White Paper) (London: HMSO, 1991).

House of Commons, *Eleventh Report from the Estimates Committee, Session 1966–67: Prisons, Borstals and Detention Centres* (London: HMSO, 1967).

House of Commons, *Fifteenth Report from the Expenditure Committee, Session 1977–78: The Reduction of Pressure on the Prison System, Vol. 1* (London: HMSO, 1978).

House of Commons, *Fourth Report from the Home Affairs Committee, Session 1980–81: The Prison Service, Vol. 1 Report with Minutes of Proceedings* (London: HMSO, 1981).

House of Commons, *Fourth Report from the Home Affairs Committee, Session 1980–81: The Prison Service, Vol. 2 Evidence and Appendices* (London: HMSO, 1981).

May, Justice, *Report of the Committee of Inquiry into the United Kingdom Prison Service*, Cmnd 7673 (London: HMSO, 1979).

Parliamentary All-Party Penal Affairs Group, *Too Many Prisoners: An Examination of Ways of Reducing the Prison Population* (Chichester: Barry Rose, June 1980).

Scarman, Lord, *The Brixton Disorders 10–12 April 1981: Report of an Inquiry by the Rt Hon. The Lord Scarman OBE*, Cmnd 8427 (London: HMSO, 1981).

Scottish Home and Health Department, *Report of the Review of Suicide Precautions at HM Detention Centre and HM Young Offenders Institution Glenochil* (Chiswick Report) (Edinburgh: HMSO, 1985).

Woolf, Rt Hon. Lord Justice and Tumin, His Hon. Judge S., *Prison Disturbances April 1990: Report of an Inquiry*, Cmnd 1456 (London: HMSO, 1991).

Appendix
Calendar of Prison Riots

No attempt to list incidents in the form of this calendar can claim to be complete. The most that can be said for the following calendar is that it provides a reference point for the reader, regarding the more newsworthy riots. Particular features of some incidents are noted, as much to draw attention to the variety of circumstances which may attract the label of 'riot' as to attempt to label them thus. Additional details are given in cases where they are noteworthy or where these are typical of the incidents in a particular period.

IN THE UNITED STATES

1774	Copper mines, Simnsbury, Connecticut, Texas
1815	Walnut Street jail
1857	New York State, Auburn prison
1895	New York State, Ludlow Street jail
1907	New York State, Plattsburg prison New Jersey, Rahway reformatory
1909	New Jersey reformatory
1911	Tennessee, Bushy Mountain mines prison Tennessee State prison
1912	Wyoming State prison: lynching and mass escape Sing Sing prison: strike California, San Quentin prison: food riot Michigan, Jackson prison
1913	Sing Sing prison
1914	New York City, Blackwells' Island

	Sing Sing prison Trenton State prison
1915	New York State, Auburn prison New York City, Bronx County jail
1916	New York City, Bronx County jail
1917	Illinois, Cook County jail Illinois, Joliet Penitentiary: riot suppressed with great force
1919	New York, Clinton prison, Dannemora Kansas, Leavenworth: strikes by military prisoners Connecticut State prison
1923	Banner coal-mining camp
1926	Washington, Walla Walla state penitentiary
1927	Kansas mine camp Illinois State prison California, Folsom prison: eight prisoners and one guard die in riot
1929	New York, Clinton prison, Dannemora New York State, Auburn prison: two riots Kansas, Leavenworth prison Colorado State prison: prisoners barricade themselves in Holmsbury Alabama State prison California, State Narcotic Hospital, Spadra
1930	Ohio State Penitentiary Howard State prison, Rikers Island Joliet penitentiary
1934	Washington, Walla Walla state penitentiary
1936	California, United State Penitentiary, Alcatraz Island

1942	Puerto Rica, San Juan prison: five-day hunger-strike
1944	Atlanta federal prison
1945	Georgia, Brunswick: camp riot, July Wisconsin, Wanpun State Prison: sit-down strike by 69 prisoners
1946	California, United State Penitentiary, Alcatraz Island
1947	Brunswick convict highway camp Wisconsin, Wanpun State prison
1948	Mexico City penitentiary New Mexico state penitentiary, Santa Fe
1950	Margette prison: hostage taken in jail-break New Mexico, State Prison: riot by 100 prisoners New Jersey, State Prison: strikes by prisoners, November–December
1951	Puerto Rico, Rio Piedras: prison riot, January Los Angeles, State Prison farm, Angola: protesting prisoners slash heel tendons Alabama, Mobile Prison: hunger-strike in protest at alleged unfair treatment by black prisoners, March Utah State Prison: riot, May Los Angeles, Passaic County Jail: riot, June Colorado, State Prison, Canon City: riot, July Utah, State Prison, Draper: two riots Oregon State Prison, Salem: strike by prisoners, August West Virginia, Moundsville state prison: protest by 1300 prisoners, about dirty cooking and inadequate clothing, October Alabama, Kilby prison, Montgomery: riot, November Idaho State penitentiary Louisiana State Penitentiary: protest by slashing heel tendons New Mexico State Penitentiary, Santa Fe West Virginia penitentiary

1952 New Jersey State prison, Trenton: two riots
New Jersey State prison farm, Rahway
Southern Michigan, State prison, Jackson: two riots
Louisiana State Penitentiary, Angola: two riots
Idaho State Penitentiary, Boise
North Carolina Central Prison, Raleigh
Kentucky State Penitentiary, Eddyville
California State Prison, Soledad
Massachusetts Reformatory, West Concord
New Mexico State Penitentiary, Santa Fe: two riots
Massachusetts State prison, Charleston
Ohio, Federal Reformatory, Chillicothe
Oklahoma, Federal Reformatory, El Reno
Illinois State penitentiary, Menard: two riots
Ohio State Penitentiary, Columbus
Montreal State prison: three riots
New Jersey State prison, Trenton
Utah State Prison, Draper

1953 Pennsylvania, Western State Penitentiary: 1100 prisoners riot, January
Pennsylvania, Eastern State Penitentiary, Pittsburgh: two riots
Allegheny County Institution, Pennsylvannia: inmates burn factory, January
Pennsylvania, Rockview Penitentiary: 575 riot, January
Arizona State Prison, Florence: second strike by prisoners, February
Oregon, Salem State Penitentiary: rebellion by prisoners, February
California, US Federal Penitentiary, Alcatraz: riot, April
Minnesota, Stillwater State Prison: riot over food, April
New Jersey, Essex County Jail: strike by prisoners, March
California, United State Penitentiary, Alcatraz Island
New Mexico, Santa Fe Penitentiary: 30 rioting prisoners took hostages, two prisoners dead, June
Oregon, Salem, State Penitentiary: 1100 prisoners in sit-down strike, July

Washington, State Reformatory, Monroe: 300 riot, August
Washington, State Penitentiary, Walla Walla: riot, September
Maryland, State Reformatory, Breathedsville: riot, September

1954   Nebraska, Lincoln Penitentiary: riot, January
Illinois, Pontiac State Penitentiary: 450 riot, one prisoner killed, June
New Jersey, Trenton Prison: 13 prisoners on hunger-strike for a week, in 'death house', July
Chicago prison: riot over food, September
New York City, Women's House of Detention: riots over disciplining of one woman for remark to guard, September
Missouri, State Penitentiary: riot, seven prisoners killed, 15 hurt, September
South Dakota, Sioux Falls State Penitentiary: riot, three guards taken hostage, October
Missouri, State Penitentiary: riot: one prisoner killed, 36 injured, October

1955   Massachusetts, State Prison: three-day siege, five guards taken hostage, January
Nebraska: rebellion by 12 prisoners, two guards taken hostage, March
Nevada State Prison: revolt by 200 prisoners, July
New York, Rikers Island reformatory: sit-down strike by 300 prisoners, July
Washington, Walla Walla state penitentiary: rebellion, nine hostages taken, July
Wyoming, State Penitentiary: 75 armed prisoners revolt, demanding dismissal of two guards for brutality, nine taken hostage, July
Ohio, London Prison Farm: sit-down strike by prisoners, August
Massachusetts, Women's Reformatory, Framingham: 50 riot, August
Nebraska, State Penitentiary: 200 riot, burn five build-

ings, August

Washington, Walla Walla state penitentiary: riot, hostages, August

New Mexico, State Penitentiary, Santa Fe: sit-down strike, September

Nebraska, Lincoln Men's Reformatory: riot after ousting of superintendent, who had criticised penal administration, September

Ohio, London Prison Farm: strike by prisoners, November

Missouri, St Louis Workhouse: riots by young prisoners, November

Massachusetts, State Prison: one day hunger-strike by 16 prisoners, November

Missouri, State Penitentiary: demonstration by prisoners, December

1956	West Vancouver, State Penitentiary: riot by 20 prisoners, one guard taken hostage, January

Illinois, Chicago County jail: riot and fire started by nine prisoners under sentence of death, March

Connecticut, State Prison: 200 in five-hour sit-down, July

Indiana, Pendelton Prison: riot about conditions, July

Georgia, State Prison: 36 prisoners inflict leg-breaks and other injuries on each other in protest at prison conditions, August

North Carolina, Central Prison

New York State, Women's State Prison, Raleigh: 18 prisoners riot, September

Georgia, State Prison: five more prisoners injure legs, November

1957	Colorado, state reformatory: riot by 125 prisoners, one killed

Connecticut, state prison

Montana, state penitentiary, Jefferson City: prisoners' demonstration

Montana, Deer Lodge: nine-hour riot by prisoners

Texas, Bexar county jail, San Antonio

Utah, point-of-the-mountain prison: riot by 500 prisoners

Washington, Walla Walla

1958   Arizona, 46 prisoners riot, 11 critically injured, December

Kansas, Leavenworth penitentiary: hunger strike, June

Massachusetts, State Reformatory: riot, prison shop burned, April

Montana Prison: riot, January

New York County, Women's House of Detention: riot, protesting short rations, April

New York County, Women's House of Detention: further disturbances, overcrowding blamed, July

Tennessee, State Prison, Petros: riot, guards use teargas, one prisoner killed, March

1959   United State Penitentiary, Alcatraz Island, California: five prisoners cut heel-tendons in protest at discipline, January

Georgia, State Prison, Reidsville: hunger-strike, July

Massachusetts, Walpole State Prison: prisoners in six-hour battle, five guards hostage, plus governor and chaplain, March

Montana, State Prison: riot, deputy warden killed, April

Tennessee, Fort Pillow Prison Farm: 150 prisoners riot, two guards hostage, May

Texas, Bascar County Jail: riot, May

Washington, State Reformatory, Monroe: riot, July

1960   California, San Quentin: hunger-strike over complaints about food, June

Connecticut, Weathsfield State Prison: 400 riot, June

Hawaii, Oahu State Prison: riot, July

Maryland, State Prison: Correction House and Reformatory prisonerstrike on withdrawal of outside workers' time off sentence, August

Minnesota prison: National Guard called to halt prison sit-down, August

New York County, Bronx Youth House: girls riot, 30

escape, overcrowding blamed, December
New York County, Bronx Youth House: demonstration by 40 girls, July
South Dakota, State Prison: hunger strike by 21 maximum-security prisoners, protest at new security rules; three later shot for interfering with firemen in shop fire, July

1961 California, San Quentin: hunger strike by 32 prisoners on 'death row', April
New York State: 1451 or 1747 prisoners in Sing Sing refused to leave cells, in demand for time-off for good behaviour to be made mandatory, November
Pennsylvania, Eastern State Penitentiary: 30 prisoners revolt, stab five guards, surrender to state troopers, January

1962 Dakota County: 40 prisoners in Youth Corrections Centre riot after Muslim members protest at the preparation of food, August
Illinois, Penal Colony Farm, Vandalia: 100 prisoners on hunger strike, November
Kansas, Kansas Reformatory: 100 prisoners rioted for one hour, August
New York State: 160 Green Haven prisoners sit-in, protesting against parole legislation affecting time-off for good behaviour, March
New York State: the parole protest strike spreads to Sing Sing, Green Haven and Auburn prisons; mainly against Section 1 of bill proposing to make paroled prisoners subject to supervision till maximum of sentence expires

1963 Indiana, State Penal Farm: riot by prisoners, eight injured and seven escape

1964 Iowa, Men's Reformatory, Anamosa: 200 prisoners in riot, quelled by tear-gas
Maryland, House of Correction, Jessup: 800 prisoners riot

Montana: 20 delinquents, intoxicated by fumes from
fingernail polish, riot in State Vocational School for
Girls, Helena, November
Texas, Dallas County jail: 160 prisoners riot, April

1965   New York State: 17 men occupy Sing Sing condemned
cells, February
Tennessee, Bushy Mount State Prison: sit-down strike,
June
Los Angeles, Angola State Prison: sit-down in protest
at use of prisoners as guards, one day, August
Maryland, Baltimore: 500 prisoners involved in brief
sit-down strike in workshop, October
Michigan, Southern Michigan prison: four prisoners
seeking narcotics invade prison hospital, hold two prisoners and three guards hostage then surrender, October
Massachusetts, State Prison, Walpole: riot by 300 prisoners for two hours
Illinois, Menard State Penitentiary: riot, three guards
killed, five stabbed, three held hostage, November
Hawaii, State Prison: riot, attributed to dispute among
rival groups of narcotics peddlers, three prisoners
killed, two by other prisoners, December

1968   Indiana state prison: 25 prisoners take guards hostage
Maryland, Hagerstown correctional institution: riot by
300 prisoners
New Jersey, Essex County jail, Newark: nearly 200
prisoners set fire to jail
North Carolina, Gaston County jail
North Carolina, Central prison, Raleigh: five prisoners
killed, 78 wounded in riot
Ohio, Columbus state penitentiary: two riots
Oregon, state penitentiary, Salem: 700 prisoners riot
and set fire to buildings, over $2m damage
Puerto Rico, Commonwealth prison, San Juan: riot by
1200 prisoners
South Carolina, state prison, Columbia: two riots
California, San Quentin: strike by 500 prisoners

1970   California, Soledad State Prison: hunger-strike by black

prisoners, following the killing of three and wounding
of one prisoner when guard fired on prisoners in exercise yard, January
Nevada Prison: seven prisoners with guns and home-
made bombs hold three guards hostage for two hours
demanding freedom; hostages released and prisoners
'subdued', April
Nebraska State Penitentiary: 13 prisoners riot, free
hostage when guards fire into cell block, May
New York City, Rikers Island: 1500 of 2200 prisoners
on hunger-strike and work-stoppage, protesting against
law which halves time off for good behaviour, May
Virginia, Lorton Reformatory: fires started by prisoners
after power-cut, four guards and one prisoner injured,
May
New Jersey, Borden Town Reformatory: 300 prisoners
refused to leave auditorium in response to national
strike by correctional officers, June
Iowa, Des Moines prison: death of black escaped prisoner triggers rock-throwing and looting by others, June
Pennsylvania, Homesburg State Prison: riot when black
prisoner attacks white guard, 86 injured; reportedly
caused by poor conditions and racial tensions, July
New York City, Federal House of Detention: prisoners
break windows and throw light-bulbs and toilet paper
into street. July
Washington, Walla Walla prison: work stoppage for
five days, July
Kansas, Leavenworth Penitentiary: prisoners on strike
and refusing to work because of hot weather, August
Nevada, Carson City: uprising by black prisoners for
stabbing of black by white prisoner, August
New York City, Tombs prison riot, August
New York State, Eastern New York Correctional
Facility, Napanoch: several hundred prisoners refused
to return to cells for nine hours, protesting at what they
called inadequate medical treatment, following death of
a sick prisoner
New Mexico State Penitentiary, Santa Fe: August
New York State, Auburn Correctional Facility: prison-

ers seize control of prison for eight hours, before halting to discuss grievances, August
California, San Quentin: 1000 prisoners strike, protesting at shifting of court proceedings to prison, set fire to offices; guards use tear-gas to regain control, August
New York City, Manhattan House of Detention: 30 black prisoners hold two white prisoners hostage, demanding return of black prisoner, removed for allegedly hitting a guard, August
New York City, Manhattan House of Detention: 94 prisoners, six days later, refused for two days to leave cells or make court appearances by end of August; plans made to shift 670 prisoners elsewhere to ease overcrowding
New York City: wave of prison riots began in Queens House of Detention, spread to three other municipal jails, plus the Manhattan House of Detention, October
Arkansas, Cummins Prison Farm, Pine Bluff: group of armed prisoners seize four hostages and threaten to kill, trying to escape, November

1971   New York State, Attica correctional facility: riot by over 1000 prisoners, at least 28 prisoners and nine hostages killed when over 1000 state troopers, guards and sheriffs' deputies use tear-gas and guns to storm prison, July
New York State, Great Meadow Correctional Facility: riot by about 75 prisoners, September

1972   Pennsylvania, Federal penitentiary, Lewisburg: over 1300 prisoners locked in after refusing to leave cells for work, February
New York City, Rikers Island: adolescent remand shelter, several incidents, including non-violent and violent protests
Connecticut, Federal correctional institution, Danbury: peaceful strike by over 400 prisoners, February
Connecticut, correctional institution, Somers: hunger strike by about 900 prisoners, February
Massachusetts, Walpole state prison, March

Massachusetts, Concord prison, November
Kentucky, La Grange state reformatory, June
New Jersey, Rahway state prison, June
Maryland, house of correction, July
Maryland, state penitentiary, Baltimore, July
New York State, Attica Correctional Facility: about
900 prisoners refuse to leave their cells, July
New York State, Green Haven correctional facility,
September
Michigan, Jackson State Prison: three-day strike by
prisoners, September
New Jersey, Trenton state prison, September
Massachusetts, State Prison, Norfold: 300 prisoners
demonstrate, October
New Jersey, Burlington county jail, October
New Jersey, Essex county correctional center, October
New Jersey, state correctional institution for women:
protest by work-stoppage
New Jersey, youth correctional unit, Bordentown,
December
Illinois, Pontiac state prison: gang-fight, December

1973   California, San Quentin State prison: one-day strike by
1200–1450 prisoners staying in cells, demanding sentences and right to grow long hair, January
Hawaii, State prison: prisoners refuse to eat or return to
cells for three days, while guards search for weapons
and drugs, October
Hawaii State prison: 180 prisoners riot, demanding better medication and recreational facilities, November
Arizona State prison, uprisings in recent months, June
Georgia, State prison, Readsville: riot, four guards
taken hostage for six hours, January
Florida, Sumter Correctional Institution: riot-control
guards stop fighting between black and white prisoners
and free five white hostages; 39 prisoners injured, May
Illinois, Menard State prison: riot by 46 prisoners
ended by state police with 'stinging gas', May
Stateville Penitentiary, Joliet III: forcible suppression
of prisoners who demand amnesty for involved, end of

isolation units, release of prisoners in special isolation units, September

Indiana, State prison: prisoners seize three blocks, three guards hostage, with ten demands, including changes in mail privileges, disciplinary procedures, September

Kentucky, State Penitentiary: three prisoners hold four hostages for 17 hours, until granted transfer to medium-security reformatory, June

Kentucky State Penitentiary: three hostages taken by five prisoners, suppressed with tear-gas and plastic bullets, March

Massachusetts, Walpole State prison: prison riot quelled by plastic bullets; much damage, including fire, apparently sparked by announced drug searches, May

New Mexico state penitentiary, Santa Fe

New York State, Great Meadow Correctional Facility: further non-violent action to complain over harassment, request minimum wage, better medical services and food, and refusal to participate in program, so 700 (50 per cent) locked in cells, February

New York State, Great Meadow Correctional Facility: further non-violent protest over lack of locked mail boxes, diet, medical facilities and frequency of showers. February

New York State, Oneida County Jail, Utica, NY: disturbances over food, three staff and one prisoner injured, September

New York State, Jefferson County Jail: 20 prisoners protest against food-preparation and lack of recreation by throwing mattresses but without violence, September

New York State, New Jersey prisons: two years of disorders reported, culminating in legal protests by 22 prisoners at Trenton and Rahway State prisons, alleging unfairness in state procedures for disciplining prisoners, October

New York State, Rockland County Jail: prisoners rip plumbing out of cells and flood two tiers of building, December

Oklahoma, State Penitentiary: hunger-strike, about con-

ditions, January
Oklahoma, State Penitentiary: prison riot, buildings
burned, three prisoners dead, 19 injured, six guards
injured, July
Oklahoma, State Penitentiary: more rioting, July
Pennsylvania, Rhode Island, Adult Correctional
Institution: uprising, four guards injured, fire damage,
April
Pennsylvania, Homesburg prison and Philadelphia
House of Correction: petition regarding 80 per-cent
prisoners held 'illegally' i.e. unconvicted, 31 May;
riot in Homesburg prison, June

1974   Hawaii, State Prison: five prisoners take hostages and
prisoners remain barricaded, January
Rhode Island, Adult Correctional Institute: 55 prisoners
refuse to return to cells, demanding more recreation,
until concessions made, January
Nevada, State Prison: 15–20 riot, quelled by 70 guards
and Highway Patrol, February
Texas, Federal Detention Headquarters: three prisoners
hold three guards hostage after revolt, March
New York State: four armed Black Liberation Army
sympathisers attempt to free three BLA prisoners from
Manhattan House of Correction ('Tombs'), April
New Jersey, Trenton State Prison: 260 prisoners seize
wing, four guards injured, April
Missouri, St Louis prison: 13 white prisoners slash
wrists in protest at integration with black prisoners,
April
Connecticut, Mead Hall, Bridgeport: juvenile detention
centre, invaded by four armed youths, escaping with
three boys and three girls after shooting matron, June
New Jersey, Trenton Psychiatric Hospital, maximum-
security prison wing: prisoners refuse to leave recreation yard, 11 guards and five prisoners injured, July
New York State, Queens House of Correction: violence
between prisoners, one guard injured, July
New York State, Brooklyn House of Correction: petition and 15-minute protest demanding dismissal of

guard for alleged racism, July

Mexico City Jail: hunger strike, July

Texas, Huntsville, State Prison: seven armed
prisoners hold ten hostages for two days, July

Colorado, State Prison: three escape, kill two and take
two hostages, August

New York State, Bedford Hills Correctional Facility:
45 women prisoners hold seven staff for 2 ½ hours,
over detention of prisoner who assaulted another,
August

Minnesota, Stillwater State Prison: fighting among prisoners, over Indian tom-tom playing, September

New Jersey, Rahway State Prison: 58 Black Muslims
barricaded in protest at transfer of two to another
prison, December

Virginia, Bland Correctional Farm: 24 prisoners in
two-hour riot, wrecking dormitories and facilities, one
dead, December

1975   Washington State Penitentiary: 24-hour lockup of prisoners who rioted and seized 13 hostages, January

New York State Prison, Duchess County Jail,
Poughkeepsie: prisoners rebel for one hour during two
suicide investigations, March

Tennesee, State Prison, Nashville: 11 maximum-security prisoners hold eight prisoners and four staff counsellors hostage until authorities agree to study grievances,
April

Washington, DC, City Jail: 18-hour hold-out by prison-
ers with 12 hostages, until head of Corrections
Department promises their demands will be considered,
April

Illinois, Joliet State Penitentiary: over 200 prisoners
seize cell block and take 12 hostages; five hours before
police quell with tear-gas, one prisoner dead, April

Rhode Island, Adult Correction Institution, Cranston:
disturbance between black and white prisoners quelled,
April

New Mexico, State Penitentiary, Santa Fe: nine prisoners on 'death row' protesting at living conditions, May

Oklahoma, Okla Reformatory, Granite: about 20 prisoners armed with clubs and knives seize 11 hostages, protesting at lack of action on poor visiting opportunities, vocational rehabilitation and training, among other demands, ending after seven hours, June

Illinois, Vandalia III Correction Center: 37 leaders of 40 hours' hunger-strike transferred to another prison, May

New Jersey, Leesburg State Prison: about 275 prisoners refuse to work, over suspension of furlough privileges, June

New York State, NC Women's Prison, Raleigh: women with concrete and hoe handles fight guards over grievances, before agreement, June

Virginia, James River Correctional Facility, Goochland: sit-down strike by 40 prisoners, protesting death of prisoner; peaceful end when staff promise investigation, July

Massachusetts, Charles Street jail, Boston: 150 police quell fires and racial fighting by 75–100 prisoners, August

New York City, Rikers Island prison: about 100 prisoners set fires and refuse to return to cells, protesting at meal delays caused by guards' 'stick-out' protest at lay-offs over high overtime and other costs, July

Alabama, Mount Meigs prison: 17 prisoners injured in disturbance; quelled by state troopers, September

Tennessee, State Prison, Nashville: riot over shortages of pork chops, nearly 50 prisoners injured, two guards injured, one prisoner dead; prison population at record level, October

New York State, Erie County Holding Center, Buffalo: prisoners end hunger-strike over food, when promised improvements, October

New York City, Rikers Island House of Detention for Men: rioting prisoners seize two cell blocks, hold five officers hostage, November

New York State, Onondaga Penitentiary, Syracuse: riot demanding dismissal of six correctional officers and complaining of whites being favoured; riot squad quells, no injuries reported, December

1976   New Jersey, Trenton State Prison: one prisoner killed
and three guards and prisoners injured in attempted
take-over of maximum security wing, January
California, San Quentin Prison: 43 prisoners on 'death
row' begin hunger-strike for more access to prison
library and better medical care
Colorado, State Penitentiary, Canon City: 120 protest -
ing prisoners armed with home-made clubs, subdued
with tear-gas, March
New York State, Great Meadow Correctional Facility:
disturbance, 30 prisoners and guards injured, May
New York City, Rikers Island Adolescent Remand
Detention Center: 'minor race riot', involving black
and Puerto Rican prisoners, June
New Jersey, Middlesex County Workhouse: strike by
120 prisoners for two days, July
New York State, Attica, State Penitentiary: eight
guards, one prisoner injured in disturbance over cell-
searching, July
Wisconsin, State Prison, Madison: 87 rebellious prison
ers release 14 hostages unharmed, in exchange for
amnesty and promise from state of investigating grievances, July
New York State, Attica, State Penitentiary: six-day
peaceful strike, refusal by most prisoners to leave cells,
protesting conditions, August
New York State, Great Meadow Correctional Facility,
Comstock: two-thirds of prisoners refuse to leave cells
in peaceful protest, August
New York State, Green Haven Correctional Facility:
protests apparently linked with convening of inquiry
into unrest at Attica, September
New York City, Bronx House of Detention: prisoners
begin peaceful strike protesting visiting restrictions,
excessive bail, cases too slow coming to trial, for two
days until many demands met, September
New York City, Queens House of Detention for Men:
more than 350 prisoners awaiting trial refuse to be

locked in cells, in non-violent protest at court delays
and use of bail, October
New York City, Bronx House of Detention for Men:
more than 200 guards from Rikers Island force
rebelling prisoners back into cells in protests over
same issues as previous month, November
Colorado, State Penitentiary, Canon City: short protest
over time off for good behaviour, food handling and
other grievances, November
New Mexico State Penitentiary, Santa Fe

1977   Washington, Walla Walla State Penitentiary

1978   California, Wayside Honor Farm, Castaic: riot, prisoners burn infirmary, ransack six barracks, February
Rhode Island, Adult Correctional Institution, Cranston:
about 150 prisoners protest, claiming extra visiting
hours and exercise times have not been given as
promised, April
Rhode Island, Adult Correctional Institution, Cranston:
70 guards refuse work because knee-deep in garbage
thrown by prisoners in maximum-security protest over
conditions, April
Georgia, Reidsville prison: disturbances involving
racial violence, one prisoner killed, five injured, July
Illinois, State Penitentiary, Pontiac: 600 prisoners riot,
burn cell house, three guards stabbed to death, three
injured, July
Georgia, Reidsville prison: riot, one guard, two prisoners dead, July
West Virginia, Huttonsville Correctional Center: 16-
hour weekend riot, smashed furniture and fires in 10 of
12 dormitories, September
Delaware, County Prison: five-hour protest at prison
conditions by four prisoners who then release three
hostages, December

1979   Washington, State Penitentiary, Walla Walla: prisoners
take nine hostages, negotiate, all released unharmed,
May
California, Folsom Prison: racial disturbance, one pris-

oner killed, nine injured, May
Tennessee, Bushy Mountain State Penitentiary: 50
guards quell riot over food, June
Washington, State Penitentiary, Walla Walla: over 200
prisoners kept in yard after throwing sinks and toilets
round cell-blocks in demand for showers, July
Washington, State Penitentiary: 150–160 prisoners
begin hunger-strike protesting lock-in cells since fatal
stabbing of guard in June, July
Massachusetts, Walpole State Prison: correctional officers strike protesting unsafe working conditions in segregation unit; prisoners hold five correctional officers
hostage protesting living conditions, July
California, Soledad State Prison: 20 prisoners and two
guards injured in racial clash, August
Nevada, Las Vegas Jail: armed prisoners take three
guards hostage demanding improved conditions,
August
New York State, Orange County Jail: over 150 prisoners protest dismissal of temporary guards, October
New York State, Green Haven State Correctional
Facility: disturbance, over 100 prisoners, seven prison-
ers injured, quelled with tear-gas, November
Washington, State Reformatory: riot, four youths hurt,
November
California, Soledad State Prison: two prisoners killed,
17 injured, December
Oregon, State Correctional Institution, Salem: 200 pris-
oners riot, set books and clothing on fire, locked in, no
injuries reported, December

1980   New Mexico prison riot: 32 prisoners killed, 50
injured, including five staff, February

1981   California, Rehabilitation center, Norco: fighting
quelled by guards firing at prisoners
Connecticut, maximum-security prison, Somers: armed
guards and state troopers quell riot
Florida, Synter correctional institution, Bushnell
Georgia, state prison, Reidsville

Hawaii, Oahu community correctional center, Honolulu
Illinois, Stateville correctional center, Joliet
Indiana, St Joseph county jail
Iowa, state penitentiary
Louisiana, Lafayette parish prison
Louisiana, Vermilion parish prison, Abbeville
Massachusetts, Deer Island house of corrections
Michigan, Southern Michigan prison, Jackson
Michigan, Marquette state prison
Nevada, state prison, near Carson City
New Jersey, Monmouth county correctional center
New Jersey, Bergen county jail
New Jersey, Trenton state prison
New York City, Rikers Island: attacks by Hispanic
prisoners on black prisoners
New York State, Westchester county prison, Valhalla
Washington State, corrections center, Shelton
Puerto Rico: protests at Puerta de Terra, Guayama and
Vega Alta prisons
Pennsylvania, state prison, Graterford

1982   New Jersey, federal correctional institution: three-day
riot by over 200 prisoners
Michigan, Huron Valley correctional facility
Montana state prison
Illinois, Menard correctional center. Chester
Georgia, Coastal correctional institution, Savannah

1983   New York State, Ossining correctional facility
New York State, Auburn correctional facility: prisoners
refuse food in fear of AIDS
New York State, Attica state prison: 1500 prisoners
protest at prison conditions by refusing to leave their
cells

1984   Georgia, federal penitentiary, Atlanta
Hawaii, Honolulu prison

1985   Virginia, Mecklenburg correctional center, Boydton
New York State, Attica state prison

1986   Virginia, Lorton reformatory: two riots
                Puerto Rico, penitentiary
                Indiana, state reformatory, Pendleton
                Indiana state prison: two riots
                South Carolina, Kirkland correctional center
                New York City, Rikers Island correctional institution:
                two riots
                Arizona state prison: fighting among 200 prisoners
                West Virginia penitentiary, Moundsville

1987   Pennsylvania, state prison, Pittsburgh
                Clinton correctional facility, New York
                Louisiana, Oakdale federal prison: riot by Cuban pris-
                oners
                Georgia, federal prison, Atlanta: riot by Cuban prison
                ers

1988   Louisiana, Avoyelles parish jail, Marksville: protests
                by Cuban detainees
                New York State, Rikers Island prison
                Oklahoma, Stringtown prison
                New Jersey, Trenton state prison
                New York State, Coxsackie correctional facility
                Massachusetts, Billerica prison
                Massachusetts, Lawrence county jail: prisoners set fire
                to buildings
                Oregon, Salem prison
                Puerto Rico penitentiary
                Puerto Rico, Guayana regional prison: riot by 400 pris-
                oners, warden hostage,13 shot and injured
                Georgia, Hall county prison

1989   Illinois, maximum-security prison, Chester
                California, Folsom prison
                Columbia, district prison
                Banning Road camp rehabilitation center, California
                Chester prison, Illinois
                New York State, Rikers Island prison
                Camp Hill prison, Philadelphia: two riots

Hudson county jail, Jersey City

1990   Arizona state prison: prisoners wounded after fights
                between Hispanic and black prisoners

1991   Alabama, federal prison, Talladega: siege
                New York State, Southport correctional facility, Pine
                City, May

1992   Kansas, federal penitentiary, Leavenworth, July

IN BRITAIN

1796   England, London, Newgate prison: November,

1810   England, Dartmoor prison: disturbance, September

1810   England, Dartmoor prison: riot, September

1816   England, London, Newgate prison: riot,
                August–September

1950   England, Portland borstal: disturbances, January

1954   England, London, Wandsworth prison: riot by 50 pris-
                oners, May

1955   England, Dartmoor prison: hunger-strike by 14 prison-
                ers, January

1959   England, Birmingham and Cardiff prisons: distur-
                bances

1968   England, Durham prison: prisoners in security prison
                barricade themselves in, Spring

1969   England, Parkhurst prison: riot, October

1971	England, Albany prison: several demonstrations

1972   England, Brixton prison: several demonstrations, May
England, Albany prison: disturbances, August
England, Parkhurst, Camp Hill, Albany, Chelmsford
England, Gartree prison, disturbances, November

1975   England, Wormwood Scrubs prison: rooftop protest, November

1976   England, Hull prison: riot, August
England: 31 prisons had disturbances, May–September

1978   England: Irish prisoners protest at several jails, July
England, Gartree prison: riot at treatment of prisoner, October; more disturbances, October
England, Durham prison: hunger-strike in protest at conditions, November
England, Nottingham prison: 85 prisoners protest at the transfer of one, November
England, Parkhurst prison: 200 prisoners protest at food, December

1979   England, Liverpool, Walton prison: prisoners destroy books and furniture, protesting locking up 22 hours a day during officers' dispute, February
England, Liverpool Walton prison: five prisoners barricade themselves in cells in protest, March
England, Parkhurst prison: five prisoners in rooftop protest, March
England, Hull prison: riot, April
England, London, Wormwood Scrubs prison: riot protesting overcrowding, quelled by first use of MUFTI squad

1980   England, London, Wormwood Scrubs prison: rooftop demonstration by five prisoners, June
England, London Wormwood Scrubs prison: barricades by six prisoners, August

1984	Nine prisoners in hunger strike, protesting 'harassment' by prisoners and staff, January
	Twelve prisoners in riot and rooftop protest, January
	England, Wormwood Scrubs prison: two prisoners hold three hostages, end voluntarily December
1986	England: disturbances in 46 prisons, April to May, ten remand prisoners hold prisoners hostage, May
	Scotland, Saughton prison: officer taken hostage by five prisoners, March
1987	Youth Custody centre: protest, July
	Scotland, Shotts prison (ST), September
	Scotland, Peterhead prison: siege ended by SAS
	Scotland, Perth prison: siege, October
1988	Scotland, Perth prison: officer taken hostage by prisoners, May
	Scotland, Bairlinnie prison disturbance: two officers injured, May
	Army camp, temporary prison, riot ends, May
	16 remand prisoners riot in police station cell block, July
	England, Lindholme prison: 250 prisoners, riot (ST), July
	Scotland, remand centre: prisoners riot, July
	Prisoners confined to cells after dirty protest at insanitary conditions, July
	England, Ashwell prison: riot (ST), August
	Scotland, Saughton prison: disturbance, two prisoners take instructor hostage, October
	England, Havering prison, Cumbria: mass breakout during riot, June
1989	England, Northeye prison: riot investigation begins, January
	England, Ashwell prison: rooftop protest, May
	England, Gloucester prison: Kurds hunger-strike over delays in processing applications for political asylum, October

1990   England, Dartmoor prison: riot by 90 prisoners after
               goal disallowed at football match, January
               England, Strangeways prison: riot, April
               England, Dartmoor prison: hostage taken during inci-
               dent, April
               England, Long Lartin prison: 13 hour siege, April
               England, Pucklechurch prison: riot, April
               Scotland, Shotts prison: rioters hold officer hostage,
               April
               England, Remand Centre, Risely: fighting female pris-
               oners attack staff, May
               England, Norwich prison: attempted escape during dis
               turbances, December

1992   England, Highpoint prison, Suffolk, riot with estimated
               £1m damage, November
               Scotland, Perth prison
               England, Reading prison
               England, Long Lartin prison, riot quelled by 150 offi-
               cers in riot gear, December

Index